The Signs of the Times

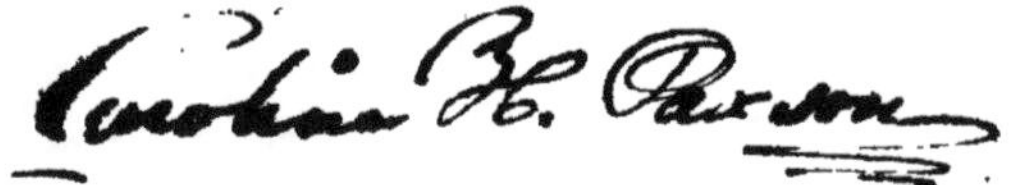

THE

SIGNS OF THE TIMES,

AS DENOTED BY THE FULFILMENT OF

HISTORICAL PREDICTIONS,

TRACED DOWN

FROM THE BABYLONISH CAPTIVITY TO THE PRESENT TIME.

BY THE

REV. ALEXANDER KEITH,

MINISTER OF ST. CYRUS,

AUTHOR OF "THE EVIDENCE OF PROPHECY."

"At the end it shall speak, and not lie.—*Hab.* *ii.* 3.

"Ye can discern the face of the sky; but can ye not discern the signs of the times.—*Matt.* *xvi.* 3.

IN TWO VOLUMES.

VOL. II.

NEW YORK:

PUBLISHED BY JONATHAN LEAVITT, 182 BROADWAY.

BOSTON:

CROCKER & BREWSTER, 47 WASHINGTON-ST.

1832.

NEW YORK:
PRINTED BY R. & G. S. WOOD, 261 PEARL-STREET.

THE SIGNS OF THE TIMES,

&c.

CHAPTER XX.

The previous visions bring us down historically till we have passed the period of the siege of Constantinople, its capture by the Turks, and the extinction of the Eastern empire. The *second woe* was not ended when Mahomet II. occupied the throne of Palæologus; and other events were yet to intervene before it should be *past.* The overthrow of the Western empire of Rome served to exalt the papacy; and the papal yoke was not broken with the last sceptre of the Cæsars, which had been swayed in Constantinople for eleven hundred years. The Turkish empire in Europe and Asia was divided into Pachalics. The nations of Europe, which were not subjected to the Turkish sway, continued the unrepentant worshippers of idols and workers of iniquity. And from the year 1453 to the end of that century, the prophetic character of the times continued unchanged—and the fact is notorious in history that, during that period, men did not repent of their corrupt worship or of their evil deeds, and that these together grew to such an excess, that the papal yoke could no longer be borne. But with a new century a *new era* began.

The first four trumpets, before which the Western empire fell, and the two woe-trumpets on apostate Christendom, by the last of which the empire of the East was subverted, followed in close succession, and the events which they respectively represent were immediately connected. The Goths, the Vandals, the Huns, and the Lombards, gave no pause to the downfall of Rome; nor was any event interposed between the wars which they waged, to merit a peculiar page in history or a word in prophecy. Alaric, Genseric, Attila, opened a way for the first barbaric king of Italy: and the sun of Rome was set. The first and second *woes*, though perfectly distinct, were not only of a kindred character, but they came into immediate contact, and there was a bond between them: The caliph invested the sultan, and put the great sword in his hand. But it is not thus in the course of the second woe, for other scenes are introduced before it is past, and before it is then said that the third woe cometh quickly. A pause is interposed, and a new description is introduced after the fall of Constantinople and the continued impenitence, immediately after that event, of the European nations which were not subjugated by the Turks.

It is also peculiarly observable, that the first sounding as well as the whole burden of each and all of the former trumpets, indicate, by the most expressive symbols and signs, the judgments that were to come generally or partially on the earth. These were all of fearful import—such as fire and hail mingled with blood cast upon the earth—the effect of which was burning,—a great mountain burning with fire cast into the sea,—a great star falling from heaven, burning as it were a lamp, and whose name was wormwood,—the smiting of the third part of the sun and of the moon and of the stars, with the consequent darkness. These were also followed in like manner, under the very name of *woes*, by the opening of the bottomless pit, and the rising of a smoke, enough to darken the sun and the stars, and out of which issued locusts upon the earth; and also by the loosing of the four angels, that were bound on earth and did not descend from heaven, whose time of preparation to *slay the third part* of men was already measured and begun. All these, however dissimilar in form, are the same in kind. And it needs but the slightest observation to discern that the next vision is altogether of a different order; and that in conformity with the symbol, the next great event which it typifies, is necessarily different in nature and in character, as all these various forms of wars and woes are different from the descent of an angel from heaven.

Reaching then, the very dawn of the Reformation, and looking on a new prophetic scene, may we not regard history as again the interpreter, and draw all our illustrations of the whole from it alone? Was there nothing then seen like ANOTHER mighty angel —the angel of the reformation—coming down from heaven—was there not something like a rainbow on his head, a sign that the world was no longer to be deluged with darkness,—was not his face seen to shine as the sun, when Jesus as the sun of righteousness, again became the light of the world,—did not his feet shine as pillars of fire, enlightening the place on which he stood—was it not on the sea, the shores of the Baltic and the island of Britain, that he set his right foot, the brightest regions of protestantism, and on the earth, in inland Europe, that, somewhat less firmly and brightly, he placed his left? What else was in his hand, as he came down from heaven and lighted on the earth, than the only little book that ever came from thence; and how did he hold it but *open*—as, after the lapse of a thousand years, it was once again open—but never a second time to be shut to the world, that each man in his own tongue might look and read? The preceding storm that humbled imperial Rome, and gave its power and glory to the winds, had indeed been terrible. And how did the other mighty angel cry, who on coming down from heaven, shook the kingdom of darkness to its centre, but with a loud voice, as when a lion roareth? or, is that vision to be for ever unintelligible, which is thus, only in part, anticipated?

And I saw another mighty angel come down from heaven, clothed with a cloud; and a rainbow was upon his head; and his face was as it were the sun, and his feet as pillars of fire; and he had in his hand a little book open: and he set his right foot upon the sea, and his left foot on the earth, and cried with a loud voice as when a lion roareth: and when he had cried, seven thunders uttered their voices. And when the seven thunders had uttered their voices, I was about to write: and I heard a voice from heaven saying unto me, seal up those things which the seven thunders uttered, and write them not. And the angel which I saw stand upon the sea and upon the earth lifted up his hand to heaven, and sware by him that liveth for ever and ever, who created heaven, and the things that therein are, and the sea, and the things which are therein, that there should be time no longer: but in the days of the voice of the seventh angel, when he shall begin to sound, the mystery of God should be finished, as he hath declared to his servants the prophets. And the voice which I heard from heaven spake unto me again, and said, go and take the little book which is open in the hand of the angel which standeth upon the sea, and upon the earth. And I went unto the angel, and said unto him, give me the little book. And he said unto me, take it, and eat it up;

and it shall make thy belly bitter, but it shall be in thy mouth sweet as honey. And I took the little book out of the angel's hand, and ate it up; and it was in my mouth sweet as honey: and as soon as I had eaten it, my belly was bitter. And he said unto me, Thou must prophecy again before many people, and nations, and tongues, and kings. Chap. x.

And I saw another mighty angel come down from heaven, clothed with a cloud: The last tidings of the former angel were that, after the full time of preparation by the Turks should be accomplished, and the third part of men be slain by the fire, the brimstone, and the smoke, yet the rest of the men that were not killed by these plagues would not in any way repent. But the next great event, on the coming down of *another* mighty angel from heaven, was of *another* kind; and all the nations were not then to be enveloped in the same gross darkness any more, nor to continue in impenitent idolatry and wickedness. Woes had been loosed from the south and from the north, after tempests had arisen on every part of the earth. But another angel, different from the former, even a heavenly visitant, came down. He was clothed with a cloud. When Jesus ascended into heaven, a *cloud* received him out of the sight of the apostles. The Lord makes the clouds his chariots. The clouds are the dust of his feet. The Son of Man shall come in the clouds of heaven, and all his holy angels with him. And, thus clothed with a cloud, the mighty angel came down from heaven, in angelic vesture, or in such a form as the angels of light and mercy visit a dark world like ours. The clothing with a cloud may imply that there was yet to be darkness around, only partially dissipated from the earth.

But, though clothed with a cloud, *a rainbow was upon his head;* a proof that light was again reflected from the sun, and, in spiritual significancy, a more glorious vision, and the token of brighter glories, than the mere mortal eye can see. The import of the rainbow, in reference to the Reformation, may be deduced from the scriptural record of its first being set as a sign in the skies. On the establishment of his covenant with Noah and his seed, after the deluge, "God said, this is the token of the covenant which I have made between me and you, and every living creature that is with you, for perpetual generations. I do set my bow in the cloud, and it shall be for a token of a covenant between me and the earth. And it shall come to pass, when I bring a cloud over the earth, that the bow shall be seen in the cloud: and I will remember my covenant which is between me and you, and every living creature of all flesh; and the waters shall no more become a flood to destroy all flesh. And the bow shall be in the cloud; and I will look upon it, that I may remember the everlasting covenant between God and every living creature of all flesh that is upon the earth. And God said unto Noah, this is the token of the covenant which I have established between me and all flesh that is upon the earth," Gen. ix. 12—17. But the rainbow seen in prophetic vision by John, himself one of the heralds of a better and everlasting covenant, rested not on floating atmospheric vapour, but on the head of the mighty angel who, at that special era, came down from heaven. It was a token from heaven that was given by the Lord. They who had been saved, as in an ark, from the flood of idolatry that had overspread the earth, looked at length on the Reformation as the rainbow of their hope—the pledge which their God, who had established his covenant with them, gave them from on high, that He remembered his lasting covenant; and that, in a spiritual, as well as in a natural sense, there should no more be a flood to destroy all flesh. And, looking back on the dawn of the Reformation, after the long night of darkness which preceded it, it still appears in the retrospect of the past, as when the rainbow is seen, when after the earth is enshrouded in blackness, the clouds are broken and scattered, on the subsiding of a thick tempest, and the rainbow gives a sure token that the sun shines in the heavens.

But the Reformation was more than a sign that God remembered his everlasting covenant, and that every region on the earth would finally be enlightened by the glorious gospel. The light shone upon the earth. "The light of the Reformation" is an historic term, as the *yoke* is the badge of popery. And the angel who came down from heaven, in his season, had not only a rainbow on his head, but *his face was as it were the sun*. Christ, the sun of righteousness, is the true light which enlighteneth every man that cometh into the world. And it seemed as if the light of the world was then about to enlighten it all. "*The dawn of truth*," says the ecclesiastical historian, "arose upon other nations besides Germany. *The light of the Reformation spread itself far and wide*; and almost all the European states welcomed its *salutary beams*, and exulted in the prospect of an approaching deliverance from the *yoke* of superstition and spiritual despotism."* It seemed as if the millennium was at hand; and that the reign of Christ was then to have been extended over all the nations of the earth. The light of the Reformation was that which Christ himself had revealed, which again broke forth on the world. The angel was but the messenger of the truth as it is in Jesus—his face shone not merely as an angel's, but as it were the sun. The Reformation, in its origin, was, *as it were*, the rising of the sun of righteousness on the nations, with healing under his wings.

* Mosheim's Eccles. Hist. Cent. xvi.

Not only had the angel a rainbow upon his head, and *his face also was as it were the sun,* but *his feet were as pillars of fire*—not a spreading blaze or a falling star to scorch the earth, but pillars of fire to enlighten all around the place where he stood. But the light wherewith he was to enlighten a portion of the world emanated not from any angelic being; he was but the messenger of light to bear it from heaven to the earth.

And he had in his hand a little book open. No man in heaven, or in earth, nor under the earth, was able to open and to read the book, neither to look thereon, which He who sat on the throne of heaven held in his right hand. There is but one book of the Revelation of Jesus Christ. "I testify unto every one that heareth the words of the prophecy of THIS BOOK," saith the Spirit, "if any man shall add unto these things, God shall add unto him the plagues that are written in *this book:* and if any man shall take away from the words of *the book of this prophecy,* God shall take away his part out of the book of life, and out of the holy city, and from the things that are written in *this book.*" No mention is ever made of two *books of Revelation.* And the little book, held in the angel's hand, is but one of many symbols characteristic of that time, or, if we do not greatly mistake, of the great events which, when previously brought into close contact with that period, marked the Reformation. How then did the Reformation rise like a rainbow on the world in its darkness; how did it look like the descent of a mighty angel; wherefore did it shine as it were the sun over the moral world; and why was there light, like a pillar of fire, wherever it rested? but because, in the providence and grace of God, the sacred scriptures were then opened or translated, even as the mighty angel that came down from heaven—held, and held only, in his hand a little *open* book. Before closed, it was then brought open to the earth. And so significant and expressive is the simile, that it has actually been adopted as the most significant of the event, in a manner that, as denoting the very fact, cannot be misunderstood; for the common picture of the heads of the Reformers, has, as their symbol, an *open Bible** beside them, of which scarcely a child needs ask the meaning. The Bible literally means *the book*. And the translation or, by the simplest figure, the opening of it, especially of the New Testament unfolding the precepts of Jesus and the doctrines of the gospel, gave a character to the time, which, in respect to the wide extended diffusion of the scriptures by the then recent art of printing, the days of the apostles scarcely equalled. The gospel, as *a book*, may be said to have been for the first time *open* to the world. And coming, as every good and perfect gift cometh from on high, it may well be said to have come down from heaven, and to have been brought open to the earth by the hand of an angel, one of the ministering spirits to them that believe in that very book.

And he set his right foot upon the sea, and his left foot on the earth. The face of the mighty angel was as it were the sun; but though the light came from heaven and was the gospel of Jesus, yet it did not at that time shine with equal and unobscured brightness, from the one end of heaven to the other. The radiance was yet chiefly local, as that of light round pillars of fire. But though partial, it was ex-extensive; and the place of the angels' feet—the regions on which the Reformation settled, were specially marked. The Reformation was not like the spungy stalk of a mushroom rising from the earth in a night and fixed to an inch of ground, but like pillars of fire, resting on separate portions of Europe—and occupying a portion of the globe. The *right*

---

* See frontispiece of Mosheim's Eccles. Hist. Glas. ed.

foot of the angel was set upon the sea. In the downfall of Rome, the ravages of Genseric along the coast of Africa, and the shores of Italy and Spain, as well as over the island of Sardinia, were like unto a burning mountain cast into the sea. Maritime regions, and islands, were the scene of the desolation. And the shores of the Baltic, or the northern coasts of Europe, and an island of the German Ocean, distinguished in like manner from inland territories, or the earth, by the name of *sea*, became the chief seat of Protestantism, when it first settled down, and was most firmly fixed.

The Baltic sea is imbayed by Sweden, which is separated by it from the rest of Europe; and the Gulf of Finland, the large lakes of Ladoga and Onega, with the rivers and marshes in the narrow intervening space, almost cut off Sweden from the continent, till the White Sea, which mingles with the northern ocean, divides the great peninsula from the government of Archangel. The capital of Denmark, situated, like that of Sweden on the *sea*, lies in an island; and that kingdom may be said to have its place in the bosom of the ocean. Maritime Holland, insular Britain need not be described. Although the Reformation originated in the interior of Europe, it is universally known that these, from first to last, have been the chief settlements of Protestantism; and that these kingdoms have mainly contributed to its establishment. But a few illustrations may not, in respect to the former, be deemed superfluous, as drawn from the same page of ecclesiastical history.

* "The reformed religion was propagated in Sweden, soon after Luther's rupture with Rome, by one of his disciples whose name was Olaus Petri; and who was the first herald of religious liberty in that kingdom. The zealous efforts of the missionary were powerfully seconded by that valiant and public-spirited prince, Gustavus Vassa Erickson, whom the Swedes had raised to the throne. This generous and patriotic hero had been in exile and prison,—but having escaped from his confinement, and taken refuge at Lubec, he was there instructed in the principles of the

Reformation, and looked upon the doctrine of Luther, not only as agreeable to the genius and spirit of the gospel, but also as favourable to the temporal state and political constitution of the Swedish dominions. The prudence, however, of this excellent prince was equal to his zeal, and accompanied it always. And as the religious opinions of the Swedes were in a fluctuating state, and their minds divided between their ancient superstitions, recommended by custom, and the doctrine of Luther, which attracted their assent by the power of conviction and truth, Gustavus wisely avoided all vehemence and precipitation in spreading the new doctrine, and proceeded in the important undertaking with circumspection, and by degrees in a manner suitable to the principles of the Reformation, which are diametrically opposite to compulsion and violence. Accordingly, the *first object of his attention was the instruction of his people in the sacred doctrine of the Holy Scriptures*; for which purpose he invited into his dominions several learned Germans, and spread abroad through the kingdom the Swedish *translation of the Bible*, that had been made by Olaus Petri. Some time after this, in the year 1526, he appointed a conference at Upsal between this eminent reformer and Peter Gallius, a gallant defender of the ancient superstition, in which these two champions were to plead publicly in behalf of their respective opinions, that it might thus be seen on which side the truth lay. This dispute, in which Olaus obtained a signal victory, contributed much to confirm Gustavus in his persuasion of the truth of Luther's doctrine, and to promote the progress of that doctrine in Sweden. In the year following, another event gave the finishing stroke to its propagation and success, and this was the assembly of the states of Westwaas, where Gustavus recommended the doctrine of the reformers with such zeal, wisdom and piety, that after warm debates, fomented by the clergy in general, and much opposition on the part of the bishops in particular, it was unanimously resolved, that the plan of reformation proposed by Luther should have *free admittance among the Swedes.* This resolution was principally owing to the firmness and magnanimity of Gustavus, who declared publicly that he would lay down his sceptre and retire from his kingdom, rather than rule a people enslaved to the power and authority of the pope, and more controlled by the tyranny of their bishops than by the law of their monarch. *From this time the papal empire in Sweden was entirely overturned.*

"*The light of the Reformation* was also received in Denmark, and that so early as the year 1521, in consequence of the ardent desire by Christiern, or Christian II., of having *his subjects instructed* in the principles and doctrines of Luther.—His successor Frederick, permitted the Protestant doctors to preach publicly the opinions of Luther. He contributed greatly to the progress of the Reformation, by his successful attempts in favour of religious liberty, at the assembly of the states that was held at Odensee in the year 1527. But it was here that he procured the publication of that famous edict which declared every subject of Denmark free, either to adhere to the tenets of the church of Rome, or to embrace the doctrine of Luther. Encouraged by this resolution, the Protestant divines exercised the functions of their ministry with such zeal and success, that the greatest part of the Danes opened their eyes upon THE AUSPICIOUS BEAMS OF SACRED LIBERTY, and abandoned gradually both the doctrines and jurisdiction of the church of Rome. But the honour of finishing this glorious work, of destroying *entirely* the reign of superstition, and breaking asunder the bonds of papal tyranny, was reserved for Christiern III., a prince equally distinguished by his piety and prudence. He began by suppressing the despotic authority of the bishop, and by restoring to their lawful owners a great part of the wealth and possessions which the church had acquired by the artful stratagems of the artful and designing clergy. This step was followed by a wise and well-judged settlement of religious doctrine, discipline, and worship, throughout the kingdom. The assembly of the states at Odensee, in the year 1539, gave a solemn sanction to all their transactions, and thus the *work of Reformation was brought to perfection in Denmark.*"*

In the year 1534 the doctrines of the Reformation made great progress in Britain, in consequence of the publication of "English books against the corruptions of the church of Rome—but it was *a translation of the Scriptures* by Tindal that was esteemed the most dangerous to the established faith."† Queen Elizabeth, A. D. 1558, "broke anew the despotic yoke of papal authority and superstition, and delivering her people from the bondage of Rome, established that form of religious doctrine and ecclesiastical government which still subsists in England."

"The seeds of the Reformation were very early sown in Scotland, by several noblemen of that nation, who had resided in Germany during the religious disputes that divided the empire.—The first and most eminent opposer of the papal jurisdiction was John Knox, a disciple of Calvin, whose eloquence was persuasive, and whose fortitude was invincible. This resolute Reformer set out from Geneva for Scotland, in the year 1559, and in a very short space of time inspired the people, by his private exhortations and his public discourses, with such a violent aversion to the superstitions of Rome, that the greatest part of the Scottish nation aban-

* Mosheim's Eccl. Hist. Cent. xvi. chap. ii. § 30, 32.
† Hume's Hist. of England, chap. 31.

doned them entirely, and aimed at nothing less than the total extirpation of popery.*

"The Reformation had not been long established in Britain, when the Belgic provinces, united by a respectable confederacy, withdrew from their spiritual allegiance to the Roman pontiff."†

The Reformation spread partially into Italy, Spain and Portugal; but these kingdoms were not ripe for freedom from dark superstition and the papal yoke. The darkness did not comprehend the light; and the watchful clergy of Rome, aided by the civil authorities, and armed with inquisitorial powers, suppressed the Reformation—and the angel who had winged his flight over them set not his foot, as a pillar of fire, on any of these kingdoms, where darkness still maintained its reign for a season. The edict of Nantz gave freedom to Protestants, which its revocation disannulled. The paleness of death, in respect to religion, has recently passed over these countries, and rests upon them still, which would not then receive, or were shut out from the light of the gospel. Neither the pillar of fire that rested on the sea, nor that which was set upon the earth, diffued its light, except by a momentary gleam, beyond the Pyrenees or the Alps.

But the mighty angel did set his left foot upon *the earth.* Switzerland, Saxony, Prussia, Bavaria, Bohemia, Hungary, are partly Protestant countries, and on them, as on the earth, the left foot of the mighty angel rested.

The angel that came down from heaven is not only denominated *mighty*, but *he cried with a loud voice as when a lion roareth.*—The first six trumpets completed the fall of the imperial power in Rome and Constantinople, but the the sixth trumpet, or second woe, had not ceased to sound or to afflict at

* Mosheim. Ibid. chap. iv. 9, 10. † Ibid. § 12.

the close of the fifteenth century. And the next great event after the taking of Constantinople, and the continued impenitence of the Roman Catholic church throughout the interval, was the Reformation; and how it was typified, as in all other respects, by a mighty angel who cried with a loud voice as when a lion roareth, may best be seen in the same record of history, and is a fact of which the world can never lose the remembrance.

"The *most momentous event* that distinguished the church *after* the fifteenth century, and, we may add, the most glorious of all the revolutions that happened in the state of Christianity, since the time of its divine and immortal founder, was that happy change introduced into religion which is known by the title of the blessed Reformation. This grand revolution, which arose in Saxony from small beginnings, not only spread itself with the utmost rapidity through all the European provinces, but also extended its efficacy more or less to the more distant parts of the globe, and may justly be considered *as the main aud principal spring which has moved the nations from that illustrious period, and occasioned the greatest part both of the civil and religious revolutions that fill the annals of history down to our times.* The face of Europe was, in a more especial manner, changed by this great event. The present age feels yet, in a sensible manner, and ages to come will continue to perceive, the inestimable advantages it produced, and the inconveniencies of which it has been the innocent occasion. The history, therefore, of such an important *revolution*, from whence so many *others* have derived their *origin*, and whose relations and connexions are so extensive and universal, demands undoubtedly a peculiar degree of attention, and has an unquestionable right to the principal place in such a work as the history of the church."*

The mighty angel had a little open book in his hand. And it is equally manifest, that the translation of the Scriptures was the great moving power in this "*grand revolution.*"

"The different parts of Luther's German translation of the Holy Scriptures, being successively and gradually spread among the people, *produced sudden and almost incredible effects*, and extirpated, root and branch, the erroneous principles and superstitious doctrines of the church of Rome, from the minds of a prodigious number of persons."†

---

* Mosheim, xvi. Cent. Introduction. † Ibid. c. i. 18.

"The charm," to use the words of Dr. Robertson, "which had bound mankind for so many ages, was broken at once. The human mind, which had continued long as tame and passive as if it had been formed to believe whatever was taught, and to bear whatever was imposed, roused of a sudden, and became inquisitive, mutinous, and disdainful of the *yoke* to which it had hitherto submitted. The wonderful ferment and agitation which, at this distance of time, appears unaccountable, or is condemned as extravagant, was so general, that it must have been excited by causes which were natural and of powerful efficacy. The kingdoms of Denmark, Sweden, England, and Scotland, and almost one half of Germany, threw off their allegiance to the Pope, abolished their jurisdiction within their territories, and gave the sanction of laws to modes of discipline and systems of doctrine which were not only independent of his power, but hostile to it. Nor was this spirit of innovation confined to those countries which openly revolted from the pope; it spread through all Europe, and broke out in every part of it with various degrees of violence. The number of converts to the opinions of reformers was so great, their zeal so enterprising, and the abilities of their leaders so distinguished, that they soon ventured to contend for superiority with the established church, and were sometimes on the point of obtaining it. In all the provinces of Germany which continued to acknowledge the papal supremacy, as well as in the Low Countries, the Protestant doctrines were secretly taught, and had gained so many proselytes that they were ripe for revolt, and were restrained merely by the dread of their rulers from imitating the example of their neighbours, and asserting their independence. Even in Spain and in Italy, symptoms of the same disposition to shake off the *yoke* appeared. The pretensions of the Pope to infallible knowledge and supreme power, were treated by many persons of eminent learning and abilities with such scorn, or impugned with such vehemence, that the most vigilant attention of the civil magistrate, the highest strains of pontifical authority, and all the rigour of the inquisitorial jurisdiction, were requisite to check and extinguish it."*

Every attempt at reconciliation with the Catholics having proved abortive, liberty of conscience having been denied to the Protestants, and a severe decree of the emperor, the signal of excommunicating bulls, having been issued against them, they entered into a league at Smalkald, and the Protestant states of Germany combined for their mutual defence. So rapidly were the doctrines of the Reformation spread, and so earnestly were they embraced, that

* Robertson's Hist. of Charles V. vol. ii. pp. 472, 473.

the league of Smalkald was formed only thirteen years after the first preaching of Luther; and in the year 1546, when alarmed at the designs of the emperor, some of the Protestant princes of Germany assembled an army of nearly a hundred thousand men, "the most numerous, and undoubtedly the best appointed, of any which had been levied in Europe during that century."* The pacification of Passau, commonly termed the *religious peace*, without a battle, secured to the Protestants the free exercise of their religion; and the Reformation might then be considered as consolidated. It forms one of the most illustrious and eventful revolutions which the world has ever witnessed; and is discriminated from them all, as in its origin it was symbolized by the descent of a mighty angel from heaven, who cried with a loud voice, as when a lion roareth.

And when he had cried, seven thunders uttered their voices. And when the seven thunders had uttered their voices, I was about to write; and I heard a voice from heaven, saying unto me, Seal up those things which the seven thunders uttered, and write them not. Ver. 3, 4. Interpreters are almost uniformly agreed that thunders denote war, and the symbol is peculiarly appropriate after the introduction of fire arms and artillery in the art of war. Being immediately connected and interwoven with the description of the Reformation, and introduced after the completion of the full time of preparation of the second woe on apostate Christendom, it is not diverging from the strict and straight line of prophetic interpretation to imagine, that these successive wars, or periods of warfare, bear some reference to the Reformation to which they immediately succeed, and fill up the chasm after it, till the

* Robertson's Hist. of Charles V. vol. ii. p. 203.

time of the sitting of the judgment on the papal church, and the pouring out of the last vials of the wrath of God which *are* written or described. The number alone of the thunders is given. The time to which they referred, and the things which they uttered, as consequent on the Reformation, and associated with it, pertained to a season of peculiar light; and never perhaps in the whole history of man was there a time when the prophecies of Scripture would have been so readily held as rules of action rather than reasons of faith; and the perfection of wisdom, in respect to them, may have been, even that they were *not* written.

But as, after the mighty angel had cried, or the Reformation was established, the seven thunders uttered their voices, it *is* written in history that the Reformation was "the main and principal spring which moved the nations from that illustrious period" down to the time of another mighty revolution, which bears not the character of religious, and drew not its light from heaven. And "the civil and religious revolutions that fill the annals of history" between these most eventful eras, and of the greatest part of which the Reformation was the occasion, may perhaps, without any violence to things sacred or civil, be now viewed retrospectively, that it may be seen whether, as emanating from the Reformation, they do not, like all antecedent history, occupy their own place in the Revelation of Jesus Christ, and, exclusive of any specific definition, give palpable illustration from their origin, nature, and number, that the seven thunders which uttered their voices after the Reformation needed not to be farther written, in order that their significancy might finally be obvious without affording a seeming sanction to Christians to look on war as their calling.

In the *retrospect* of events since the Reformation, may it not therefore be warrantable to inquire, whether enough has not been written to shew, that the *thunders* dictated by the spirit of prophecy, as well as the trumpets and the woes, may not now take their place in the testimony of Jesus?

The great event that, with the intervention of a brief period of continued papal impenitence, succeeded to the taking of Constantinople, was the Reformation. The blood which it cost was on the Church of Rome and the empire of Germany. The men who were the lights of the Reformation, and who shewed no lack of boldness in a righteous cause, cherished a Christian horror of war, sought to curb the earthly passions of their more fiery associates, and though, like the men of understanding in the earliest days of the church who knew their God and instructed many, they were ready to die, yet they were not prepared to fight. The angelic likeness of the Reformation was not disfigured or destroyed by a bloody war to accomplish it. The open book was the great instrument of the godlike work.—But thunders soon began to utter their voices, and to roll successively over Christendom.—And in tracing their progress we have simply to follow history in its course, to hear the reverberation of the thunders, as well as the echo of the trumpets.

The sudden surprise of the emperor Charles V. by Maurice of Saxony, at Inspruck, led to the pacification of Passau, in 1555, without the intervention of a bloody and unseemly war. The protestants have been charged by historians with improvident forbearance, when they might have timely assaulted and defeated the army of the emperor: but the love of peace prevailed over the desire of vengeance. And the Reformation was consolidated; the free exercise of their religion was recognised and secured; and the *religious peace*, as it is commonly denominated, was established, without actually engaging in a murderous warfare, or imbruing their hands in the blood of their enemies. The Reformation was as the descent of a mighty angel from heaven—and it was altogether of *another* character and kind from the earthly commotions that had preceded it. The angel cried with a loud voice as when a lion roareth; but it was only WHEN he *had* cried—when the Reformation had first been established—that the seven thunders uttered their voices.

The pacification of Passau had not lasted long, when it was suddenly interrupted as with the voice of thunder.

"Philip II. king of Spain, apprehending the danger to which the religion of Rome was exposed from that spirit of liberty and independence which reigned in the Low Countries, took the *most violent measures* to dispel it. For this purpose he augmented the number of the bishops, enacted the most severe and barbarous laws against the innovators in religion, and erected that unjust and inhuman tribunal of the *Inquisition*, which would intimidate and tame, as he thought, the manly spirit of an oppressed and persecuted people. But his measures, in this respect, were as unsuccessful as they were absurd; his furious and intemperate zeal for the superstitions of Rome accelerated their destruction, and the papal authority, which had only been in a critical state, was reduced to a desperate one by the very steps that were designed to support it. The nobility formed themselves into an association, in the year 1566, with a view to procure the repeal of these tyrannical and barbarous edicts; but, their solicitations and request being treated with contempt, they resolved to obtain by force what they hoped to have gained by clemency and justice. They addressed themselves to a free and an abused people, spurned the authority of a cruel yoke, and *with an impetuosity and vehemence that was perhaps excessive*, trampled upon whatever was held sacred or respectable by the church of Rome. To quell these tumults a powerful army was sent from Spain under the command of the duke of Alva, *whose horrid barbarity and sanguinary proceedings kindled that* LONG AND BLOODY WAR from which the powerful republic of the United Provinces derives its origin, consistence and grandeur. It was the heroic conduct of William of Nassau, prince of Orange, seconded by the succours of England and France, that delivered this state from the Spanish yoke. And no sooner was this deliverance obtained, than the reformed religion, as it was professed in Switzerland, was established in the United Provinces: and, at the same time a universal toleration granted to those whose religious sentiments were of a different nature, whether they retained the faith of Rome, or embraced the Reformation in another form, provided still that they made no attempts against the authority of the government or the tranquillity of the public."*

In 1569 hostilities commenced between the armies of Spain and the protestants of Holland and Zealand. Such was the barbarity of the Spaniards, the desperate but unavailing defence of Haarlem was followed by the execution of two thousand of the inhabitants; and the duke of Alva boasted that, "during the course of five years, he had delivered above eighteen thousand rebellious heretics into the hands of the executioner."† But the most atrocious ferocity was met with the most desperate resolution. And siege ensued after siege, and battle followed after battle, till Spain was wearied with the contest, though the Dutch seemed repeatedly devoted to destruction. The *Union* of Utrecht in 1579, first constituted them as a nation. The alliance and aid of England revived their hopes, and divided the forces of their enemies; and, the wrathful Philip having threatened England with invasion, the peals of the first thunder, were heard in the harbours of Spain; and the defeat and dispersion of the Armada in 1588, ranked proudly, in human estimation, among the first of the bloody triumphs of Protestantism. It was not till 1606, that Holland was acknowledged as a free and independent state; and from its first rise, the thunder could not be said to cease, but with a suspension of hostilities and a truce of twelve years first entered into in the year 1607.

But the first thunder, at the same time and from the same cause, as well as in direct affinity, rolled over France with equal violence as over Holland. Under their respective leaders the prince of Condé and the duke of Guise, the Hugenots (protestants) and Catholics came to open conflict.

---

* Mosheim's Eccles. Hist. cent. xvi. chap. iv. 89.
† Hume's Hist. of England, chap. 40.

"Animosity ran high between the parties. The attendants of the duke of Guise insulted some protestants at their worship, and sixty of the latter were slain. The protestants all over France took arms; *fourteen armies* were levied in different parts of the kingdom. The conflict was carried on with the most extreme virulence. A *holy league* was formed between the courts of France and Spain: the glory of God was to be promoted, heresy in the dominions of both extirpated.—In the massacre of St. Bartholomew (August 24, 1572) no rank or age was spared; five hundred gentlemen, and ten thousand inferior persons, perished in Paris alone, and a like carnage took place in all the great towns of the kingdom.—It is computed that 60,000* persons were massacred.—At Rome and Spain the account was received with ecstasy, and public thanks returned to heaven.†

The civil and religious war in France was carried on with the most barbarous atrocity, and, according to the impartial record of Mosheim, the "contending parties committed such deeds as are yet, and always will be, remembered with horror." These dreadful commotions were at length calmed in the year 1598;—at which period liberty of conscience, full toleration, and the enjoyment of all civil rights and privileges, were secured to the protestants by the celebrated edict of Nantz, passed by Henry IV., who, although he gave up his faith for a kingdom, maintained the rights which he conferred on the protestants.

The memorable "thirty years war," formed throughout Europe another thunder, or continued season of warfare, from 1618 to 1648, and was terminated by the celebrated treaty of Westphalia. During this period the war was renewed between Spain and Holland, and was carried on as before with unrelenting barbarity, and unyielding perseverance. At the commencement of the same period, or rather in the following year 1619, the Bohemians

* Sully estimates the number at 70,000.
† Outlines of Hist. pp. 341, 343.

having elected a protestant king, incurred the wrath of the emperor, and the Austrians and Bavarians ravaged their territories with the most unrelenting and rapacious barbarity. But some of the protestant princes of Germany "confederated" anew; and, aided by the king of Denmark, withstood both the papal and imperial power. In 1629, "the emperor Frederick II., issued the terrible *restitution-edict*, by which the protestants were ordered to restore to the church of Rome all the possessions they had become masters of in consequence of the *religious peace*, concluded in the preceding century." The *thunder* extended over inland Europe. Contests for the faith became scenes of carnage, when the long-suffering and righteous strife of principle, in which the primitive Christians were ready to die but not prepared to slay, and could learn to look on no blood but their own, was contaminated by the unholy union of a strife for property, in the defence of which an arm of flesh was lifted up to kill; and heroes of another order took the field in the cause of the Reformation, than those who fought its first and most glorious battles, with no other weapon than the sword of the Spirit; and who, like the mighty angel that then had come down from heaven, held nothing but the little open book in their hands. Gustavus Adolphus, the king of Sweden, clad in human armour, and at the head of his armies, became the hero of the Reformation, and maintained its cause, linked as then it was to worldly politics, on many a bloody plain, till he fell, (in the battle of Lutzan 1632,) more like a warrior than a martyr. Yet battle followed after battle, like peal after peal, till the second thunder ceased; the peace of Europe was at last restored in 1648 by the famous treaty of Westphalia, by which the rights of protestantism were defined and established on a sure and permanent basis.

"After a war of thirty years, carried on with the most unrelenting animosity and ardour, the wounds of Germany were closed, and the drooping states of Europe were revived by the peace of Westphalia, so called from the cities of Munster and Osnaburg, where the negotiations were held, and that famous treaty concluded. The Protestants obtained from this peace privileges and advantages which the votaries of Rome beheld with much displeasure and uneasiness; and it is unquestionably evident that the treaty of Westphalia gave a new and remarkable degree of stability to the Lutheran and reformed churches in Germany. By this treaty the peace of Augsburg, which the Lutherans had obtained from Charles V. in the preceding century, was finally secured against all the machinations and stratagems of the court of Rome; by it the *Restitution edict*, which commanded the Protestants to restore to the Romish church the ecclesiastical revenues and lands they had taken possession of after that peace, was abrogated, and both the contending parties confirmed in the perpetual and uninterrupted possession of whatever they had occupied in the year 1624. The treaty was executed in all its parts; and all the articles that had been agreed upon at Munster and Osnaburg were confirmed and ratified, in the year 1650, at Nuremburg."*

In the same year in which the peace of Westphalia was concluded, the civil wars in Britain ceased; and the dark thunder-cloud that hung upon the sea was dissipated, together with those that had long rested on Europe. The Protestant and Catholic nations, exhausted with war, sunk again into repose; and the second thunder was past. But before its close, the Irish massacre (in 1641) left not that of St. Bartholomew unrivalled in bloody and ferocious cruelty.

Neither the wars between France and Spain, originating in court intrigue, and in which the opposite factions were headed by two cardinals, De Retz and Mazarin, nor the contests for territory or power between the Swedes, the Poles, and the Russians, nor yet the maritime war between Britain and Holland, springing from commercial jealousy, maintained the character or attained the magnitude of the thunders

* Mosheim, cent. xvi. chap. i. § 7.

that began to utter their voices after the Reformation. But the dark cloud that soon again covered the hemisphere, and burst in thunder over Europe, rending the air and shaking the earth, arose in France with the rising ambition of Louis XIV. He exercised all the tyranny of the state, and sought to let loose again the tyranny of the church. The unnatural union of France and of England, under the reign of the reckless Charles II., against Protestant Holland, threatened, of itself, to rise into a thunder; but the clouds were dissipated by the winds of heaven.

"The combined fleets, with an army on board, approached the coast of Holland. In a manner almost miraculous, they were carried out to sea, and afterwards prevented from landing their forces by violent storms. Those who regarded this as the interference of Providence cannot justly be accused of superstition."*

The invasion of Holland, the persecution of Protestants, and the revocation of the edict of Nantz by Louis XIV., were the preludes to that general war to which the name of another thunder too appropriately pertains.

"In the ignorance of his bigotry, he revoked the edict of Nantz, treated his Protestant subjects with all the injustice and cruelty that blind fanaticism could dictate, and thereby lost to France thousands of industrious citizens, who augmented the wealth and *armies of his enemies*. A league was formed at Augsburg, to restrain the encroachments of France. Spain and Holland joined it, as also did Denmark, Sweden, and Savoy, and finally England, now governed by William."†

The edict of Nantz was revoked in the year 1685. The league of Augsburg was formed in 1687; and the following year was the era of the glorious, and no less glorious because bloodless, revolution; from

---

* Outlines of Hist. p. 379. † Ibid. p. 383.

which period England took the lead in the cause of Protestantism.

"Louis assembled two large armies in Flanders; a third was opposed to the Spaniards in Catalonia; another entered and ravaged the Palatinate in a most barbarous and fiendish manner." "Twice during the reign of Louis XIV. was this fine country desolated by the arms of France; but the flames lighted by Jurenne, however dreadful, were only like so many torches, compared with the present frightful conflagration which filled all Europe with horror."*

The bloody war continued with varied success till 1697, when it was terminated by the peace of Ryswick. And

"scarcely had the emperor acceded to the treaty of Ryswick which re-established tranquillity in the north and west of Europe, when he received intelligence of the total defeat of the Turks, by his arms, at Zenta, in the kingdom of Hungary. Thus was *general tranquillity* restored once more in Europe. But the seeds of future discord were already sown in every corner of Christendom. It was but a delusive calm before a more violent storm."†

The third thunder, though all in the brief interval was *calm*, was rapidly succeeded by the fourth, to which the name of Marlborough is the ready index, and in the course of which the power of Louis was shattered as if by quick repeated strokes of lightning, and his ambition was prostrated in the dust, where all earthly glory must lie.

In the year 1701 "the grand Alliance" was formed against France: and, to adopt the shortest memoir of the murderous strife, "from the year 1702 to 1711, the reign of Louis XIV. was one continued series of defeats and calamities."‡ In 1713, peace was concluded at Utrecht between France, England, Portu-

* Russel's Hist. of Modern Europe, vol. ii. p. 519.
† Ibid. pp. 537, 538.
‡ Encyclop. Brit, art. *France*.

gal, the United Provinces, Prussia, and Savoy; and in the following year, at Rastadt, between Germany and Spain. Charles XII., "the madman Swede," who would not otherwise have ceased from warfare, was at that very period a prisoner in the hands of the Turks. And "Europe rested from war."*

The incessant warfare and desperate battles by which Marlborough was the instrument of humbling Louis, quashed for a time the love of war; and, from 1714 to 1739, there followed, as marked in history, "a period of comparative repose."† Alliances were formed for the preservation of peace, which was only partially interrupted and speedily restored. The pragmatic sanction, regulating the right of female succession to the imperial throne, and the disputed possession of Sardinia, were the chief objects of controversy, which did not immediately involve such principles or interests as to excite a general war, or to rouse another prophetic thunder throughout Europe. But, before the middle of that century, which had speedily introduced a history of blood, Europe was again in arms, and had witnessed another thunder. In 1739 war was declared by Great Britain against Spain, and in 1744 against France. The battles of Dettingen and Fontenoy are not forgotten in Britain. In 1740 the death of Charles VI., and the succession of Maria Theresa, laid Germany open to invasion. "Treaties of spoliation and division" became the pastime of the German and European princes. The wars of Frederick the Great began. Britons, Prussians, Dutch, Austrians, Bohemians, Bavarians, Silesians, Hanoverians, Sardinians, Spaniards, and Italians, all mingled in the warfare. And no calm was interposed till the year 1748, when peace was

* Outlines of History, p. 390. † Ibid. p. 393, title.

concluded by the treaty of Aix-la-Chapelle. A thunder-cloud passed over Britain at the time.*

The sixth thunder is defined by "the seven years' war," commencing in 1755 and concluding in the beginning of 1763. The battle of Minden, the siege of Quebec and the death of Wolfe, the taking of Belleisle, the capture of Guadalope, the Havannah, and Martinique, are memorials of it in Britain that come within the recollection of the aged. The Protestant countries of Prussia and Britain stood against a confederacy of Continental kingdoms. And America, as well as Europe, became the scene of contests, where Protestants and Catholics maintained their distinctive and discordant creeds, no less than in Britain and in France.

"England obtained all Canada, and the islands of St. John and Cape Breton, great part of Louisiana, her conquests on the Senegal, the island of Grenada: all her other conquests she restored. Prussia and Austria agreed to place themselves on the same footing they were on at the commencement of hostilities. Thus ended the seven years' war,—a war which had caused such an effusion of blood and treasure: it ended without being productive of any real advantage to any one of the parties. Europe now reposed from war."*

History is not, perhaps, greatly in fault, if, in recording wars and their desolations, it sometimes omits the mention of their benefits. And though the work of warriors be often the most fruitless of labours, as some may reckon it not the least pernicious, yet diplomatists are not always forgetful to mingle the seeds of war with treaties of peace. The interests of the greatest of Protestant and of Catholic countries were soon to be contended for anew; and the world was not long altogether ignorant how the gain of Canada by Britain might possibly be connected with the loss of America.

---

* Outlines of History, p. 408.

Europe did not repose long from war: nor did the last of the seven thunders make long delay in uttering its voice. The seven years' war terminated in 1763; in 1775 the North American war began; France declared war against Britain in 1778. The next season Spain followed her example; and in 1780, Holland was added to the enemies of England. The Spanish, the Dutch, and French fleets were defeated. Gibraltar was besieged in vain. But in another seven years' war, the Americans, after an arduous contest, maintained their independence; the troops of Cornwallis surrendered, as prisoners of war, to the French and Americans commanded by Washington, and in 1782 the American war was ended. If a jewel fell from the crown of Britannia, it soon glittered on the brow of the best child of her hope,—her eldest daughter.* And though the benefits of war be often looked for in vain, yet the blessings of the Reformation, after which the first of the seven thunders began, may yet be seen, half a century after the conclusion of the last of them, by looking to America alone, in the striking contrast between its Northern and Southern States, and the opposite effects that have followed their respective independence. The book that was held in the angel's hand is open in the one region, and shut in the other. But lately there were only three Bibles in Lima, the capital of one of the States of South America; while in one of the States in the North three houses could scarcely be found in which a Bible is wanting.

And the angel which I saw stand upon the sea and upon the earth, lifted up his hand to heaven, and sware by him that liveth for ever and ever, who created heaven and the things that therein are, and the

* A jewel fell from the crown on the coronation of George III. It has been named America.

earth, and the things that therein are, and the sea, and the things which are therein, that there should be time (delay) no longer: But in the days of the voice of the seventh angel, when he shall begin to sound, the mystery of God should be finished, as he hath declared to his servants the prophets,—ver. 5, 6, 7. Express reference seems here to be made to that which, in a manner exactly similar, was declared unto Daniel, as we read in the close of his prophecies. "But thou, O Daniel, shut up the words and seal the book, even to the time of the end: many shall run to and fro, and knowledge shall be increased. Then I Daniel looked, and behold, there stood other two, the one on this side of the bank of the river. And one said to the man clothed in linen, which was upon the waters of the river, How long (shall it be) to the end of these wonders? And I heard the man clothed in linen, which was upon the waters of the river, *when he held up his right hand and his left unto heaven, and sware by him that liveth for ever and ever, that (it shall be) for a time, times, and an half;* and when he shall have accomplished to scatter the power of the holy people, all these things shall be finished. And I looked, but I understood not: then said I, what (shall be) the end of these things? And he said, Go thy way, Daniel, for the words are closed up and sealed till the *time* of the end. Many shall be purified, and made white, and tried; but the wicked shall do wickedly; and none of the wicked shall understand, but the wise shall understand. And from the time that the daily sacrifice shall be taken away, and the abomination that maketh desolate set up, there shall be a thousand two hundred and ninety days. Blessed is he that waiteth and cometh to the thousand three hundred and five and thirty days. But go thy way till the end be: for thou shalt rest, and stand in thy lot at the end of the days,"—Dan. xii. 4—13.

In the Book of Daniel and of the Revelation it is

thus apparent that events on earth were to succeed the period, concerning which the angel, in lifting up his hand to heaven, sware that time shall be no more,—or as the words may be rendered, there shall be no more delay. As declared unto Daniel, the express time is conjoined with the *time*, *times*, and half a *time*, the exact period, as defined in the same words, during which the saints of the Most High would be given into the hand of the papal power,—Dan. vii. 25. In reference to these times, with which the solemn angelic asseveration is conjoined, there should then be *time* no more. The point in history where they were to terminate, seems in like manner to be fixed as subsequent, without a long intervening delay, to the close of the seven thunders.

Each event, in prophecy as in history, throughout a long range of time, naturally leads, as the forerunner, to that which follows it. Thus we may trace the connexion between the Persian and Grecian empires, and the last remains of the Grecian, in Syria and Egypt, with the introduction of the Roman. The Vandals were united with the Goths in the first storm that fell upon the western empire. The Huns leagued with the Vandals, and the confederacy of Italy, which was formed where Attila *fell*, subverted the empire of Rome. The exaltation of the papacy on the ruins of imperial Rome, brought down the *first woe* on idolatrous Christendom; Mahometanism arose at the time when transgressors came to the full. And, uniting the second to the first, the caliph girded the sultan with the sword. The Reformation was the descent of an angel from heaven, and took not its rise from any earthly commotions, yet it came at the time when corruption was full, and when the *rest* of Europe, that was not hurt by them, would not learn repentance from *woes*.

The same natural sequence is marked in the history of the thunders as in that of the trumpets and woes. And in like manner, the last of the thunders was the first of the revolutionary wars, and introduced a new era into the world. Trumpets had sounded over the Roman empire; and the voice of the last was the requiem of imperial Rome. The progress of the first woe, and the preparation of the second, when that time was fully come, dissolved the eastern empire, and turned the city of Constantine into the metropolis of Mahometanism. The seven thunders successively shook the mighty fabric of Catholicism; and when these had ended—there was to be time no more—the period was drawn to a olose, and about to be fulfilled, when the saints should no longer be given into the hands of an idolatrous and persecuting church—but the sounding of the seventh trumpet was announced, and the time was come when the judgment was to sit, the last vials to be poured out, and the papal kingdom to be consumed and destroyed unto the end. But no definition of the length of the time is here given; that is otherwise repeatedly told. Yet the connexion, in regard to civil history, seems to be marked between the expiry of the thunders, and, when the time of papal dominancy would be no more, the outpouring of the seven last vials of the wrath of God. It is the succession of *events* that has here to be regarded, and the time of passing from one series of wars to another, yet more momentous and appalling. We are brought to the brink of the French revolution, and may not be far from that point of vision in the march of time where the judgments of God are *manifest*. In the days of the voice of the seventh angel when he shall *begin* to sound, the *mystery* of God shall be finished, as he hath declared unto his servants the prophets.

And the voice which I heard from heaven spake unto me AGAIN, *and said, go and take the little book which is open in the hand of the angel, which standeth upon the sea and upon the earth. And I went unto the angel, and said unto him, Give me the little book. And he said unto me, Take it, and eat it up; and it shall make thy belly bitter, but it shall be in thy mouth sweet as honey. And I took the little book out of the angel's hand, and ate it up; and it was in my mouth sweet as honey: and as soon as I had eaten it, my belly was bitter. And he said unto me, Thou must prophecy again before many peoples, and nations, and tongues, and kings.*—Ver. 8, &c.

The voice of the angel who commanded John to seal up those things which the seven thunders uttered, and to write them not, spake unto him again, and told him to take the little book. The angel who held it commanded him to eat it up. Ezekiel was enjoined by an angel to eat a roll or book, who said unto him also, All the words that I shall speak unto thee, *receive in thine heart, and hear with thine ear,*—Ezek. iii. 1, 10. "Thy words were *found,*" says Jeremiah (xv. 16,) "and I did eat them; and thy *word* was unto me *the joy and rejoicing of my heart.*" John was commanded *not* to write; but it was given unto him to see and understand the vision. By his own word, recorded in scripture, we know that he was a man who had no greater joy than to hear that his children walked in truth. And it was as *honey in his mouth* to *know*, that after an age of darkness, the truths of the gospel would again be proclaimed, and the scriptures be *open* to the world. But the message that he had heard from the beginning was, that we should love one another. His epistles teem with Christian charity, in a manner which shows the spirit of the man, who bore the testimony of Jesus. And though, when he *tasted* the good word of God, and knew the meaning of the descent of the angel from heaven, it was sweet to his heart as honey in the mouth; yet, whenever he knew the ungodly rancour to which, from the wickedness of men, the Reformation would give birth, the murderous wars that would ensue, and the fierce animosity and "mutual barbarities" which even protestant historians cannot record without sorrow, grief soon succeeded to his joy; and as soon as he had eaten or understood it, *his belly was bitter*, his heart was afflicted. The cause of protestantism, it must be confessed, has not always been maintained with the Christian spirit of forbearance and love. And many a ponderous volume might supply the painful proof, that, even between protestants, in their schisms and contentions, the breaking and tearing of the bond of peace was enough to disgust and grieve the man who chose Christian love for the theme on which he dwelt so fondly, as soon as he saw and understood how Jesus, on whose bosom he had leaned, was thus wounded again in the house of his friends. Too often, it may be feared, have wrangling polemics illustrated its significancy, without understanding *the sign. It was in my mouth sweet as honey; and as soon as I had eaten it, my belly was bitter.*

And he said unto me, thou must prophecy AGAIN *before many peoples, and nations, and tongues, and kings.* Hitherto the prophecy was continuous, from the opening of the seventh seal, to the close of the seventh thunder; and the line of history was unbroken from the rise of the Goths, preparatory to the downfall of the Roman empire, to the last great event that preceded the grand revolution of modern times. But it is announced to the apostle that he must prophecy *again*,—intimating a new order, or course of predictions.

It is not the purpose of the writer to attempt a

full exposition of the Book of Revelation on many parts of which, he thinks, that history will yet throw a much fuller light. But in allusion to what appears to be already past, he deems it in some degree essential to touch briefly on the intermediate visions, recorded previously to the pouring out of the last seven vials. The thunders were *not* written: nor, in the previous prediction, was their duration, or the period of their ceasing, marked. And, as dates abound in the succeeding visions, we must look to what John prophesied again, if thereby the connexion may be established between events and their *times*, without which accordance the interpretation given to the seven thunders, would want the confirmation it may possibly receive from a comparison with other predictions. And thus, more than by any explanatory words, it may perhaps be ascertained, by the farther developement which still later histories may give to other visions of the prophet, how, or in what sense, after the seven thunders, which were manifestly to be succeeded by other events, *had* uttered their voices, it might be clear, as by the oath of an angel, what *time* would be no longer, or how there would be no longer delay.

CHAPTER XXI.

After the religious and political state of the world had separately or respectively been traced down for many ages, it was given unto John to prophecy *again.* But in commencing the immediately subsequent prophecies, or intermediate visions, the subject of them is, in the very first instance, so clearly defined that they needed not to be written in another book, but in that alone of the Revelation of Jesus Christ.

And there was given me a reed like unto a rod: and the angel stood, saying, Rise, and measure the temple of God, and the altar, and them that worship therein. But the court which is without the temple leave out and measure it not; for it is given unto the Gentiles: and the holy city shall they tread under foot forty and two months, chap. xi. 1, 2. The subject of the prediction is thus limited to the Christian church, whether nominally, or the *temple of God* (in which, as the Spirit speaketh expressly, he who exalteth and opposeth himself above all that is called God, was to sit) or the altar, the more sacred part of the temple, and those that worship therein, would seem to comprehend and include all that pertains to the professedly Christian church. But the court which was without the temple was *left out* and *not measured.* It was given to the Gentiles, to the nations of the earth; and they were to tread down the holy city forty and two months. The holy city seems here manifestly to be comprehended in the portion that was not measured; even as the *glorious land* is described by Daniel as included among the *countries* that were given unto the Turks, who were Gentiles. The very expressions are also used in which Christ foretold that Jerusalem was *to be trodden down of the Gentiles.* And while the Christian church formed the very subject of the prediction, that portion of the earth, on the other hand, which was given unto the heathen, or had permanently fallen under the dominion of the Saracens, and subsequently and more especially of the Turks, whose career had already been so fully detailed, was excluded from the present or renewed prophesying.

The first object that is presented to the view of the prophet within the church, or temple, is the prophesying of the two witnesses. *And I will give power unto my two witnesees, and they shall prophesy a thousand two hundred and threescore days, clothed in sackcloth*, ver. 3.—The saints of the Most High were to be given into the hands of the papal power, for a time, times, and the dividing of time; and as he who was to speak great words against the most High, was to wear out the saints, so also were the witnesses to prophesy in sackcloth.

These are the two olive trees, and the two candlesticks, standing before the Lord of the whole earth, ver. 4. Of Israel, as a church, it is said, "The Lord called thy name a green *olive tree*, fair, and of goodly fruit." Jer. xi. 16. The same term is applied by Zechariah to the faithful witnesses of the Christian church.—"Behold I will bring forth my servant the branch; and he said unto me, what seest thou? and I said, Behold a *candlestick* all of gold, and *two olive trees* by it. Then answered I and said unto him, what are these two olive trees upon the right side of the candlestick and upon the left side thereof? And I answered again and said unto him, what be these two olive branches which, through the two golden pipes, empty the golden oil out of themselves? And he answered and said, These are the two anointed ones, that stand by the Lord of the whole earth," c. i. 8, c. ii. 2, 3, 11, 14. The *two candlesticks* are two Christian *churches*, even as the Lord Jesus Christ did say unto John, "The seven candlesticks which thou sawest are the seven churches." Rev. i. 20.

There never have been wanting faithful *witnesses* of Jesus, who, in the spirit of faith, and in the strength of the Lord, have maintained the character and preserved the pureness and unity of the churches of Christ. In the long night of darkness, the Vaudois, or the Waldenses,* and the Albigenses—the former deriving their name from the valleys of Piedmont, and the latter from Albi, a town in the province of Toulouse—who were jointly known by the name of Leonists, and were also called Catherins, from the *purity* of their lives, and Paterins, from the severity of their *sufferings*,—were, as churches, stedfast in the faith, the candlesticks of Christendom, and lighted up the wilderness, while gross darkness rested on the world.

In proof of the purity of the doctrine of the Vaudois, and the integrity of their lives, we need not appeal even to Roman Catholic authorities, seeing that direct reference may at once be made to the testimony of an inquisitor-general, whose confession assimilates to that of Judas, though without his compunction. Such was the greatness of the mystery of iniquity and deceivableness of unrighteousness, that the hand which shed their blood wrote down their innocence, without adding that the act was murder.

" Among all the sects which still are or have been, there is not any more pernicious to the church than that of Leonists. And this for three reasons. The first is, because it is *older*; for some say that it hath endured from the time of Pope Sylvester, (fourth century,) others, from the time of the apostles. The second, because it is more general, for there is scarce any country wherein the sect is not. The third, because when all other sects beget horror in the hearers by the outrageousness of their blasphemies against God, this of the Leonists hath *a great shew of piety; because they live justly before men, and believe all things rightly concerning God, and all the articles which are contained in*

---

* 'The ancient official seal of the Waldensian Church represents a lamp or candle diffusing rays of light over a surrounding field of darkness. See Sims. Leger,' &c. *History of the Church of Christ*, vol. 3, p. 375.

the creed; only they blaspheme the church of Rome and the clergy; whom the multitude of the laity is easy to believe.*

"The causes of their estrangement from his church are thus singularly stated: 'It is because the men and women, the young and old, the labourer and the learned man, do not cease to instruct themselves; because they have translated the Old and New Testaments into the vulgar tongue, and learn these books by heart and teach them; because if scandal be committed by any one, it inspires them with horror, so that when they see any one leading an irregular life, they say to him, the apostles did not live so, nor should we who would imitate the apostles: in short, they look upon all that a teacher advances, unsupported by the New Testament, as fabulous."†

Reinerius, (as his testimony is quoted by Fox,) farther states that some of them could recite "the whole New Testament perfectly by heart," and that there were forty schools in the single parish (parœcia) of Cammach.‡ The Roman Catholic historians, Thuanus and Mezeray, cited by Newton, bear similar testimony to the purity of their doctrine. Of the Albigenses, Sismondi bears this decisive testimony, "In the exposition made by the bishop of Tournay, of the *errors* of the Albigenses, we find nearly all the principles upon which Luther and Calvin founded the reformation of the sixteenth century."* "The Paterins, the Waldenses, the Albigenses, had spread their instructions throughout all the countries which had been comprised in the western empire."§

The history of the Vaudois and the Albigenses has lately excited a renewed interest throughout Europe, as well as in Britain, to which the pen of the celebrated Sismondi has not slightly contributed. A Christian sympathy and generous interest have been roused in England on their behalf, by Acland's brief history of the Valdenses, and Gilly's Narrative

---

* Reinerius con. Heret. cap. 4. quoted by Usher, Cave, Bishop Newton, &c.

† H. D. Acland's Hist. of the Vaudois, p. 6.

‡ Fox's Martyrology, fol. p. 610. § Sismondi's Hist. p. 116.

of an excursion to the Mountains of Piedmont. Farther researches may yet disclose more abundant facts to complete the memoirs of the sufferings and virtues of the witnesses. Yet while the purity of their doctrine and the integrity of their lives may be held confessed on the word of an arch persecutor, the annals of the vatican, and the records of the inquisition, are as full of evidence corroborative of the testimony of Jesus, as any book written by an infidel, and amply illustrate the severity of the persecution of the saints, to which though our limits preclude detail, some slight allusion may here be made, in a combined view of corresponding predictions.

The witnesses were *clothed in sackcloth.* The little horn of the fourth beast, or the papal power, *was to wear out the saints of the Most High. The men of understanding were to fall, to try them, and to purge, and to make them white to the time of the end: because it is yet for a time appointed.* It is the character of the brethren of Jesus that *they loved not their lives unto the death. The great whore that sitteth upon many waters was drunken with the blood of the saints, and with the blood of the martyrs of Jesus.* Rev. xvii. 6. (See table).

The persecution, even unto the death, that the saints of the Most High and the witnesses of Jesus were to endure, is a matter of the plainest prediction: and there is no need for searching into any secret records to discover the proof; for this thing was not done in a corner. The design of papal persecution was to extirpate heresy; and the most savage torture of the martyrs was, with that intent, exhibited openly. The gospel of Jesus inculcates brotherly love, and even the love of our enemies. But the time was, while it was hid, that the stake was a scene round which the persecutors exulted with joy, and shouted with transport at each cry of the expiring victims. The history of papal persecutions leads us far beyond the period of the dawn of the Reformation; and so *drunken with blood* was the church of Rome, that the reign of the *bloody* Mary, by which they are best known in Britain, appears but as the sprinkling of a few drops from a large cup already full to the brim.

Heretics and heathens were involved, according to the papal creed, in the same condemnation. And when the perils of the desert and the sabres of the Saracens had somewhat quashed the frenzied spirit of military crusading for the recovery and possession of the Holy Land, absolution was held forth at the cheaper rate and safer charge of extirpating heresy *within* the precincts of Christendom. A new order of holy wars was proclaimed. And by the authority of the pope, the monks of Citeaux, with a zeal outrivalling that of Peter the hermit, the great preacher of the Palestine war, proclaimed a crusade against the Albigenses. In the year 1208, "in the name of the pope and of the apostles St. Peter and St. Paul, they promised to all who should perish in this holy expedition plenary absolution of all sins committed from the day of their birth to that of their death."* A campaign of forty days, in so holy a cause, was reckoned, by papal infallibility, merit enough to secure eternal salvation. "Bull after bull was fulminated from the court of Rome. And never had the cross been taken up with a more unanimous consent." "The immense preparations resounded throughout Europe, and filled Languedoc with terror."†

The preaching of a crusade against the saints of the Most High, was combined with the invention and

---

* Sismondi's Hist. of the Crusades against the Albigenses, p. 24. The history of the Crusades against the Albigenses has been extracted from Sismondi's History of the French, and translated into English in separate volumes.

† Ibid. p. 25.

active agency of the inquisition, in wearing them out. While one class of monks preached in every church a war of extermination, year after year another, with father Dominic at their head, who gave rise to the order of the Dominicans, searched out in every village the victims of papal tyranny, and the fires of the inquisition were added to all the horrors of a war, of which the barbarous atrocity never was exceeded. A few extracts from the pages of Sismondi, in depicting the cruelties of which the crusade against the Albigenses was full, will shew, beyond the wish of any heart that can be touched with humanity, how war was made with the saints, how the witnesses were clothed with sackcloth, how the churchmen of Rome sought to wear them out, and yet how they loved not their lives unto the death. Though the slaughter was often indiscriminate, the witnesses were first sought out before the crusade began, and the malignant ingenuity of demons was added to the most savage ferocity of men.

"While the Bernardins were recruiting soldiers for the cross, Innocent III. charged a new congregation, (at the head of which he placed the Spaniard saint Dominic,) to go on foot two by two through the villages, to preach the faith in the midst of them, to enlighten them by controversial discussions, to display to them all the zeal of Christian charity, and to obtain from their confidence exact information as to the number and dwellings of those who had wandered from the church, in order to burn them when the opportunity should arrive. Thus began the order of the preaching brethren of St. Dominic, or of the inquisitors."*

These apostles of the inquisition, though going out two by two, differed as much from the first preachers of the gospel of peace, as the fanatic robbers who were the apostles of Mahomet. Yet they were but the fit heralds, or rather the blood-hounds of the *war*

* Sismondi's History of the Crusades against the Albigenses, pp. 24, 25.

against the saints which, close upon their footsteps, pursued their tract.

"As the crusade approached, the bishop of Beziers delivered to the legate of the pope a list of those among his flock whom he suspected of heresy, and wished to see consigned to the flames. The citizens refused to surrender them to the avengers of the faith, notwithstanding that the assemblage of the tents and pavilions of the crusaders was so great, that it appeared as if the world was collected there. All the inhabitants of the country had taken refuge in Beziers. The city was taken. The immense multitude were massacred in the churches, whither they had fled; seven thousand dead bodies were counted in that of the Magdalen alone. When the crusaders had massacred the last living creature in Beziers, and pillaged the houses of all that they had thought worth carrying off, they set fire to the city in every part at once, and reduced it to a vast funeral pile. Not a house remained standing, not one human being alive. Historians differ as to the number of victims. The abbot of Citeaux, feeling some shame for the butchery which he had ordered, in his letter to Innocent III. *reduces* it to fifteen thousand, others make it amount to sixty."* "The legate was profoundly penetrated with the maxim of Innocent III., that *to keep faith with those who have it not*, is an offence against faith." In the siege and assault of Lavaur, 'the bishops, the abbot of Courdieu, who exercised the functions of vice-legate, and all the priests, clothed with their pontifical habits, giving themselves up to the joy of seeing the carnage begin, sang the hymn *Veni Creator*. The knights mounted the breach. Resistance was impossible; and the only care of Simon de Montfort was to prevent the crusaders from instantly falling upon the inhabitants, and to beseech them rather to make prisoners, that the priests of the living God *might not be deprived of their promised joys*. Our pilgrims,' continues the monk of Vaux-Cernay, 'collected the innumerable heretics that the castle contained, and *burned them alive with the utmost joy*. In Bernard's life of Innocent III. their number is stated at 400.† The castle of Montjoyre was abandoned, but burned by the crusaders. The castle of Cassero afforded them more satisfaction, as it furnished human victims for their sacrifices. It was surrendered on capitulation; *and the pilgrims, seizing nearly sixty heretics, burned them with infinite joy*. This was always the phrase employed by the monk who was the witness and the panegyrist of the crusade.‡

"One of the articles of the capitulation of the castle of Minerva provided, that the heretics themselves, if they were converted,

---

* Sismondi's History of the Crusades against the Albigenses, pp. 34—37.

† Ibid. pp. 76, 77. ‡ Ibid. p. 78.

might quit the castle and have their lives saved. When the capitulation was read in the council of war, 'Robert of Mauvoisin,' says the monk of Vaux-Cernay, 'a nobleman, and entirely devoted to the Catholic faith, cried, that the pilgrims would never consent to that; that it was not to shew mercy to the heretics, but to put them to death, they had taken the cross.' But the Abbot Arnold replied, 'fear not, for I believe that there will be very few converted.' The legate was not deceived in this bloody hope. The crusaders took possession of the castle of Minerva on the 22d July, 1210; they entered, singing *Te Deum*, and preceded by the cross and the standards of Montfort. The heretics were, in the mean time, assembled, the men in one house, the women in another, and there on their knees, and resigned to their fate, they prepared themselves, by prayer, for the punishment that awaited them. The abbot Guy de Faux-Cernay, to fulfil the capitulation, came and began to preach to them the catholic faith; but his auditors interrupted him by an unanimous cry—'We will have none of your faith,' said they, 'we have renounced the church of Rome, your labour is vain; for neither death nor life shall make us renounce the opinions that we have embraced.' The abbot then passed to the assembly of the women, but he found them as resolute and more enthusiastic still in their declarations. The count of Montfort, in his turn, visited both. Already he had piled up an enormous mass of dry wood. 'Be converted to the catholic faith,' said he to the assembled Albigenses, 'or ascend this pile.' None were shaken. They set fire to the pile, which covered the whole square with a tremendous conflagration. And the heretics were then conducted to the place. But violence was not necessary to compel them to enter the flames; they voluntarily precipitated themselves into them, to the number of one hundred and forty, after having commended their souls to God, in whose cause they suffered martyrdom."*

They loved not their lives unto the death; but the church of Rome *was drunken with the blood of the saints.*

"Innocent III., at first, excited the *sanguinary* spirit which then lorded it over Europe. It was but too true that the whole of Christendom then demanded the renewal of those scenes of carnage, that it prided itself on the *slaughter of the heretics*, that it was in the name of public opinion that the fathers of Lavaur required new massacres.† Kings, nobles, priests, and people

---

* Sismondi's History of the Crusades against the Albigenses, pp. 64, 65.

† Ibid. p. 95.

were all agreed in thinking that heretics must be destroyed with fire and sword.* No calculation can ascertain, with any precision, the dissipation of wrath, or the destruction of human life, which were the consequences of the crusade against the Albigenses. There was scarcely a peasant who did not reckon in his family some unhappy one, whose life had been cut off by the sword of Montfort's soldiers; not one but had repeatedly witnessed the ravaging of his property by them. Simon de Montfort was to them *the representation of the evil spirit;* the prototype of all the persecutions they had endured.† The number of the slain, in France alone, has been computed at a million."‡

They MADE WAR *with the saints, and prevailed against them.*

"Raymond VII., count of Toulouse, was compelled to promise that he would henceforth *make war* against all those who had remained faithful to him; and that he would pay to every individual who should arrest a heretic two marks for each of his subjects who might be carried before the tribunals."§

It was with the *saints* that they made war.

"The heretics supported *their doctrines by the authority of the Holy Scriptures;* the *first* indication of heresy was, therefore, considered to be *the citation either of the epistles or the gospels;* secondly, any exhortation *against lying;* and, finally, any *signs of compassion* shown to the prisoners of the inquisition. The council of Toulouse (held in November, 1229) for the first time decided, that the reading of the holy books should not be permitted to the people. 'We prohibit,' says the fourteenth canon, p. 430, 'the laics from having the books of the Old and New Testaments; unless it be at most that any one wishes to have, from devotion, a psalter, a breviary for the divine offices, or the honour of the blessed Mary; but we forbid them in the most express manner to have the above books translated into the vulgar tongue."‖

"But that which perhaps exceeded all the other calamities of the Albigenses was the establishment of the inquisition. The only expedient for maintaining the unity of the faith which the

* Sismondi's History of the Crusades against the Albigenses, p. 208. † Ibid. pp. 128, 129.

‡ Mede, in Apoc. p. 503. § Sismondi, p. 218.

‖ Labbei Consil. Tolosan. tom. v. p. 1784—1786, et seq. Flewry, Hist. Eccles. liv. lxxix. n. 58. Vide Sismondi, p. 227.

church has ever known, was to burn those who separated from it. For two hundred years the fires had been kindled, yet every day Catholics abandoned the faith of their fathers to embrace that which must conduct them to the flames."*

The Vaudois, in the secluded valleys of the mountains of Piedmont, were subjected to a like relentless persecution. The inquisition was established at Turin, the capital of the Duke of Savoy. In spots where a scanty subsistence could only be procured by laborious industry, papal tyranny sought out its victims. There every house was a house of prayer; in every family there was an altar for the worship of God, but in none was an image to be found; every child was instructed in the knowledge of Jesus, and fed with the bread of life, and they would not worship the consecrated wafer as a God; they looked on life as a time of purifying, and disowned all faith in purgatory. The craft of the priest was in danger. And the purer that was the doctrine, and the holier the lives of the witnesses of Jesus, the more surely were they *clothed in sackcloth*, and the churchmen of Rome, thirsting for their *blood*, would not be satiated till they were *drunken* with it. The emissaries of the inquisition, at first sought out their victims, who were either immured in the dungeons of Turin, and secretly tortured, or publicly executed, to intimidate heretics. But to quote the words of M. Acland,

"This was a process too slow and too partial to satisfy the unrelenting fury of the church of Rome. Bull after bull, and army after army, issued forth to the devastation of the valleys, the spirit of which may be collected from the following specimen. In 1477, Innocent VIII. having commented on the heresies of the Vaudois, commands all archbishops, bishops, vicars, &c. to obey his inquisitor, to render him assistance, and to engage the people to take up arms, with a view to so *holy and necessary an extermination*. Accordingly, he granted indulgences to all who would make a crusade against the Vaudois, and full authority to

---

* Labbei Consil. Tolosan. tom. v. p. 1784—1786, et seq. Flewry, Hist. Eccles. liv. lxxix. n. 58. Vide Sismondi, p. 246.

apply to their own use whatsoever property they could seize. Animated by these spiritual and temporal stimulants, 18,000 regular troops, and 600 uncommanded vagabonds burst upon the vallies; and had not a feeling of compunction speedily visited the sovereign, (Philip VII., duke of Savoy,) the work of destruction would probably have been complete, and his successors saved from the infamy of assisting in subsequent transactions of the same character. Such was the style of the persecutions, which, at small intervals, and in different degrees, mark the whole history of this suffering and faithful people during the 15th, 16th, and 17th centuries."*

"This persecution was carried on with peculiar marks of rage and enormity in the years 1655, 1686, and 1696, and seemed to portend nothing less than the total destruction and entire extinction of that unhappy nation. The most horrid scenes of *violence and bloodshed* were *exhibited on this theatre of papal tyranny*."† "Thousands were massacred, and many put to death with tortures of a more horrid and revolting nature than any recorded in the Spanish inquisition; and the most barbarous cruelty was united to indecency the most brutal and profligate. The very recital of these scenes would be sufficient to make the book that contained it a scorn and a horror to society."‡

An inquisitor-general testifies to the faithfulness of the witnesses; a monk records the monstrous cruelties exercised against the Albigenses; and an attested document, written by the commander of a French regiment, and which is preserved in the university of Cambridge, gives an illustration of the barbarities to which the faithful Vaudois were subjected, which were of so shocking a nature, that he resigned his command rather than be a participator or a witness of such iniquitous actions. "I was witness," says Du Petit Bourg, "to many great violences and cruelties exercised by the banditti and soldiers of Piedmont upon all of every age, sex, and condition, many of whom I myself saw massacred, dismembered, hung up, &c. with many horrid circumstances of barbarity."§

It were loathsome to tell of children smothered in the cradle, or dashed from the rocks, or suffocated,

*Acland, pp. 12, 13. † Mosheim, cent. 17, part. ii. chap. 2. sect. 5. ‡ Gilly's Narrative, p. 146. § Ibid. p. 216.

together with their mothers, in a cave; of villages burnt to ashes, and their inhabitants exterminated, of women flying by hundreds from a blazing church, and butchered by a brutal soldiery, or of the execrations of an infuriated mob, while the witnesses of Jesus were suffering martyrdom. But such allusions may here be needful, while Piedmont is in view, that it may afterwards be more clearly seen how righteous are the judgments of God. Milton describes the scene with the power, without the fiction, of a poet. And without looking alone to the righteous retribution which awaits iniquity, he has obviously in view the words of the prophet,—that higher inspiration which no poetry alone can ever reach.

Avenge, O Lord, thy slaughtered saints, whose bones
Lie scattered on the Alpine mountains cold,
E'en them that kept thy truth so pure of old,
When all our fathers worshipped stocks and stones,
Forget not; in thy book record their groans,
Who were thy sheep, and in their ancient fold
Slain by the bloody Piedmontese, that rolled
Mother with infant down the rocks. Their moans
The vales redoubled to the hills, and they
To heaven. Their martyred blood and ashes sow
O'er all the Italian fields, where still doth sway
The triple tyrant; that from these may grow
An hundred fold, who, having learned the way,
Early may fly the Babylonian woe!

MILTON.

The inquisition, which originated in the persecution of the witnesses, is too faithful an index of the sufferings which they endured. Its history, wherever it was established, is one tale of horror. Its victims were indeed clothed with sackcloth. The witnesses of Jesus were questioned by torture; and their testimony to the faith led the way to the dungeon and the stake. Yet the inquisition was but one of many modes by which, age after age, the man of sin, who exalted himself above all, sought to wear out the saints of the Most High. Power was given them to *testify*, though the invention of their enemies was racked to devise new modes of the most aggravated torture. And if ever the malignity of demons had full scope on earth, it was practised in vain against the *anointed ones* of the Lord. The shedding of their blood, that would not for ever be unavenged, served to exemplify and perfect the faith and patience of the saints. The law of the members overmastering the law of the mind, needs not a witness wherever faith is wanting. But, throughout ages, the opposite proof was given to the world, that the power which man has of killing the body, under whatever form of death, was unable to resist the faith which overcomes the world, or to extinguish in the mind the light of the gospel, or the hopes of the Christian. Manifold are the instances in which, rather than deny their Lord, the victims of papal barbarity threw themselves into the flames, and their last word was that of *witnesses*.

The persecution of the Albigenses and the Vaudois disseminated the doctrines which they preached, wherever they fled from the fiery inquisition. And notwithstanding the zeal of a corrupt priesthood in suppressing them, the seeds of the glorious Reformation were sown extensively throughout Europe, especially in Germany and Britain. The light of the gospel penetrated the gloom, and survived all the fires of the inquisition, though they were kindled in many countries. "The seed of the church," as at the first, sprung forth the most vigorously around the stake where the ashes of the martyrs were mingled with their blood. Even a war of extermination, which, as in France, did there extinguish the light, spread it the more rapidly into other regions, and prepared them for an easier riddance of the papal yoke than the fearful revolution which finally became the portion of that kingdom, whose territories were deluged with the blood of the saints, and which lent its power to extirpate them in other lands.

And if any man will hurt them, fire proceedeth out of their mouth, and devoureth their enemies; and if any man will hurt them, he must, in like manner, be killed, &c. verse 5. The saints of the Most High were to be given into the hands of the papacy, for a time, times and a half; but, it is added, the judgment shall sit, and they shall take his dominion, to consume and to destroy it unto the end. The cause of the martyrs shall finally prevail over that of the murderers. Vengeance belongs unto their Lord. They denounced against papal Rome, as Babylon the Great, the mother of harlots and the abominations of the earth, all the judgments written in the word of God against an idolatrous church. And as the Lord said unto Jeremiah, "I will make my words in thy mouth *fire*, and this people wood, and it shall devour them;" so it is said, that fire proceeded out of their mouth and devoureth their enemies. God would avenge their cause by bringing not only spiritual, but temporal judgments on their enemies. But the time of their prophesying in sackcloth had first to cease. In the charge, or threatening, to the papal church, (as symbolized by the rider on the black horse, with the yoke in his hand,) it is said, "And see thou hurt not the wine and the oil." And, in the same vision, under the representation of the saints calling from beneath the *altar*, (which is here *measured*,) they are heard exclaiming, "How long, O Lord, holy and true, dost thou not judge and avenge our blood on them that dwell on the earth?" But this appeal for the souls of them that are slain for the word of God, and for the *testimony which they held*, (the *witnesses*,) was not made till after the rise of infidelity, or till the pale form of spiritual death had stalked upon the earth, to do his work of slaughter; and the appearance of a new enemy called forth, at last, the expostulation of the saints, and made their spirits speak. Even then it was said, (chap. vii. 11,) that they should rest YET for *a little season*, until their fellow servants and their brethren, that should be killed as they were, should be fulfilled. If "the analogy of faith" warrant such an appropriation, or sanction so seemingly plain a comparison of things spiritual with spiritual, instead of turning to past history for an interpretation of the sequel of the vision, the church of Christ should not be unprepared for the fact, that though the time of the *testifying* of the witnesses may be completed, their *death* may be yet to come.

On the death and resurrection of the witnesses it is said, "*And the same* hour there was a great earthquake, and the tenth part of the city fell, and in the earthquake were slain of men (or names of men) seven thousand; and the remnant were affrighted, and gave glory to the God of heaven." The illustration is not palpable (like that of all fulfilled prophecy) in the retrospect of modern history, even since the first decline of the Turkish power, *what* revolution has yet been followed by giving glory to the God of heaven. And in the verse following it is also added, "*The second woe is* PAST, *and behold, the third woe cometh quickly.*" The Turkish empire is not yet dissolved. Greece was reconquered by the Turks *after* the battle of Zenta, in 1697; and the massacre of Scio, with many other barbarities that preceded or accompanied it, go far to invalidate the assumption, that, even at a late date, the second woe was *past*. That woe is designated by the four angels of the Euphrates,—and comparing scripture with scripture, it seems to be the more warranted opinion, if not the direct inference, that the second woe can only be said to be *past*, when the waters of the Euphrates, as under the sixth vial, are dried up.

CHAPTER XXII.

THE WOMAN CLOTHED WITH THE SUN.

In the revelation of the things that were to be, and that now have come to pass, after the days of Daniel and of John, the rise and revolution of earthly kingdoms, together with the great apostacy of Christendom, and the imposture of Mahomet scarcely less influential on the fate of the world, occupy page after page, and form the subject of vision after vision, as if the Lord of the whole earth had resigned his dominion over it, and had given it into the hands of those who take the glory to themselves, and who reject his authority or corrupt his word. But such is not the conclusion of the matter. The only language of faith here is, *How long*, O Lord? The first of the prophecies of scripture, while yet the human race were but a single pair, speaks of the bruising of the SERPENT's head. The great image which stood before Nebuchadnezzar, was indeed of a brightness that was excellent, and of a form that was terrible, but he saw till that a stone was cut out without hands, which smote the image upon his feet of iron and clay, and brake them to pieces;—and the stone that smote the image became a great mountain, and filled the whole earth. And as Daniel told the interpretation, and described the four successive kingdoms that should arise upon the earth, and made known unto the king what should come to pass thereafter, he ceased not whenever the glory of all earthly kingdoms was told, but also added, "And in the days of these kings shall the God of *heaven* set up a kingdom, which shall never be destroyed; and the kingdom shall not be left to other people, but it shall break in pieces and shall consume all these kingdoms, and it shall stand for ever," Dan. ii. 44. In the correspouding vision of the four beasts, or four kingdoms that shall arise out of the earth, the fourth, or the Roman kingdom, is described as devouring the whole earth, treading it down and breaking it in pieces; and among the *ten* kingdoms which arise out of it, another arises, which speaks great words against the Most High, and wears out the saints of the Most High; and they are given unto his hand for a time, times, and the dividing of time. Yet the judgment sits to take away his dominion, to consume and destroy it unto the end. And the kingdom and dominion, and the greatness of the kingdom under the whole heaven, shall be given to the people of the saints of the Most High, whose kingdom is an everlasting kingdom, and all dominions shall serve and obey him, Dan. vii.

The history of earthly empires is prophetically announced, their course is marked, but all their dominions finally merge into an everlasting kingdom. The kingdom of the Most High was to be set up in the days of these kingdoms, to encounter opposition for ages, to be threatened with extinction, and yet finally to be established over all the earth. These visions of Daniel represent how different is the final prospect of the cause of Christ, from what the retrospect has been; and however different any emblem of it must be from that designative of the kingdoms of the earth, yet the reader will not fail to recognise strong points of resemblance between these antecedent predictions, and a vision of the Apocalypse, which, in some respects may perhaps be termed the contest of the church, or the conflict of the kingdom of God, with the powers of darkness and the kingdoms of the world. That contest, it is obvious, had chiefly to be maintained first with the imperial, and afterwards for a defined period, with the papal power of Rome.

And there appeared a great wonder in heaven: a woman clothed with the sun, and the moon under her feet, and upon her head a crown of twelve stars: and she being with child, cried, travailing in birth, and pained to be delivered. And there appeared another wonder in heaven; and behold a great red dragon, having seven heads and ten horns, and seven crowns upon his heads. And his tail drew the third part of the stars of heaven, and did cast them to the earth; and the dragon stood before the woman which was ready to be delivered, for to devour her child as soon as it was born. And she brought forth a man-child who was to rule all nations with a rod of iron; and her child was caught up unto God, and to his throne. And the woman fled into the wilderness, where she had a place prepared of God, that they might feed her there a thousand two hundred and threescore days. And there was war in heaven: Michael and his angels fought against the dragon; and the dragon fought, and his angels, and prevailed not; neither was their place found any more in heaven. And the great dragon was cast out, that old serpent, called the devil and Satan, which deceiveth the whole world; he was cast out into the earth, and his angels were cast out with him. And I heard a loud voice saying in heaven, now is come salvation and strength, and the kingdom of our God, and the power of his Christ: for the accuser of our brethren is cast down, which accused them before our God day and night. And they overcame him by the blood of the Lamb, and by the word of their testimony; and they loved not their lives unto the death. Therefore rejoice ye heavens and ye that dwell in them. Woe unto the inhabiters of the earth and the sea! for the devil is come down upon you, with great wrath, because he knoweth that he hath but a short time. And when the dragon saw that he was cast unto the earth, he persecuted the woman which brought forth the man-child. And to the woman were given two wings of a great eagle, that she might fly into the wilderness, into her place: where she is nourished for a time, times and half a time, from the face of the serpent. And the serpent cast out of his mouth water as a flood after the woman, that he might cause her to be carried away of the flood. And the earth helped the woman; and the earth opened her mouth and swallowed up the flood which the dragon cast out of his mouth. And the dragon was wroth with the woman, and went to make war with the remnant of her seed, which keep the commandments of God, and have the testimony of Jesus Christ.— Chap. xii.

A great wonder was seen in heaven, and great is the mystery of godliness. In prophesying *again*, John still measures the temple and the altar, and them that worship therein. After having first told of the witnesses of Jesus, instead of reverting to the destiny of the kingdoms of this world, he describes, in more general terms, the rise, the history, and the fate of the kingdom that the God of heaven had set up. The beloved disciple of Jesus continues as before to fill up the outline given by Daniel, who also was a man greatly beloved. And in the Revelation of Jesus Christ, the kingdom of the Most High, spoken of by Daniel, is not without its appropriate symbol and its specific delineation. It came not in the form of a wild beast, to trample on the earth;

nor did the symbol of other empires bear any similitude to it. *A woman clothed with the sun*, covered all around with heavenly light and radiance, and *having the moon under her feet*, as if standing on Judaism, or trampling on any other form of faith, and infinitely transcending them all, is aptly significative as the most glorious of symbols could be, of the kingdom of God, which in the fulness of time was set up on earth. In the spiritual horizon Jesus alone is the sun of righteousness; his kingdom is surrounded by light, all other brightness is dim before it, and by it alone can all the world be enlightened; while the crown of twelve stars, in the same aspect of celestial objects, seems to name the twelve apostles, the stars of first magnitude and unrivalled brightness in the church, to whom the Lord Jesus said, I appoint unto you a kingdom, as my Father hath appointed me. Ye shall sit on twelve thrones, judging the twelve tribes of Israel. Even in the seven churches of Asia, the *stars* were the angels of the churches.

The light shone in darkness, but the darkness comprehended it not. Because Jesus told the truth, men would not believe him. They that were not of God would not hear God's words. And when the apostles went forth to preach the gospel, men hated and persecuted them for his name's sake. The kingdom of God was preached unto the Gentiles; and Jesus was believed on in the world. But truth finds not a ready access to the heart; and the struggle is often hard, before it be admitted. It is not easy for those to learn righteousness who are naturally prone to do evil, and averse to that which is good. If any man be in Christ Jesus he is a new creature. And the kingdom of God which he came to establish, consists not, like other creeds, in meats, or drinks, or days, or ordinances, but is righteousness, and peace, and joy in the Holy Ghost. The Author of our faith hath declared, that except a man *be born again*, he cannot enter into the kingdom of God. It was the office of his apostles to turn men from darkness to light. And in speaking of the change of heart that had to be wrought through faith, Paul, adopting the very figure which is used in the vision, says, My little children of whom I *travail in birth again till Christ be formed in you.* In similar significancy, the woman clothed with the sun, and the moon under her feet, and who had upon her head a crown of twelve stars, *being with child, cried, travailing in birth, and pained to be delivered.* Such symbolically was the first aspect of the kingdom of heaven. Jesus had a baptism to be baptized with, and how was he straitened till it was accomplished! He had to be lifted up on the accursed tree, before men would be drawn unto him. And in the very early propagation of the gospel, while the kingdom of God was beginning to be formed, we read that (Acts xiv. 21, 22) when the *apostles* had preached the *gospel* to Derbe, and had taught many, they returned again to Lystra, and to Iconium and to Antioch, confirming the souls of the disciples, and exhorting them to continue in the faith and that we must *through much tribulation* enter into the *kingdom of God.* The disciples were called Christians first in Antioch: and such, in travail and in pain, was the manner in which that kingdom began to be established.

The mutual destruction of the Roman and Persian empires, left no formidable enemy to contend with Saracen fanatics when they came forth from Arabia in armed multitudes to propagate the faith of Mahomet: and the love of plunder, as a stimulus to conquest, is a feeling which it needed not a prophet to implant in the human breast. Their success lay in their swords. But contrariwise, no sooner was the faith of Jesus preached, than the Roman empire, holding the world in subjection, and supporting with all its authority a pompous paganism, was prepared, like a ferocious monster, to devour the infant church, or to persecute unto the death those who should profess a holy faith and disown the worship of many gods. The *seven heads*, or as otherwise interpreted, the *seven mountains*, on which the imperial city was built; the *ten horns*, or according both to the Book of Daniel and the Revelation, the ten kingdoms, into which the Roman empire was divided; and the *seven crowns*, or different successive forms of government, (Rev. xix. 9, 10,) mark the empire of Rome, in its bloody persecutions, as the *great red dragon that stood before the woman which was ready to be delivered, for to devour her child as soon as it was born.* As Herod the king sought the life of the holy child Jesus, so the power of Rome was exerted in vain to stifle christianity at its very birth. And as *Satan*, in the hour of the prince of darkness, entered into the heart of Judas when he betrayed the Lord into the hands of sinners, so that *great dragon* which sought the destruction of the church is denominated, in the sequel of this prophecy, however varied may be the form he assumes, whoever may be the agent of his will, or whatever may be the instrument of his power—*that old serpent the devil, and Satan, which deceiveth the whole world.*—Men were led captive by him at his will; and the kings of the earth claimed not freedom from his sway. The purposed destruction of the church of Christ was a device worthy of the great *adversary* of God and of man. And never was there a more powerful instrument ready to his hand than Rome in all the majesty of its greatness, wholly given up to idolatry, and, though subjecting the world to its sway, enslaved to the grossest vices. Satan is repeatedly termed in scripture the prince of this world. "We wrestle not," saith the apostle, "against flesh and blood, but against principalities and powers, against *the rulers* of the darkness of *this world, against spiritual wickedness in high places.*" That sin and death reign upon the earth, can scarcely be hid from the blindest. Such truths need not any revelation from heaven to declare them. Each individual has given witness to the one, and must therefore bear witness to the other. The scriptures reveal how sin came into the world, and the gospel proclaims redemption from its guilt, and salvation from its power to them that obey it. And thus though there be a mystery of iniquity at work on earth, there is a mystery of godliness at work against it. The contest, begun in Eden, is not closed. It may be long; but the issue is not doubtful. He by whom all things were made has not given up the world to be for ever ruled and desolated by sin; but righteousness shall reign on the earth, and be established for ever. In the days of earthly kingdoms, over which idolatry and sin domineered, did the God of heaven set up his kingdom. And that kingdom, symbolized by the stone cut without hands, which shall finally smite the image till it fall into dust, was not itself to be crushed or to be sunk for ever in the earth by the Roman empire, though then concentrating in itself all human power, and lorded over by the prince of darkness. The disciples of Jesus wrestled not in vain with all principalities and powers. But the dragon sought in vain to devour the child so soon as it was born. *The man child was brought forth who shall rule all nations with a rod of iron.* And if the kingdom of God be indeed symbolized by the woman clothed with the sun, having the moon under her feet, and upon her head twelve stars, (the gospel of the kingdom, of heavenly brightness, eclipsing every other faith, and propagated by the twelve apostles,) then *the children of the kingdom,* as the name is given them in scripture, the true believers of the gospel, may well be esteemed her progeny, brought forth as they were, in pangs and throes, and manifold tribulations. The words of Jesus are spirit and are life. The symbol is an express similitude. It is as being born again that men enter into the kingdom of God; as well as by tribulation that they then approved themselves as its children. And there is the same relation between the gospel and believers, as between a mother and a child. The people that did know their God were strong and did exploits. And they that understood among the people instructed many; yet they fell by the sword, and by flame, and by captivity, and by spoil many days. The dragon could not devour them. The Roman empire could not destroy the church,—"the body of Christ,"—of which true believers are the members. A church was formed by the preaching of the gospel. *A man-child was brought forth, who shall rule all nations with a rod of iron.* Not only is it written of Jesus that he shall thus rule, and that God will give him the heathen for a heritage, and the uttermost part of the earth for a possession; but the Spirit also saith unto the churches, "He that overcometh and keepeth my works unto the end, to him will I give power over the nations, and *he shall rule them with a rod of iron;* as the vessels of a potter shall they be broken to shivers; even as I received of my Father, Rev. ii. 27. The kingdom of God shall break in pieces and consume all these kingdoms, and they shall become as the chaff of the summer threshing floors. Looking from the first conflict to the final triumph of the church, the apostle, in this vision, *heard a loud voice saying in heaven, now is come salvation, and strength, and the kingdom of our God;* in like manner as it is said in the book of Daniel, "And the kingdom and the dominion, and the greatness of the kingdom under the whole heaven, shall be given to the people of the saints of the Most High, whose kingdom is an everlasting kingdom, and all dominions shall serve and obey him." He shall finally bruise the *serpent's* head.

But Christianity was not destined to triumph, till many subjects, throughout many ages, should first be gathered to the kingdom of God. Farther identifying his people as his own, it is said that the man-child was caught up to God and to his throne, even as Jesus after his exaltation on high, said—To him that overcometh will I give to sit with me in my throne, even as I also overcame, and am set down with my Father on his throne.

But the pangs of child-birth were not the only perils of the woman clothed with the sun. After the man-child was brought forth, new dangers arose. And after a Christian church was formed, a long period was to elapse, and new dangers to be encountered, before the prince of darkness and of this world would cease to exercise his malignity, or be deprived of his power. After the emperor of Rome "should be removed out of the way, that wicked one would be revealed, whose coming is after *the working of Satan*, with all powers, and signs, and lying wonders," &c. And as Daniel represents the church passing from one state of tribulation, that inflicted by the Roman empire after the subversion of Judaism, to enter on another, that of papal persecution, to endure throughout an appointed time, so, after the man-child was born, and survived in defiance of all the power of the dragon, the woman fled into the wilderness, and, under another form, and even directly named, the serpent again was her persecutor. In the things noted in the scripture of truth, an "appointed time" of persecution succeeds to the early tribulation of the Christians, during which second and defined period, many were to fall, to be tried, and to be purged, and to be made white. And the period to the end of the wonders is declared to *be a time, times, and a half.* Dan. xii. 7. The saints of the Most High were to be given into the hands of the papacy (the little horn of the fourth beast) until a time, times, and the dividing of time, (half a time,) Dan. vii. 25. The two witnesses were to testify *a thousand two hundred and threescore days.* It is specially to be noted that BOTH these forms of expression, or different modes of determining the same period, are repeated, in the exact terms, in the vision now before us, whereby all those prophecies are linked together, and identified as descriptive of the same power, retaining, as otherwise they do, a manifest uniformity and entire accordance (see Table). *And the woman fled into the wilderness, where she had a place prepared of God, that they should feed her there a thousand, two hundred and threescore days,* ver. 6. *And to the woman were given two wings of a great eagle, that she might fly into the wilderness, into her place, where she is nourished for a time, and times, and a half a time, from the face of the serpent,* ver. 14.

Some evidence will afterwards be adduced to show the probable commencement and termination of the 1260 years.

The dragon, during the second great period of persecution, and after a christian church had been formed, is spoken of under another form: and it was from the *face of the serpent* that the woman fled into the wilderness. As, at the beginning, believers had to wrestle with the rulers of the darkness of this world, and with spiritual wickedness in high places, or against *the great red dragon which stood ready to devour the man-child* at his birth, so even in the days of the apostles the mystery of iniquity began also to work in another form; and *that wicked one* was to be *revealed in his time,* or after the subversion of the western empire, whose coming is after the WORKING OF SATAN, with all *powers, and signs, and lying wonders, and all deceivableness of unrighteousness,* &c. *And the great dragon is that old serpent, called the devil, and Satan, which deceiveth the whole world.* The same prince of darkness had but separate agents, and wrought but by other means. The persecution against the saints was not less satanic, under papal than under imperial Rome. The knights or kings who slaughtered them at the dictation of a monk, were not more humane than Roman lictors, and Simon de Montfort was, in cruelty, another Nero. He was, as the philosophical historian relates, "*the representative of* THE EVIL SPIRIT; *the prototype of all the persecutions they had endured.*" Nor when he forebore from the more gentle slaughter by the sword, that, in committing the saints to the flames, the priests might not be deprived of their expected joy, were they less fiendish than he. *The old serpent, called the devil, and Satan, which deceiveth the whole world,* wanted not incarnate demons as the agents of his will, against those who would despoil him of his reign. But the *brethren overcame him by the blood of the Lamb, and by the word of their testimony, and they loved not their lives unto the death.*

While the church of Christ, who came to dispossess Satan of his kingdom, lay obscure in *the wilderness* in a depressed and suffering state, it may be remarked, that it was with *two wings of a great eagle* that the woman, who was clothed with the sun, fled thither. There was no abode or resting place in Judea, nor in the lesser Asia, nor in Greece, where first she had flourished; nor was she suffered to remain in the rich plains of southern France;*

* The Albigenses may be traced to a remote region of the earth, as well as to an early age of the church. The Paulicians, or dis-

but on the remote Alps, in some of the most sequestered of the villages of Piedmont, amidst the fastnesses of rocks and the wilds of the desert, and literally in an Alpine region where eagles dwell, the existence of the gospel was preserved, in active and embodied form, and the church of Christ had there her seat in the *wilderness*. But even there the trial of the faith of the *brethren* was, that *they loved not their lives unto death;* and peaks of mountains seemingly inaccessible, and caves in the rocks, were frequently their only resort, in *the place which the Lord* had *prepared for them.*

These few observations have been hazarded, in the hope that they may not altogether tend to mystify mystery, or to obstruct the understanding of what has been called the most difficult part of the book of Revelation. But that which cannot yet be seen clearly in *all* its parts, cannot be fully defined. And it is not on such themes that we should dare to give scope to any vain imaginations. It were folly, not wisdom, to attempt to be wise above what is

---

ciples of Paul, were first established in Armenia and Pontus. And after suffering severe persecutions, they were transplanted, about the middle of the eighth century, from Armenia into Thrace. "A confession of *simple worship and blameless manners* is extorted from their enemies; and so high was their standard of perfection, that the increasing congregations were divided into two classes of disciples, of those who practised, and of those who aspired. It was in the *country of the Albigeois*, in the southern provinces of France, that the Paulicians were most deeply implanted; and the same vicissitudes of martyrdom and revenge which had been displayed in the neighbourhood of the Euphrates, were repeated in the thirteenth century on the banks of the Rhone. The laws of the eastern emperors were revived by Frederic the Second. The insurgents of Tephrice were represented by the barons and cities of Languedoc. Pope Innocent III. surpassed the sanguinary fame of Theodora. It was in cruelty alone that her soldiers could equal the heroes of the crusades, and the cruelty of her priests was far excelled by the founders of the inquisition; an office more adapted to confirm than to refute the belief of an evil principle. The visible assemblies of the Paulicians, or Albigeois, were extirpated by fire and sword," &c.—Gibbon's Hist. vol. x. p. 187, c. 54.

written. And to tear asunder that which time may not yet have fully unfolded or unsealed, were to do violence to the word of God. Yet we may *read*, that besides the long period during which the woman remained in the wilderness, mention is made of war in heaven, of the discomfiture of Satan and his being cast unto the earth—of his great wrath at last, because he knows that he has but a short time—of woe to the inhabiters of the earth and of the sea—of the flood cast out of the serpent's mouth after the woman—of the earth helping the woman and swallowing up the flood, and finally of the wrath of the *dragon*, and his making war with the remnant of her seed, which keep the commandments of God, and have the testimony of Jesus.

The contest of the church is not yet over; nor can all the forms of its warfare be yet literally described. Time may not yet have unfolded that by which alone the prophecy can be unsealed. The *judgments* of God may be manifest, and yet his *strange* work may remain to be done. But while thus there may still be needful exercise for the *patience* as well as the faith of the saints, there may, at the same time, be some warrant for believing that the expiry of the twelve hundred and sixty years is not a period of repose to the church or to the world. It is the ceasing of the time during which the witnesses were to *testify*, and in which the kingdoms of the western empire were to be given into the hands of the church of Rome. But it is not said that they were to be easily, or in a moment, wrenched from its grasp. There was still to be war in heaven—great wrath on the earth—and there is the announcement of another woe. The papal kingdom was not to rest in peace, after wearing out the saints of the Most High. Nor was the strife of the kingdoms of this world against the kingdom of Christ at an end, that they should all serve and obey him. On the termination of the 1260 years, the judgment, as often repeated, and as still remains to be shown, was to sit upon the papacy, which was to be consumed and destroyed until the end.

The infidel power, which was at last to arise, was destined to kill with sword, and with hunger, and with death, and with the beasts, or kingdoms, of the earth. Whatever the flood may be that the serpent cast out of his mouth against the woman, that he might cause her to be carried away of the flood, we know that against the church of Christ all the gates of hell never shall prevail. Superstition shall be swept from off the earth. That which destroys it, may seem to overwhelm the church; but yet the truth shall be established for ever. "Now he hath promised, saying, Yet once more I shake not the earth only, but also heaven. And this word, Yet once more, signifieth the removing of these things that are shaken, as of things that are made, that those things which cannot be shaken may remain." —Heb. xii. 27, 28.

The conclusion of this vision shows the last struggle of the church, the death, perhaps, of the witnesses. But, even though the woe, that is announced to the inhabiters of the earth, unlike to the two former, reach to the *sea* as well as to the earth (v. 12,); and although the *dragon*, spoken of in the first part of the vision, reappear at its close, yet, looking to the original formation among the children of men of a church to Christ amidst manifold tribulations, and unto witnesses that afterwards, under another form of persecution, testified successively for 1260 years, who overcame by the blood of the Lamb, and by the word of their testimony, and who loved not their lives unto the death; and waiting farther for a *little season*, the faithful need not fear that the last war and brief triumph of their wrathful enemies, shall dispossess the saints of their faith and patience, or extirpate the religion of Jesus from the world. The man-child whom the Roman empire, like a dragon, sought in vain to devour, *shall rule all nations with a rod of iron.* However *great* may be the *wrath* of the *devil*, it is but the last sting of the serpent before the crushing of his head. *And the kingdom of God and his Christ shall come.*

Thus partly has the progress of history been anticipated, in order to view, in connexion, the one subject of the vision, the conflict of the church; and thus, as well as in preceding prophecies, it may be seen, that momentous events, if not a series of judgments, follow the expiry of "the appointed time," during which the church of Rome was to wear out the saints of the Most High. And their termination may therefore be marked by other wars.

The fate of the church having been noted in the preceding vision, the next, we apprehend, fills up the history of her enemies, pagan and papal Rome, till those judgments begin to sit upon the latter, which subsequent prophecies specially define.

CHAPTER XXIII.

THE FIRST AND SECOND BEAST.

And I stood upon the sand of the sea, and saw a beast rise up out of the sea, having seven heads and ten horns, and upon his horns ten crowns, and upon his heads the name of Blasphemy. And the beast which I saw was like unto a leopard, and his feet were as the feet of a bear, and his mouth as the mouth of a lion; and the dragon gave him his power, and his seat, and great authority. And I saw one of his heads as it were wounded to death; and his deadly wound was healed: and all the world wondered after the beast. And they worshipped the dragon which gave power unto the beast; and they worshipped the beast, saying, who is like unto the beast? who is able to make war with him? And there was given unto him a mouth speaking great things, and blasphemies; and power was given unto him to continue forty and two months. And he opened his mouth in blasphemy against God, to blaspheme his name, and his tabernacle, and them that dwell in heaven. And it was given unto him to make war with the saints, and to overcome them: and power was given him over all kindreds, and tongues, and nations. And all that dwell upon the earth shall worship him, whose names are not written in the book of life of the Lamb slain from the foundation of the world. If any man have an ear, let him hear. He that leadeth into captivity, shall go into captivity: he that killeth with the sword, must be killed with the sword. Here is the patience and the faith of the saints. And I beheld another beast coming up out of the earth; and he had two horns like a lamb, and he spake as a dragon. And he exerciseth all the power of the first beast before him, and causeth the earth, and them that dwell therein, to worship the first beast, whose deadly wound was healed. And he doeth great wonders, so that he maketh fire come down from heaven on the earth in the sight of men, and deceiveth them that dwell on the earth by the means of those miracles which he hath power to do in the sight of the beast, saying to them that dwell on the earth, that they should make an image to the beast which had the wound by the sword, and did live.

And he had power to give life to the image of the beast, that the image of the beast should both speak, and cause that as many as would not worship the image of the beast should be killed. And he caused all, both small and great, rich and poor, and free and bond, to receive a mark in their right hand, or in their foreheads: and that no man might buy or sell, save he that had the mark, or the name of the beast, or the number of his name. Here is wisdom. Let him that hath understanding count the number of the beast; for it is the number of a man; and his number is six hundred threescore and six.

It seems to be universally admitted, that the first beast in this vision represents Rome; but whether pagan or papal has been disputed by Roman Catholic and Protestant commentators: we adhere to the opinion of the former. The beast, like the four beasts in the vision of Daniel, *rose up out of the sea.* It had seven heads, or seven kings, seven forms of government which successively ruled over it. Rev. xvii. 10. Like the fourth beast also, he had *ten horns,* and upon his horns *ten crowns,* even as these are similarly interpreted by Daniel as *ten kings* or kingdoms. *A leopard* in the vision of the prophet, represented the Grecian empire, a *bear* the Persian, and a *lion* the Babylonian—and these were all to be subdued by the Roman, the fourth empire, which is described as a beast great and dreadful and strong exceedingly; and which devoured and brake in pieces, and stamped the *residue* with the feet of it. *And the beast which I saw in the vision,* says John, *was like unto a leopard,* and his feet were as the feet of a *bear,* and his mouth as the mouth of a *lion.*

Upon his heads were the names of blasphemy.—And the dragon gave him his power, and his seat, and great authority.—Romulus, the son of a vestal, the reputed suckling of a wolf, the murderer of his brother, and the chief of a band of robbers and ravishers, gave to Rome its existence and its name. Narrow and irregular lines of huts resting on the ground, and, when completed, not exceeding a thousand in number, and a thatch-covered dwelling formed of rushes, were the city and palace of Romulus.* From such beginnings, how mighty was the *power*, how celebrated the *seat*, and how *great* the *authority* of the empire, or the *beast*. Babylon, Persia, and Greece, yielded to Rome; and the fragments and residue of these kingdoms were but a portion of its greatness. From the sides of the Grampians to the banks of the Euphrates, the Roman legions held the world in awe; and its *great authority* is told in 'the majesty of the Roman name.' But it was not founded in righteousness. An all-holy God was not worshipped there. It upheld idolatry throughout the world. The names of blasphemy were upon the heads of the beast, and Satan gave him his power, and seat, and great authority.

The vision further represents the power, the idolatry, the period of the continuance of the Roman empire, the wounding of one of the heads, and the healing of the wound, and the grievous persecutions which it exercised against Christians. *All the world wondered after the beast.* Never was an imperial authority greater or more *wonderful* than that of Rome. And long was the period during which the question might have been asked, but could not be answered throughout the world, *Who is like unto the beast? who is able to make war with him? Power was given unto him over all kindreds, and tongues, and nations.*

And they worshipped the dragon which gave

* Val. Max. B. 4.

power unto the beast. And he opened his mouth in blasphemy against God, to blaspheme his name and his tabernacle, and them that dwell in heaven. And it was given unto him, to make war with the saints, and to overcome them. In the wilderness, where Christ was tempted of the devil, the arch-deceiver, shewing him all the kingdoms of the world, and all the glory of them, said, "All these things will I give thee, if thou wilt fall down and worship me." "Thou shall worship the Lord thy God, and him only shalt thou serve," was the answer of the Son of God. But while the Romans tolerated every form of idolatry, they persecuted unto the death the worshippers of the only living and true God. Under their authority Christ was crucified, and by imperial edicts saints were martyred. An *odium* was attached to the Christian name. They worshipped the dragon and *bowed down* to idols, and, doing the work of the adversary of God and the enemy of the souls of men, they were led captive by Satan at his will. Idolatry alone was the religion of the empire. *He opened his mouth in blasphemy against God.* The holy One of Israel was the only God they disowned and dishonoured. The whole system of idolatry was a repudiation of his worship, and blasphemy against the only living and true God. *They blasphemed his name and his tabernacle, and those that dwell in heaven.* The first testimony on record concerning the Christian faith in Rome, is that it was everywhere *spoken against*, as blasphemy literally implies. The edicts of the emperors designate it in the most opprobrious terms. Even the refined and elegant Tacitus describes it as a pernicious or pestilent (exitiabilis)* superstition—

* Tacit. Ann. lib. xv. 44.

applying to it the same term in which he otherwise describes a pestilent disease; and he ranks the Christian faith among the atrocious and shameful things (atrocia aut pudenda) which flowed from every quarter in Rome. The humane Pliny, as compared with other Roman governors he may be called, terms Christianity a wicked and extravagant superstition (pravam et immodicam superstitionem); he too, as well as more modern inquisitors, could interrogate by torture, though he could discover nothing but a piety, a purity, an innocence, brotherly-kindness, and charity, that mocked all the pomp of paganism, and might well have put the best of heathens to the deepest blush. And to prove the difference of their faith, as well as of their virtue, he brought forth before Christians the *image* of the emperor, and the *images* of the gods; and those who would not worship them, and offer oblations of frankincense and wine, and *blaspheme* Christ, (maledicerent Christo,) were punished for their inflexible obstinacy.* As the governor of Bithynia, he expressed, in an epistle to the emperor Trajan, his *doubts* whether in punishing Christians, no distinction should be made between the old and the young, the feeble or the strong, the penitent or the impenitent, or whether the *name alone* was worthy of punishment. But he cherished not a thought of religious toleration in the truest sense, nor a doubt of his duty as a Roman governor of punishing all who would not bow down and offer oblations before the *image* of a mortal, and worship those that are not gods. The lenity of the emperor reached not farther than to pardon those who abjured their faith. *Idolatry* was the very test. Those only could escape who supplicated the gods, and wor-

* Pliny, lib. x. Ep. 97.

shipped an idol. Such was the answer of Trajan; such the boasted toleration of paganism; such the union between idolatry and persecution, between the *worship of the dragon* and *war with the saints;* and such the mildest specimen of Roman and imperial legislation against the church of Christ. The blood of many martyrs, many imperial and bloody edicts, and ten successive persecutions, are a portion of the reckoning on behalf of the church against the ancient empire of Rome. *There was given unto the beast a mouth speaking great things, and blasphemies. And it was given unto him to make war with the saints, and to overcome them. And all that dwell upon the earth shall worship him, whose names are not written in the book of life.* They whose names *were* written there would *not* worship him.

And power was given unto him, to continue forty and two months. The presumed coincidence of this period, with the twelve hundred and sixty years, or the time, times, and a half, has induced protestant commentators in general, to identify the beast having seven heads and ten horns, &c. with *papal* Rome. Yet the analogy is not only wanting in other respects, (except in their joint power, and persecution of the saints,) but it is also obvious, that a different mode of computation, or *measure* of time, is here adopted, and that a different period may therefore be designated. One kingdom might even possibly have subsisted 1260 years as well as another; and different empires, or forms of government, *might* have been marked, though the same space has been specified as their duration, and though it had been defined even in the same manner. But both, there is reason to presume, are here different—the period itself, as well as the form of defining it. The Jewish month bore no fixed, uniform, or positive relation to a year, which sometimes consisted of twelve, and sometimes of thirteen months. Previous to the giving of the law, the month consisted solely of thirty days, five months being equivalent to 150 days. Gen. vii. 11; viii. 4. But, after the institution of their ritual observances, their months consisted alternately of thirty and twenty-nine days. To appeal to the familiar authority of Cruden, "that which had *thirty days* was called *a full or complete month;* and that which had but *twenty-nine* days was called *incomplete or deficient.*" A *single* full and complete month, or the period that was marked by the name of one *month,* consisted of thirty days. Every third year contained an additional month, or thirty days;* and when, instead of a single month, several were included, some of them were necessarily "incomplete or deficient." Forty-two months (including twenty-two full and twenty incomplete months) thus amounted to 1240 days, prophetically years.

Rome, according to Varro, was founded in the year before Christ 753. But Fabius Pictor dates its foundation five years later, or in the year before Christ 748. The power of the Roman emperor, continued in Rome till the 493d year of the Christian era. After the dethronement of Augustulus, Zeno reigned as *sole emperor,* and consuls and senate exercised their wonted authority under the Roman emperor in Constantinople, according to their repeated practice from the days of Constantine. Odoacer, though the conqueror of Rome, abstained from the use of the purple and diadem, and, claiming only the title of patrician, scrupulously transmitted to the emperor all the insignia of royalty.† The purple, the ensign of Roman authority, was for the first time assumed by Theodoric, the king of the Ostrogoths, in the year 493. His "*royalty* was proclaimed by the

* Brewster's Encyclop. vol. vi. p. 403. Art. Chronology, Table.
† Gibbon's Hist. vol. vi. pp. 226, 228.

Goths, with the tardy, reluctant, ambiguous consent of the emperor of the east.—From the Alps to the extremity of Calabria, Theodoric *reigned* by the right of conquest."*

Foundation of Rome, B. C. - - - -	753 or	748
Authority of emperor ceased in Rome, A. D.	493	493
It *continued* either - - - - - -	1246 or	1241 years.

For so long a period the Roman authority was recognized and obeyed *in Rome,* and the successor of Romulus was its master. By the *latter* computation, the forty two prophetic months, or 1240 years, had then exactly expired, and the utmost variation by the former period, as denoting the continuance from the foundation of the city, amounts only to the sixth part of a prophetic month, and could, therefore, as measured by *months,* denote no other number than that which is stated in the prophecy. *Power was given him to continue forty and two months.* Another *month* would have *exceeded* the period of the *continuance* of his power, either twenty-three or twenty-eight years. The twelve hundred and forty-first year behoved to be entered on, before the twelve hundred and forty years were completed.

And I beheld ANOTHER *beast coming up out of the* EARTH; *and he had two horns like a lamb, and spake as a dragon.* The first beast, like the successive *temporal* kingdoms described by Daniel, arose *out of the sea,* from the midst of commotions and revolutions; but the second beast rose out of the *earth,* as the Roman empire itself is repeatedly denominated in the previous visions. It sprung not up by war, but in another form, within the territories of the Roman empire.

The second beast manifestly succeeds to *the first*

---

* Gibbon's Hist. vol. vii. 15, 16.

beast before him. And the prophecies of Daniel and Paul may help to expound the vision. Having described the Roman empire, or the fourth beast, (corresponding in every particular, as well as in the manner of its origin, with the first beast in the present vision,) he adds, "I considered the horns, and behold there came up among them ANOTHER little horn, before whom there were three of the first horns plucked up by the roots." And, by interpretation, "the ten horns out of this kingdom are ten kings (or kingdoms) and shall arise, and *another* shall rise after them, and he shall be diverse from the first, and he shall subdue three kings. And he shall speak great words against the Most High," &c. "Now ye know what withholdeth," saith the apostle, "that he might be *revealed* in his time. For the mystery of iniquity doth already work: only he that now letteth (hindereth) will let, *until he be taken out of the way; and* THEN *shall that wicked one be revealed*," &c. 2 Thess. ii. 6—8.

Another beast, or kingdom, was to arise after the *first;* and to be revealed when the first was taken out of the way. The second beast was to arise also after the first beast *before him*, and may therefore be presumed to come up in his place, when he should be *taken out of the way*. That event happened towards the close of the fifth century; and early in the sixth, in the year 508, the first religious war began.

"In the fever of the times," says Gibbon, "(A. D. 508–518,) the sense, or rather the sound of a syllable was sufficient to disturb the peace of an empire.—Vitalian, with an army of Huns and Bulgarians, for the most part idolators, declared himself the champion of the Catholic faith. In this pious rebellion he depopulated Thrace, besieged Constantinople, exterminated sixty-five thousand of his fellow Christians, till he obtained the recall of the bishops, the *satisfaction of the pope*, and the establishment of the council of Chalcedon, an orthodox treaty, reluctantly signed by the dying Anastasius, and more faithfully performed to the uncle of *Justinian*.

And such was the event of the FIRST *of the religious wars, which have been waged in the name, and by the disciples, of the God of peace."**

In tracing the connexion between historical events, Gibbon is the man who leads us on step by step in the illustration of historical predictions. And immediately consecutive to the preceding extract is a description of "the *theological* character and government of *Justinian*." It was *always* the object of that emperor to preserve the unity of the church, without which, such was the temper of the times, the empire in all likelihood would have been torn asunder by violent commotions, and the first religious war" might have been the prelude to many more. To have raised the patriarch of Constantinople to the supremacy of the church, would have set a rival, or more than a rival, close beside the throne. And when the authority of the emperor had ceased over Rome, or when Italy could only be a conquered province, nothing hindered the emperor from *giving* the church *into the hands* of the pope. And to become the "judge of controversies," and "head of the churches," and "corrector of heretics," was to be armed with a power, and to exercise an authority, which future ages testified that the prerogative of kings did not equal. The pontifical power was not then consolidated, nor the yoke fully imposed or even formed, as afterwards it hardened into iron; and a long period elapsed before the pope became a temporal prince, or ere his spiritual dominion was turned into *blackness*. But striking facts seem to warrant the conclusion, that at that time, in the age of Justinian, that wicked one was *revealed*, and that the church was *given into his hands*. His gradual rise is told by the prophet, *and I beheld another beast* COMING UP *out of the earth; and he had two horns*

* Hist. vol. viii. p. 320, c. 47.

like a lamb, and he spake as a dragon. Among the ten kingdoms of the Roman empire, another, diverse from them all, was to arise—another *little horn.* The papal power, though *diverse* from the rest, is symbolized by a *horn,* as well as the rest, which thus represents power, or a form of government, whether temporal or spiritual. And there is no greater incongruity—that is, there is none—between the representation of the spiritual and temporal power of the pope, by two horns, (each distinct of itself, and both united in his person,) than between the little *horn* of the fourth beast (so called before any of the others were rooted up before it) representing the papacy, and the ten other kingdoms, represented in like manner by ten horns. Spiritual as well as temporal power, when supreme, are both alike represented by a *horn,* or denominated a *king.* The pope possessed both. To his supreme spiritual authority an earthly kingdom was added, by the extirpation before him of three of the first kings.

He had two horns. "The *ecclesiastical power* that was obeyed in Sweden and Britain had been ultimately derived from the suffrage of the Romans. The same suffrage gave a *prince* as well as a *pontiff* to the capital,"* &c.—"A Christian, a philosopher, and a patriot, will be equally scandalized by the *temporal kingdom* of the clergy," &c.† "In an age of superstition it should seem that the *union* of the *regal* and *sacerdotal* characters would mutually fortify each other; and that the keys of paradise would be the surest pledge of earthly obedience," &c.‡

He had two horns *as a lamb.* The pope subscribes himself the servant of servants. Once every year in mock imitation of the meek and lowly Jesus, he washes the feet of twelve pilgrims. The name of *pope* implies that his government and authority are only *paternal.* And as prophecy adopted the

* Gibbon's Hist. vol. xii. p. 260, c. 69.
† Ibid. p. 391, c. 70. ‡ Ibid. vol. xii. p. 261.

arms of Macedon (the *he-goat*), and of Persia (a ram with two horns, the one higher than the other), and used the designation of *eagle*, in allusion to the imperial power, so the pope has adopted his own prophetic symbol of a *lamb*. Among the different flags of all the kingdoms of the world, as may be seen by reference to Danville's Atlas, on the edge of a map, there is one *a lamb* at the foot of the cross, thus,—

But though a lamb was his adopted symbol, yet *he spake as a dragon*. The bulls that were subscribed "the servant of servants" were often interdicts to kingdoms, sentences of excommunication against princes, or deposition of kings. However meek the pretence, the words of the father of the church were the acts of him who spake marvellous words against the Most High, *as those of a dragon*, and of the man of sin who exalted himself above all.

"In the *ambitious contests* which the popes maintained *for the rights of the church*, their sufferings or their success must equally tend to increase the popular veneration. They sometimes wandered in poverty and exile, the victims of persecution; and the apostolic zeal with which they offered themselves to martyrdom must engage the favour and sympathy of every catholic breast. And sometimes *thundering from the vatican*, they created, judged, and deposed the kings of the world: nor could the proudest Roman be disgraced by submitting to a priest, whose feet were kissed, and whose stirrup was held by the successor of Charlemagne."*

He had two horns like a lamb, and he spake as a dragon.

---

* Gibbon's Hist. vol. xii. pp. 261, 262.

And he exerciseth all the power of the first beast before him.

"After the loss of her legions and provinces, the genius and fortune of the popes *again* restored the *supremacy of Rome*."*—"Under the *sacerdotal monarchy* of St. Peter, the nations began to *resume* the practice of seeking, on the banks of the Tiber, their *kings, their laws*, and the oracles of their fate."†—"The *sovereignty of Rome* no longer depended on the choice of a fickle people; and the successors of St. Peter and Constantine were invested with the purple and prerogatives of the Cæsars."‡

The *first beast* was wounded to death, but his deadly wound was healed; and the second beast *causeth the earth, and them that dwell therein, to worship the first beast whose deadly wound was healed.*

"On the festival of Christmas, the last year of the eighth century, Charlemagne appeared in the church of St. Peter's, and, to gratify the vanity of Rome, he had exchanged the simple dress of his country for the habit of a patrician. After the celebration of the holy mysteries, Leo (the pope) suddenly placed a precious *crown* on his head, and the dome resounded with the acclamations of the people, 'Long life and victory to Charles, the most pious *Augustus*, crowned by God the great and pacific EMPEROR OF THE ROMANS!' The head and body of Charlemagne were consecrated by the royal unction; after the example of the Cæsars, he was saluted or *adored* by the pontiff; his coronation oath represents a promise to *maintain the faith and privileges of the church*; and the first fruits were paid in his rich offerings to the shrine of the apostle. The appellation of *great* has been often bestowed, and sometimes deserved; but CHARLEMAGNE is the only prince in whose favour the title has been indissolubly blended with the name. That name, with the addition of *saint*, is inserted in the Roman calendar, and the saint, by a rare felicity, is crowned with the praises of the historians and philosophers of an enlightened age. Without injustice to his fame, I may discern some blemishes in the sanctity and greatness of THE RESTORER OF THE WESTERN EMPIRE."§

"When Otho, the king of Germany, restored and appropriated the western empire, (A. D. 962,) after the fall of the Charlovignian race, at the head of a victorious army he passed the Alps, subdued the kingdom of Italy, delivered the pope, and (for ever) fixed the imperial crown in the name and nation of Germany. From that

* Gibbon's Hist. vol. ix. p. 131, c. 49. † Ibid. p. 151.
‡ Ibid. p. 161. See above, p. 96, &c. § Ibid. pp. 173—175.

memorable era, two maxims of public jurisprudence were introduced by force, and ratified by time. I. That the prince who was elected at the German diet, acquired from that instant the subject kingdoms of Italy and Rome. II. But that he might *not legally assume the titles of emperor and Augustus till he had received the crown from the hands of the Roman pontiff.*"*

"In the beginning of the twelfth century, the era of the first crusade, Rome was revered by the Latins, as the *metropolis of the world, as the throne of the pope and the emperor;* who, from the eternal city, derived their title, their honours, and the right of exercise of temporal dominion. After so long an interruption, it may not be useless to repeat, that the successors of Charlemagne and the Othos were chosen beyond the Rhine in a national diet; but that these princes were content with the humble names of kings of Germany and Italy, *till they had passed the Alps and the Appenines, to seek* THEIR IMPERIAL CROWN *on the banks of the Tiber.* At some distance from the city, their approach was saluted by a long procession of the clergy and people, with *palms and crosses;* and the terrific emblems of wolves and lions, *of dragons and eagles,* that floated in the military banners, *represented the departed legions and cohorts of the republic.* The royal oath to maintain the liberties of Rome, was thrice reiterated, at the bridge, the gate, and the stairs of the Vatican; and the distribution of a customary donative feebly imitated the magnificence of the first Cæsars. *In the church of St. Peter,* the coronation was performed by his successor; the voice of God was confounded with that of the people; and the public consent was declared in the acclamations of 'Long life and victory to *our lord the pope!* Long life and victory to *our lord the emperor!* Long life and victory to the Roman and Teutonic armies!' The name of Cæsar and Augustus, the laws of Constantine and Justinian, the example of Charlemagne and Otho, established the supreme dominion of the emperors; *their title* and IMAGE was *engraved on the papal coins;* and their jurisdiction was marked by the sword of justice, which they delivered to the prefect of the city, &c. Once, and once only in his life, each emperor, with an army of Teutonic vassals, descended from the Alps."†

The restoration of the western empire, or that of Rome, by the pope, scarcely requires any farther illustration; but the following extract from the pen of an able lawyer, shews so tersely and distinctly how the nations of Europe were connected, and forms so obvious an elucidation of the prophecy, as descriptive both of papal and imperial Rome, that

---

* Gibbon's Hist. vol. ix. pp. 190, 191.
† Ibid. vol. xii. pp. 258, 259, c. 69.

such testimony may be associated with that of Gibbon.

"There was no general connexion existing between the states of Europe, till the Romans, in endeavouring to make themselves masters of the world, had the greatest part of the European states under their dominion. From that time there necessarily existed a sort of connexion between them, and this connexion was strengthened by the famous decree of Caracalla, by the adoption of the Roman laws, and by the influence of the Christian religion, which introduced itself insensibly into almost all the subdued states. *After the destruction of the empire of the west*, the *hierarchical system* naturally led the several christian states to consider themselves in ecclesiastical matters as unequal members of one great society: Besides the immoderate ascendant that the *bishop of Rome* had the address to obtain, as *spiritual chief of the church*, and *his consequent success in elevating the emperor to the character of temporal chief*, brought such an *accession of authority to the latter*, that most of the nations of Europe showed for some ages *so great a deference to the emperor*, that in many respects Europe seemed to form but *one society*, consisting of unequal members subject to *one sovereign*."*

And he doth great wonders, so that he maketh fire to come down from heaven upon earth in the sight of men, and deceiveth them that dwell upon the earth by means of those miracles which he hath power to do in the sight of the beast, saying to them that dwell on the earth that they should make an image to the beast which had the wound by a sword and did live. And he had power to give life unto the image of the beast, that the image of the beast should both speak, and cause that as many as would not worship the image of the beast should be killed.

It was a realm of darkness over which popery reigned; its power lay in the pretence of *miracles*, its art in *deceiving* the people; and not only did it restore the empire of *Rome*, and healed its deadly wound, but gave life also to the *image* of the beast, and re-established the *idolatry* of the pagan empe-

* Brewster's Encyclop. vol. xii. p. 618. Art. Law, by the late James Bell, Esq. Advocate.

rors. The connexion between miracles and the revival of *image-worship*, may be seen in the very titles of immediately succeeding paragraphs of Gibbon's history, thus following in close order,—"*fabulous martyrs and relics—miracles—revival of polytheism—introduction of pagan ceremonies.*"*

"In the long period of twelve hundred years, which elapsed between the reign of Constantine and the reformation of Luther, the *worship* of saints and relics corrupted the pure and perfect simplicity of the Christian model. The progress of superstition would have been less rapid and victorious, if the faith of the people had not been assisted by the seasonable aid of visions and *miracles*, &c. The tombs of the martyrs were the perpetual theatre of *innumerable miracles*. The sublime and simple theology of the primitive Christians was gradually corrupted; and the MONARCHY of heaven, already clothed with metaphysical subtleties, was degraded by the introduction of a *popular mythology*, which tended to *restore* the REIGN OF POLYTHEISM. The *same uniform* original spirit of superstition might suggest, in the most distant ages and countries, the same methods of DECEIVING the credulity, and of affecting the senses of mankind; but it must ingenuously be confessed, that the ministers of the Catholic church *imitated the profane model*, which they were impatient to destroy. The most respectable bishops had persuaded themselves, that the ignorant rustics would more cheerfully renounce the superstition of paganism, if they found some *resemblance*, some compensation in the bosom of Christianity. The religion of Constantine achieved, in less than a century, the final conquest of the Roman empire; but the victors themselves were insensibly subdued by the arts of their vanquished rivals."† "The *pagan* rites of genuflexion, luminaries, and incense, *again* stole into the Catholic church."‡

The connexion between the establishment of images, the coronation of Charlemagne, and the restoration of the western empire is, in a similar manner, as manifest, even in these very words, from the index, or contents, of another chapter of the same history, when thus set down at length.

* Gibbon's Hist. vol. v. pp. 127—136, four concluding paragraphs of chap. 27.

† Ibid.

‡ Ibid. vol. ix. p. 115.

Introduction, *worship*, and persecution of *images*.—Revolt of Italy and Rome.—*Temporal dominion of the popes*.—Conquest of Italy by the Franks.—*Establishment of images*.—Character and *coronation of Charlemagne*.—*Restoration* and decay of the *Roman empire in the West*.—Independence of Italy.—*Constitution of the Germanic body*.*—"In the eighth century of the Christian era, a religious quarrel, the worship of images, provoked the Romans to assert their independence: their bishop became the *temporal* as well as the *spiritual* father of a free people; and of the western empire, which was restored by Charlemagne, the title and *image* still decorate (decorated) the singular constitution of modern Germany."†

Such is the rise and character of the second beast, the revival of the first, and their joint connexion. The power of popery lay in *deceiving* the nations. His coming was after the working of Satan, with all powers and signs, and lying wonders, and all *deceivableness* of unrighteousness. The pretended miracles were innumerable, and need not to be recorded. The causing of fire to come down from heaven is still a superstitious act, and is yet deceitfully practised, even where Jesus preached. "The *same methods* of DECEIVING the credulity of mankind," which pagans had originated, were adopted anew by "the ministers of the Catholic church, who imitated the profane model;" and *deceived them that dwell upon the earth.* The deadly wound of the first beast was healed. The emperorship of Rome was restored by the pontiff; and the existence of the authority and title was made dependant on coronation by his hand. It was he who elevated the emperor to the character of temporal chief, and set him over kings. The idolatry of paganism was renewed, and with it the persecution of the worshippers of God. They who refused to worship an image, became, as before, the martyrs of Jesus. The temporal power was sub-

* Gibbon's Hist. vol. ix. p. 115. c. 49. † Ibid. vol. xii. p. 287

servient to the spiritual, and they who had not the badge of popery were victims of the most relentless persecution.

And he caused all, both small and great, rich and poor, free and bond, to receive a mark in their right hand and in their foreheads, and that no man might buy or sell, save he that had the mark, or the name of the beast, or the number of his name. Here is wisdom. Let him that hath understanding count the number of the beast: for it is the number of a man; and his number is six hundred threescore and six.—Wherever the papal authority was disowned, or the creed of the church of Rome rejected, or its infallibility brought into question, nations were laid under an interdict, kings excommunicated, and the secluded heretic was searched out. Wherever the fearful *anathema* of the church fell, all interchange of kindly or common offices of duty, friendship, or charity were prohibited; the *great* had no longer authority over the *small*, nor did the small pay any deference to the *great;* the rich had no longer any pity on the *poor*, nor would the poor take a bribe from the hands of the *rich;* the *free* could no longer command the personal duties of the *bond;* and the bondsman heard unheeded the mandate or entreaty of his master. The brand of the church was as the spot of a leper; and the father of a family was as a stranger, or an enemy, in his household; and a king was as an alien in his kingdom. Whenever the inquisitor's coach was at the door, and so soon as the name of the denounced was uttered, the menials turned their master from his house, or the husband led forth the wife of his bosom, or the parent gave up the hope of his family or the child of his love, to be carried to the dungeon where no eye could see them, or unto the stake where none could save. With those on whom the sentence of excommunication was passed, all communication was interdicted, and, as even a sentence against a king of England shews, all were ordered to avoid them, on pain of *excommunication*. The very term implies the cessation of all friendly intercourse; all ties were broken, and all distinctions lost in the overwhelming sensation, under the dominion of dark superstition, of a sentence pronounced by an infallible judge, and involving eternal reprobation. No doctrine was more rife throughout Europe than this, that out of the church there is no salvation. The words were those of the man of sin, who himself goeth into perdition; the earthly power that dealt out damnation, must itself de destroyed: but such for ages was the supremacy of its dominion, that *no man might buy or sell save he that had the mark, or the name of the beast, or the number of his name.*

The connexion and union between imperial and papal Rome form the subject of the vision, and they are not divided at its close. Letters being equivalent to figures, *Romiith*, the Roman, (agreeing with either beast, or kingdom,) *Lateinos*, the Latin, (the number of a man,) and Apostates, apostate,—the Roman kingdom, the Latin apostate—contain *each* the precise number *six hundred sixty and six**—the *name*, the *number*, and *the mark* of the beast.

Such, in past history, is the Roman empire and papal power—giving, we apprehend, no vague or ambiguous commentary to the words of the prophet. The significancy, at least, of the first and second beast, may not be held doubtful. But the whole of their history may not yet be told, nor the whole of the prophecy be developed. The great red dragon, the symbol of the Roman empire as the enemy of the church, reappears at the close of the preceding

---

* See Evidence of Prophecy, Appen. iii.

vision. The witnesses have also to be *killed*. And in the judgment against the papacy, (chap. xvii.) its character and power, as well as fate, together with those of the *empire*, are yet more fully defined; the ten-horned beast, rising at last out of the bottomless pit and going into perdition, is again upon the scene. And things noted in scripture, and, perhaps, not to be expounded yet, may possibly be reserved as the signs of other times. And therefore it may remain for that time to disclose an infinitely clearer illustration of the last form of government of imperial Rome, (though now, it *is not*,) than all human ingenuity can devise.

Having thus glanced respectively, in brief review, at those separate visions which John saw, when, after having delineated the political history of the world down to the close of the seven thunders, it was told him by the angel that he must prophesy again, and when, in the renewed prophesying, he was commanded to measure the temple of God and the altar and them that worship therein, we may here, before entering on the consideration of a new series of predictions, give heed to the *time* which, in these visions, is *measured* and thrice repeated by the prophet, in precise accordance with the same prophetic period, which is also twice announced by Daniel.

There are other periods, not yet expired, connected with that of the twelve hundred and sixty years, during which the various kingdoms into which the Roman empire was subdivided, was given into the hands of the papacy. And it is not, perhaps, yet possible to determine, with *absolute* precision, the commencement or termination of that period. But in respect to the time when religious persecution (if so sacrilegious a term may be used) was sanctioned and established in the church by civil authority, when he that *letted* had been taken out of the way, and the pope's authority was submissively deferred to, by the Roman emperor then reigning at Constantinople, as that of the Head of the Church, no era in history seems to be more marked, than that of the age of Justinian, whether we look into the pages of the ecclesiastical or civil historian.

"The emperor Justinian," says Dupin, "may be justly ranked among ecclesiastical writers, for NEVER *prince did meddle so much with what concerns the affairs of the church, nor make so many constitutions and laws upon this subject.* He was persuaded that it was the duty of an emperor, and for the good of the state, to *have a particular care of the church, to defend its faith, to regulate external discipline, and to employ the civil laws and the temporal power to preserve in it order and peace.* Upon this account he did not only make *a collection of the laws* made by the princes, his predecessors, about ecclesiastical discipline, *but he added many to them.*"*

"Justinian," says Gibbon, in summing up his character and reign, "has been already seen in the various lights of a prince, a conqueror, and a lawgiver: the theologian still remains, and it affords an unfavourable prejudice, that *his theology should form a very prominent feature of his portrait.* The sovereign sympathized with his subjects in their *superstitious reverence for living and departed saints;* his *code,* and more especially his *novels, confirm and enlarge the privileges of the clergy;* and in every dispute between the monk and the layman, the partial judge was inclined to pronounce, that truth, and innocence, and justice are always on the side of the church. In his public and private devotions, the emperor was assiduous and exemplary; his prayers, vigils, and fasts displayed the austere penance of a monk, his fancy was amused by the hope, or belief, of personal inspiration; he had secured the *patronage of the virgin,* and St. Michael the archangel; and his recovery from a dangerous disease was ascribed to the miraculous succour of the holy martyrs Cosmas and Damian. The capital and the provinces of the East were decorated with the monuments of his religion; and, though the far greater part of these costly structures may be attributed to his taste or ostentation, the zeal of the royal architect was probably quickened by a genuine sense of love and gratitude towards his invisible benefactors. Among the titles of imperial greatness, the name of *Pious* was most pleasing to his ear; *to promote the temporal and spiritual interest of the church, was the serious business of his life;* and the

---

* Cent. vi. vol. v. p. 37.

duty of father of his country was often sacrificed to that of *defender of the faith.* While the barbarians invaded the provinces, while the victorious legions marched under the banners of Bellisarius and Narses, the successor of Trajan, unknown to the camp, was content to vanquish *at the head of a synod.*

"Toleration was not the virtue of the times, and indulgence to rebels has seldom been the virtue of princes. But when the prince descends to the narrow and peevish character of a disputant, he is easily provoked to supply the defect of argument by the plenitude of power, and to *chastise* without mercy the perverse blindness of those who wilfully shut their eyes against the light of demonstration. *The reign of Justinian was an uniform yet various scene of* PERSECUTION; *aud he appears to have surpassed his indolent predecessors, both in the contrivance of his laws and rigour of their* EXECUTION. The insufficient term of three months was assigned for the conversion or exile of all *heretics;* and if he still connived at their precarious stay, they were deprived, under his iron yoke, *not only of the benefits of society, but of the common birthright of men and Christians.*"*

From this evidence, it appears that never did prince meddle so much with the affairs of the church as did the Emperor Justinian; that he esteemed it a duty to defend the faith of the church, and to employ the civil laws and temporal power; that he confirmed and enlarged the privileges of the clergy; and that his reign was an uniform yet various scene of persecution, &c.

Such was the man who, perhaps more than any other, may be said to have given the church into the hands of the pope. Though more ambitious of vanquishing at the head of a synod than at the head of an army, he owned and maintained the supremacy of the pope, expressed his devotion to the Roman see, and *subjected and united to his holiness* all the priests of the whole east. But the supremacy of the pope was not then confined to the east. Under the same date in the age of Justinian, it is recorded by Gibbon,—

"The perseverance of the popes insensibly transferred to their

* Gibbon's Hist. vol. viii. pp. 321—324.

adversaries the appellation of schismatics; the Illyrian, African, and Italian churches were *oppressed by the civil and ecclesiastical powers*, not without some effort *of military force; the distant barbarians* TRANSCRIBED THE CREED OF THE VATICAN."*

In the answer of the pope to the epistle of Justinian, previously quoted, he declares, that, among the virtues of the emperor, "one shines as a star, his reverence for the apostolic chair, to which he has subjected and united all the churches, it being truly the head of all." Though the emperor's epistle was dated in 533, yet in it he states, that he not only did, but always *had* rendered honour to the apostolic chair, and honoured his holiness as a father. Here we would only submit a few historical facts and dates to the reader, and leave it to his determination whether there be not a rational presumption that the twelve hundred and sixty years, during which period the church was given into the hands of the pope, did not commence in the reign of Justinian, while their termination was correspondingly marked by the French Revolution, which, alike rejecting every form of faith, broke the charm by which popery had spell-bound the nations, when infidelity, armed with power, first assumed an active form, and, becoming the scourge of superstition, unconsciously avenged the blood of the saints, and, while disavowing every form of faith, proclaimed religious toleration, unknown among Roman Catholics since the days of Justinian.

Justinian ascended the imperial throne in the year 527. In the year 529 the Code of Justinian was published, and the order of Benedictine monks, afterwards the most extensive and influential in Christendom, was instituted. The new CODE of Justinian was honoured with his name,

* Ibid. vol. viii. p. 331. chap. 47.

and confirmed by his royal signature; authentic transcripts were multiplied by the pens of notaries and scribes; they were transmitted to the magistrates of the European, the Asiatic, and afterwards the African provinces; and "the law of the empire was proclaimed on solemn festivals at the doors of churches.*" Twelve hundred and sixty years subsequently to the first publication of the Code of Justinian, the French Revolution began in 1789, and before the close of that year it was decreed "that the estates of the church were at the disposal of the nation."†

The Pandects, or digest, were composed from the 15th December, A.D. 530, to December 16, A.D. 533, in which year the Institutes were also published. In the year 1790, or twelve hundred and sixty years subsequent to the former of these dates, (before which time the code of Justinian could scarcely have been proclaimed throughout all the Roman empire,)

"the Assembly had determined, that, all prejudices apart, the property of the church should come under confiscation for the benefit of the nation, and decreed the assumption of the church lands. A motion was made for decreeing that the holy and apostolical religion was that of France, and that its worship alone should be permitted; but all who favoured it were insulted, beat, and *maltreated by a large and furious multitude, and it was withdrawn in terror and despair.* Any experiment on the church might be tried with effect, since the religion which it taught seemed NO LONGER *to interest the national legislators. A civil institution was framed for the clergy, declaring them* TOTALLY INDEPENDENT OF THE SEE OF ROME, *and vesting the choice of bishops in the departmental authorities. To this constitution each priest and prelate was required to adhere by a solemn oath.* A subsequent decree of the Assembly declared forfeiture of his benefice against whomsoever should hesitate."‡

---

* Gibbon's Hist. vol. viii. p. 38. c. 44.

† London Annual Register, 1791, p. 68.

‡ Sir Walter Scott's Life of Napoleon, vol. i. pp. 221—224 Annual Register, ib. p. 101.

About four thousand five hundred religious houses were suppressed in France* in the same year, 1790.

An incident recorded in the *Memoirs of Lavalette* supplies a curious, if not striking, illustration, as a note of the time.

> "The events that preceded the grand drama of 1789 took me by surprise in the midst of my books and my love of study. I was then reading 'L'Esprit de Lois,' a work that charmed me by its gravity, depth, and sublimity. I wished also to become acquainted with *code of our own laws;* but Dommanget, to whom I mentioned my desire, laughed, and pointed to the *Justinian code, the common law code of the kingdom,*" &c.† "I thought I should do well to unite, with the meditations of my closet, the observations of those scenes of disorder which were *harbingers of the revolution.*"‡

In the year 533 the Institutes of Justinian were published. "The *Code*, the *Pandects*, and the Institutes, were declared to be the legitimate system of civil jurisprudence; they alone were admitted in the tribunals, and they alone were taught in the academies of Rome, Constantinople, and Berytus."§ And in the same year, in the case of an appeal by the emperor to the ecclesiastical decision of the pope, (which itself implies the supremacy of the pontiff,) he had addressed the pope as the Head of all the holy Churches. And as the recognition of the supremacy of the pope seemed thus to be *complete* in the year 533, on the part of the emperor who put the power into his hands, so, in like rapid, and yet graduated progress, with the same appointed space intervening, the dominion of the papacy was destroyed and disannulled in that kingdom which had been its chief stay for ages, in the year 1793,

---

* Brewster's Encycl. vol. vi. p. 455. Chron. Table, 1790.
† Lavalette's Memoirs, vol. i. p. 4. ‡ Ib. p. 5.
§ Gibbon's Hist. vol. viii. p. 39, c. 44.

the power was wholly taken out of the hands of the pope, and infidelity, or rather atheism, was proclaimed, and popery abolished.

*"The churches were in most districts of France closed against priests and worshippers—the bells were broken, and cast into cannon—and the whole ecclesiastical establishment destroyed."**

The papacy was *to wear out the saints of the Most High, for twelve hundred and sixty* years; and the *judgment was to sit and consume and destroy it unto the end.* The papal power *began* to be destroyed; and the time was come for *the last vials of the wrath of God to be poured out.* From the last of the seven thunders to the first of the seven vials, a very brief space intervened; and there was then *no longer delay.* Another link may, perhaps, thus be seen to connect the various prophecies, and to show the coherence of the system.

A tabular view of parallel predictions may present to the reader at a glance,—1st, The prophetic description of the Roman empire as the papacy emerged from it. 2d, The rise of the papal power. 3d, Its exaltation. 4th, Its blasphemous assumptions. 5th, The persecution it inflicted on the saints. 6th, The change of times and laws which it introduced or enjoined. 7th, The honouring of guardian saints, or idolatry, which formed so large a portion of its worship. 8th, The gorgeous ornaments of its churches, and rich offerings to the saints. 9th, Its miraculous pretensions. 10th, The period of the duration of its power. And, 11th, the consequent sitting of the judgment, to take away his dominions, to consume and to destroy it unto the end.

* Scott's Life of Napoleon, vol. ii. p. 306.

CHAPTER XXIV.

THE SEVEN VIALS.

From the previous visions, both of Daniel and John, it may be inferred, in a manner neither doubtful nor indistinct, that a season of *war* and not of peace, succeeds to the termination of the twelve hundred and sixty years. After that period, as remains to be seen, there is a time for the sitting of the judgment, and also for the cleansing of the sanctuary. And that the appointed time of papal persecution was to be succeeded in like manner as Daniel foretold, by a period during which *they shall take away his dominion, to consume and destroy it unto the end*, is plainly intimated in the vision introductory to the seven last plagues, in which they that *had gotten* the victory over the beast and over his image are seen standing with the harps of God, and it is said, as if noting the sequence and the time, AFTER THAT the seven last plagues, or the vials of the wrath of God, are poured upon the earth.

And I saw another sign in heaven, great and marvellous, seven angels having the seven last plagues; for in them is filled up the wrath of God. And I saw as it were a sea of glass mingled with fire; and them that had gotten the victory over the beast, and over his image, and over his mark, and over the number of his name, stand on the sea of glass having the harps of God. And they sang the song of Moses the servant of God, and the song of the Lamb, saying, Great and marvellous are thy works, Lord God Almighty; just and true are thy ways, thou King of saints. Who shall not fear thee, O Lord, and glorify thy name? for thou only art holy: for the nations shall come and worship before thee; for thy judgments are made manifest. And after that I looked, and, behold, the temple of the tabernacle of the testimony in heaven was opened: And the seven angels came out of the temple, having the seven plagues, clothed in pure and white linen, and *having their breasts girded with golden girdles; and one of the four living creatures gave unto the seven angels seven golden vials full of the wrath of God, who liveth for ever and ever. And the temple was filled with smoke from the glory of God and from his power; and no man was able to enter into the temple, till the seven plagues of the seven angels were fulfilled.* Chap. xv.

The last sight of the expiring martyrs, in human view, was on the gibbet or in the flames. And all that man could farther do was to disperse their mutilated limbs, or scatter their ashes in the air. But in the heavenly vision, they are seen standing on a sea of glass, and singing praises unto God, the song of Moses and the song of the Lamb. And at the very time when men were lifting up their voice against heaven, renouncing all faith in Him that sitteth upon the throne, and in the Lamb that once was slain, and deeming it wisdom to deny the gospel, and to deride all the evidences of its truth, the saints in heaven were proclaiming that in the acts that were passing, and about to pass on the earth, even the *judgments* of God were *made manifest.* The interpretation of these judgments, therefore, should not be less clear and precise, than that of any, or of all, that have preceded them.

Many vague and discordant interpretations have given a seeming sanction to the prevalent suspicion and distrust respecting the application of prophecies to modern and existing events. Great caution, indeed, is requisite; but it may at least be questionable

n sit
beast,
re seven mountains. And there are
horns are the ten kings.—The woman
at great city, which reigneth over the
12, 18.

ry of
beast
d seven heads and ten horns, 7.

had

saw- She hath glorified herself—
teth, she hath said in her heart, I sit

whether a careless incredulity savours of wisdom. The whole enigma of the world's history has yet to be solved by the Revelation of Jesus Christ. The varied and changeable fancies of men are not chargeable on the word of Him, who is the same yesterday, to day, and forever. The blessing promised to those who read and understand the words of this prophecy is not taken from them, because some, involving it in tenfold mystery, may have held forth extravagant imaginings of theirs as tantamount to the dictates of inspiration. And although it be possible that another Uzzah may have rashly put forth his hand to touch the ark in which the testimony is kept, as if it needed to be upheld by human power, and that some may have drawn their interpretations rather from the air than from the earth, or more from fancies than from facts, yet it behoves all to remember that the book of Revelation is the ark of the *testimony*, from which it becomes us not to turn away, but towards which we may reverently inquire, knowing that of itself it is *Revelation*, that it is given to be read and understood, and that there is a time when the *judgments* shall be *made manifest*. Christians, therefore, may well consider not merely whether they be warranted to hear, but whether they be warranted to forbear from hearing; whether it becomes them to close their eyes or to shut their ears against the word that the Lord hath spoken; or whether, looking to the promised blessing on the deed, it does not rather behove them to hear and understand, whoever may wrest any portion of Scriptures, or whoever may be silent, or whoever may sneer. If in our days,—full as they are of events not less critical and marvellous, nor yet less influential on the fate of the world, than any of the past,—as in all that have preceded them, the judgments of God be abroad on the earth, whether does the wisdom lie in considering or disregarding them? Nay, as touching hypocrisy itself, a word so carelessly bandied from mouth to mouth, is it not made chargeable by Jesus, (who taught men to pray always and not to faint,) on others than on those who *for a pretence* make long prayers? Or who is it, that, appealing to an ordinary exercise of reason, and pointing to the earth and to the sky, did say, Ye hypocrites! ye can discern the face of the earth and of the sky, but how is it that ye do not discern the signs of the times? Are we to have less faith in the words of the prophets, and in the revelation of Jesus Christ, than in a cloud, or in the colour of the sky? and are we to regard their indications less than that of these changeful things? Caution, nay, extreme caution, is requisite on the part of any writer who adventures on so serious a task, lest, on so sacred a theme, he should be greatly guilty of the slightest misrepressentation; and caution, nay, extreme caution, there also should be, on the part of the reader, lest he should be seduced to give heed unto a fable. But not less cautious or watchful should men be, that they do not copy the example of that generation whom the Lord Jesus thus charged with hypocrisy, and to whom, after disregarding many, no sign was given. It may not be always safe to let signs from heaven pass unheeded. And if the matter contained in the preceding pages be not a wild and reckless speculation; if there be reason to presume that nearly half a century is past, since *the judgment* began *to sit* upon the papacy, and *the vials of the wrath of God* began *to be poured out upon the earth;* and if the season thus be come concerning which it is announced that *the judgments of God are made manifest*, then *the time now is*, that the marvellous convulsions of which the earth has been recently the scene, may re-echo in the ears of men, on the passing of the last plagues, what the living creatures from around the altar said unto John, on the opening of each seal—come and see. There is at least a distinctiveness in the description of the seven last plagues, or the seven vials of the wrath of God, which demands some attention.

And I heard a great voice out of the temple, saying to the seven angels, go your ways, and pour out the vials of the wrath of God upon the earth. And the first went, and poured out his vial upon the earth; and there fell a noisome and grievous sore upon the men which had the mark of the beast, and upon them which worshipped his image. And the second angel poured out his vial upon the sea; and it became as the blood of a dead man: and every living soul died in the sea. And the third angel poured out his vial upon the rivers and fountains of waters, and they became blood. And I heard the angel of the waters say, Thou art righteous, O Lord, which art, and wast, and shalt be, because thou hast judged thus: for they have shed the blood of saints and prophets, and thou hast given them blood to drink, for they are worthy. And I heard another out of the altar say, Even so, Lord God Almighty, true and righteous are thy judgments. And the fourth angel poured out his vial upon the sun; and power was given unto him to scorch men with fire. And men were scorched with great heat, and blasphemed the name of God, which had power over these plagues: and they repented not to give him glory. And the fifth angel poured out his vial upon the seat of the beast; and his kingdom was full of darkness; and they gnawed their tongues for pain, and blasphemed the God of heaven because of their pains and their sores, and repented not of their deeds. And the sixth angel poured out his vial upon the great river Euphrates; and the water thereof was dried up, that the way of the kings of the east might be prepared. And I saw three unclean spirits like frogs come out of the mouth of the dragon, and out of the mouth of the beast, and out of the mouth of the false prophet. For they are the spirits of devils, working miracles, which go forth unto the kings of the earth, and of the whole world, to gather them to the battle of that great day of God Almighty. Behold, I come as a thief. Blessed is he that watcheth, and keepeth his garments, lest he walk naked, and they see his shame. And he gathered them together into a place called in the Hebrew tongue Armageddon. And the seventh angel poured out his vial into the air; and there came a great voice out of the temple of heaven, from the throne, saying, it is done. And there were voices, and thunders, and lightnings; and there was a great earthquake, such as was not since men were upon the earth, so mighty an earthquake, and so great. And the great city was divided into three parts, and the cities of the nations fell: and great Babylon came in remembrance before God, to give unto her the cup of wine of the fierceness of his wrath. And every island fled away, and the mountains were not found. And there fell upon men a great hail out of heaven, every stone about the weight of a talent: and men blasphemed God because of the plague of the hail; for the plague thereof was exceeding great, chap. xvi.

Before entering minutely on the subject of the "seven last plagues, in which is filled up the wrath of God," it may not be amiss, as tending to shew the intimate connexion and systematic coherence of the whole, to take a retrospective glance at those which have preceded them.

The golden magnificence of Babylon the great; the union of Media and Persia into one dominant empire, which subverted and succeeded the Babylonian; the conquest of Persia by the Greeks; the establishment of their dominion; the subsequent rise and extension of the iron empire of Rome, great, terrible, and strong exceedingly; the setting up of the kingdom of God, by superhuman means, in the days of these kingdoms, or while the last of them was at the height of its glory, and in the fulness of its strength; the subdivision of the empire of Rome itself into various kingdoms; the rise among them of the papal power, diverse from the rest, attaining a secular dominion over a large portion of Italy, and exercising a high control over all the other kingdoms which Rome had ruled; the similar and nearly co-eval rise of Mahometanism; the sway which it acquired over the countries of the east; the long continued prevalence of both; and the things noted in the scripture of truth, the Persian invasion of Greece, and the Grecian invasion and subjugation of Persia; the immediate partition, without the intervention of a single reign, of the kingdom of Alexander into four notable ones; the history of Egypt and Syria, under the Ptolmies and Seleucidæ; the subversion of the Jewish polity and state, and the desolation of Judea by the Romans; the preaching of the gospel, or the instruction of many by men of understanding who knew their God, and confirmed their doctrine by marvellous works; their grievous and multiform persecutions during a long period the little help which was all that, after three centuries of violent opposition, the conversion of an Emperor could give to the cause that was of God and not of man; the consequent hypocritical profession, by many, of the Christian faith; the renewal, for a long and appointed time, of the persecution of the servants and true worshippers of God; the rise and character of the papacy, its exaltation, splendour, blasphemous pretensions, and idolatrous practices; the speedy and enduring rod that was laid on an apostate and idolatrous church, first by the Saracens from the south, and afterwards perpetuated by the Turks from the north; the irruption of the former, and the settlement of the latter, within the bounds of the Roman empire; the permanent subjugation of the world for ages, to popery, the great apostacy of the west, and to Mahometanism, the great imposture of the east (thus set forth before the world as the two last horns, both of the fourth beast, and of the ram and the he-goat); and, though springing thus from the ruin of their empires, like horns from the head of a beast, the more than imperial despotism by which the earth has been held and divided between them in thraldom and in bondage, not altogether yet rid of and broken, which mocked the sovereignty of Alexander and the Cæsars; are events which, linking ancient to modern times, for the space of twenty-four centuries, without the want of a single essential fact, or the transposition of a word, are as prominently marked in the book of Daniel, as in the history of the world. In the Revelation of Jesus Christ, on the opening of the seals, we may come and see on earth what John saw prefigured in heaven; and the whole view of the religious state of man, within the compass and even without the limits of all the kingdoms which Daniel foretold, and in the long retrospect of more than seventeen centuries, since the Revelation was given, is open before us; and we see a pure and primitive Christianity; a murderous Mahometanism; the dark superstition and spiritual tyranny of the Romish church, till all was black; and infidelity, in its livid paleness, till, spiritually, all was death; together with the persecuted followers of the Lamb, till even in their faith and patience they could not forbear from crying out, How long, O Lord? Again, looking to the political state of the world, and the various phases of such a changeful thing, we see, as if eclipses, whether partial or full, were noted in a book and calculated to their time, how, after a period of silence in heaven, and of suspended judgments on earth, and also of commotions preparatory to the downfall of Rome, the Goths and Vandals, like a storm of hail and fire, overspread and desolated the Roman world;—how Genseric ravaged the coasts and burned the fleets of the Romans, and was like unto a burning mountain cast into the sea; how Attila, burning cities in his course, and blazing like a star, ravaged the land of a thousand streams, spread his devastations within the borders of Italy, along the Po and its tributary waters, between the Alps and the Appenine, falling upon the fountains and rivers of waters. And part after part having thus been dismembered from the empire, looking upon the imperial city, no longer a terror to the world, we see the seditious hosts, under rebellious chiefs, severing the north of Italy from the diminished empire, and establishing a rival metropolis in Milan. From hence, too, from the waters that were made bitter, the western empire was extinguished, till the sun, the moon and the stars were smitten, and the emperor, the consuls, the senate were no more. Where the emperor had reigned the pope arose; and a kingdom, or spiritual domination, diverse from all others, was gradually established on the earth. Instead of trumpets which sounded for a moment, or wars that speedily effected their objects, *woes* that endured for ages, came upon Christendom. As previously earthly warriors, seeking to establish an earthly dominion, devastated and finally demolished an empire, which was itself built up by war and cemented by blood, so, in like appropriate judgment, a false religion became the scourge of an apostate church. The coincident exhaustion of the eastern empire, which had first conferred on the pope the supremacy of the churches, and the fall of the great king, who had threatened the last remnant of the empire of the Cæsars, with annihilation,—by which mutual destruction, the power and pride of Persia was humbled in the dust, and the blaze of its glory turned into blackness, smoothed the path of the Mahometans from the deserts of Arabia to the banks of the Indus and the shores of the Atlantic. The period of the two first woes was marked by centuries. The first hurt and tormented, from the one end of Europe to the other; the second became a settled woe, and, after a preparation of nearly four centuries, the sultan of the Turks occupied the throne of the Cæsars. From the taking of Constantinople, half a century, marked by continued impenitence in Western Europe, intervened till the time of the Reformation, which descended upon the earth like a mighty angel from heaven, with a little open book in his hand. After the establishment of the Reformation, itself of angelic likeness, and resplendent with light like pillars of fire amidst surrounding darkness, seven great successive wars ensued, affecting the interests of protestantism, and from which the political settlement of Europe and America took the form of it maintained at the eve of the French Revolution. After the seven thunders had uttered their voices, time was to be no longer; and it was given to John to prophesy *again*.

The various forms of religion, and commotions or revolutions of kingdoms, having thus successively passed in vision before him, a reed, like unto a rod, was put in his hand, and he was commanded to measure the temple of God and the altar, and them that worship therein. The testifying of the witnesses, clothed in sackcloth; the contest of the church from first to last; the enemies that consecutively arose to destroy or subvert the kingdom of God and of his Christ, are described or measured, as if they had been a platform at his feet, over which he had only to stretch the measuring line in his hand. . To us, its termination may not yet be distinctly seen, after eighteen centuries have, in a large measure, filled up the space, which then had no local habitation but in the eye of the prophet, and which nothing on earth could then touch but the reed that was given him. Yet the oft-repeated limits of one space in time, and one eventful period in history, supply the more abundant data for warranting the presumption, if not confirming the opinion, that the 1260 years, from the time that the churches were given into the hands of the pope till the time that the judgment began to sit, comprised a period which, taking its date in the reign of Justinian, terminated in the revolution of France. If such a presumption be borne out by Scripture and by facts, then so far as hitherto brought down, the prophetic, political, and ecclesiastical records would jointly bring us to the same point, and lead us to the entrance on a new order of events. These, however, like all that preceeded them, have not to be tried by verisimilitude alone, but each must exhibit its own defined character, as well as occupy its appointed place, if the judgments of God be indeed so manifest that not a word could be wrested in accordance with a fancy, without distorting the figure set before us in the oracles of God.

Returning, then, to the exact point to which history had brought us down, we may trace the analogy anew, but in a defined and more distinctive form, between the words of prophecy and the records of history. The "*state of Europe*," in respect both to the character of the philosophy which prevailed at that very period, and the political excitements which betokened an approaching convulsion, is thus summarily described;—of the former, it is said,

"A set of men, many of them of talents of the first order, arrogating to themselves the exclusive title of philosophers, and actuated at first, perhaps, by a zeal for the truth, *carried on an incessant warfare against all that they were pleased to designate as superstition and vulgar prejudice*. But theirs was not that philosophy which elevated above all low and grovelling passions, and irradiated by light from heaven, views with pity rather than contempt the aberrations of man, and seeks by mild and gentle method to lead him into the way of truth. *It was heartless, cold, and cheerless:* its *summum bonum* was sensual indulgence or literary fame, and few of its professors displayed any real dignity of soul; its favourite weapon was ridicule; *it attacked not only the absurdities of the popular faith, but it levelled its shafts at the sublimest truths of religion; it shook the firmest bases of social order,* and sought to rob man of all lofty hopes and aspirations. Every mode of composition, from highest science and most serious history, down to the lightest tale, with which was often joined a sickly affected sensibility, calculated to gain it admittance into the female bosom. The consequence was, as might be expected, a general laxity of principle.

"The chief seat of this philosophy was France, where a court corrupt and profligate, beyond, perhaps any which Europe had yet witnessed, had utterly degraded the minds of the upper classes of society. The efforts of the virtuous Louis XVI. to stem this torrent was unavailing; *national vice was not to escape its merited chastisement.* The middle orders were disgusted and galled by the privileges of the *noblesse,* and their excessive pride and insolence; the writing of the philosophers, and the scandalous lives of many of the clergy, had shaken their reverence for religion; and abuses and oppression of arbitrary and extravagant government were keenly felt; the glorious struggle of the English for liberty in the last century, and the dignity and prosperity consequent on it, awakened the aspirations of the better disposed; the achievement of American independence filled the minds of many enthusiasts with vague ideas of freedom and happiness beneath republican institutions; and the lower orders in general looked forward to any change as a benefit.

"IT WAS A TIME OF INNOVATION, TURMOIL, AND VIOLENT CHANGE. The English colonies had thrown off the bridle of the mother country, whom she curbed too straitly. The kingdom of Poland had been most nefariously dismembered. Gustavus III. of Sweden had overthrown the aristocracy, and made himself absolute. A contest arose in the United Provinces, between the party of the stadtholder and those who wished to make the government of a more republican form, which drew the attention of all the principal powers; the respective parties appealed to arms, and by the Prussian aid the republicans were crushed. *All these were but preludes to the storm that was soon to burst over Europe.*"*

"The peace concluded at Versailles in 1783, was reasonably supposed," says Sir Walter Scott, "to augur a long repose to Europe." But the oracles of God spake not of repose as suited to the time. And only ten years elapsed, marked as a time of innovation, turmoil, and violent change, till a revolution, characterised by "unheard-of enormities," and affecting the destinies of the world, more, perhaps, than any single event in history, was perfected in one of the chief nations of Europe. The whole history of the world would be searched in vain for any parallel to such a period. Never was such a combination heard of against altars and thrones. But it came not without a cause, nor without an object to fulfil. And the historian can scarcely refrain from regarding it as the manifestation of judgment, without any allusion to the word of Revelation; nor can he withhold the admission that the

* *Outlines of History*, Lardner's Cyclop.

judgment was righteous. The unasked concession is extorted by facts. And, while innumerable witnesses, trained up in scepticism, were actors in the scene, a modern writer, of unequalled popularity and fame, who is not prone to introduce religion, takes up, when needful, the task of commentator.

"*The Catholic church had* GROWN OLD, and unfortunately did not possess the means of renovating her doctrines, or improving her constitution, so as to keep pace with the enlargement of the human understanding. The lofty claims to infallibility which she had set up and maintained during the middle ages,—claims which she could neither renounce nor modify,—now threatened in more enlightened times, like battlements too heavy for the foundation, to be the means of ruining the edifice they were designed to defend. *Vestigia nulla retrorsum*, continued to be the motto of the church of Rome. *She could explain nothing, soften nothing, renounce nothing, consistently with her assertion of impeccability.* The whole trash which had been accumulated *for ages of darkness* and ignorance, whether consisting of extravagant pretensions, incredible assertions, absurd doctrines which confounded the understanding, or puerile ceremonies which revolted the taste, were alike incapable of being explained away or abandoned. Infidelity, in attacking the absurd claims and extravagant doctrines of the church of Rome, had artfully availed herself of those abuses, as if they had been really a part of the Christian religion; and they whose credulity could not digest the grossest articles of the papist creed, thought themselves entitled to conclude, in general, against religion itself, from the abuses engrafted on it by ignorance and priesthood.*

"The mask of religion has been often used to cover more savage and extensive persecutions, but *at no time* did the spirit of intrigue, of personal malice, of slander and circumvention, appear more disgustingly from under the sacred disguise; and in the eyes of the thoughtless and the vulgar, the general cause of religion suffered in proportion.

"Partaking of the licence of its professors, the degraded literature of modern times called into its alliance that immorality, which not only Christian, but even heathen philosophy had considered as the wise, great, and happy state of existence. The licentiousness which walked abroad in such disgusting and undisguised nakedness, was a part of the unhappy bequest left by the Regent Duke of Orleans to the country which he governed. The conduct of Orleans and his minions was marked with *open infamy, deep enough to have called down in the age of miracles an immediate*

---

* Scott's Life of Napoleon, vol. i. pp. 26, 27.

JUDGMENT *from heaven; and crimes which the worst of the Roman emperors would have at least hidden in the solitary isle of Caprea, were acted as publicly as if men had no eyes and God no thunderbolts.*

"From this filthy Cocytus flowed those streams of impurity which disgraced France during the reign of Louis XV., and which continued in that of Louis XVI. to affect society, morals, and above all, literature. Religion cannot exist where immorality generally prevails, any more than a light can burn where the air is corrupted; and, accordingly, infidelity, was so general in France, as to predominate in almost every rank of society. The errors of the church of Rome, connected as they are with her ambitious attempts towards dominion over man, in their temporal as well as spiritual capacity, had long become the argument of the philosopher and the jest of the satirist; but in *exploding these pretensions*, and holding them up to ridicule, the philosophers of the age involved with them the general doctrines of Christianity itself; nay, some went so far as not only to deny inspiration, but to extinguish by their sophistry the lights of natural religion, implanted in our bosoms as a part of our birthright. Like the disorderly rabble at the time of the Reformation, (but with infinitely deeper guilt,) they not only *pulled down the symbols of idolatry*, which ignorance or priestcraft had introduced into the Christian church, but sacrilegiously defaced and desecrated the altar itself. This work* the philosophers, as they termed themselves, carried on with *such unlimited and eager zeal*, as plainly to show that *infidelity* as well as divinity, hath *its fanaticism*. *An envenomed fury against religion and all its doctrines;* a promptitude to avail themselves of every circumstance by which Christianity could be misrepresented; an ingenuity in mixing up their opinions in works, which seemed the least fitting to involve such discussions; above all, a pertinacity in slandering, ridiculing and vilifying all who ventured to oppose their principles, distinguished the correspondents in this celebrated *conspiracy* against a religion, which, however it may be defaced by human inventions, breathes only that peace on earth, and good will to the children of men, which was proclaimed by Heaven at its divine origin."

The age of miracles indeed was past, and pretension to them was one of the marks of an apostate church. Yet God had not left himself without a witness; nor, at the time when infidelity gave proof of its fanaticism, and even the literature of the age was distinguished by an "*envenomed fury against religion and all its doctrines,*" did the Father refrain

* Scott's Life of Napoleon, vol. i. p. 39.

from bearing witness of the Son. There was no Elisha on earth to call down fire from heaven. Nor did there live a man on whom an apostle of Jesus had laid his hand, and thereby invested with the power of working miracles. But before the age of miracles ceased, the spirit of prophecy, in speaking of the things that were to be thereafter, kept not silence concerning the latter times; and when fanatical atheists, with envenomed fury, were plotting, in their frenzy, against the Lord and his anointed, the testimony of Jesus, though unheeded on earth, sounded the louder, and was at last to be seen the clearer, and even then the judgments of God were declared to be made manifest. *And I saw another sign in heaven, great and marvellous, &c. And I heard a great voice out of the temple saying to the seven angels, Go your ways, and pour out the vials of the wrath of God upon the earth. And the first went and poured out his vial upon the earth, and there fell a noisome and grievous sore upon the men which had the mark of the beast, and upon them which worshipped his image*, chap. xvi. 1, 2.

It was not till open infamy was deep enough to have called down, in the age of miracles, an immediate *judgment* from heaven, that, in fulfilment of prophecy, *judgment did sit*, and the last plagues began to be fulfilled, and the first vial of the wrath of God was poured out on the land where the blood of saints had been most freely shed, where one witnessing church had been exterminated, and where the guilt and open infamy, at the time, were such as to have put the worst of pagan emperors to shame. Long-suffering as God is, he will by no means acquit the guilty; and when men lived as if God had no thunderbolts, the voice of his thunder was in the heavens; and when their iniquity was ripe for judgment, and when the angel had lifted up his hand to heaven, and sworn by him that liveth for ever and ever,—whose existence men began as openly to disown as they defied his wrath,—that there would be delay no longer, "he gave them up to hot thunderbolts; he cast upon them the fierceness of his anger, wrath, and indignation, and trouble, and he made a way to his anger."

Close to its time, and true to its character, the first vial of the wrath of God was poured upon the earth, and the revolutionary wars in Europe began. Yet so righteous are the judgments of God, that whether in chastisement of national or individual transgressions, the wicked reap but the fruit of their own doings. Their own wickedness corrects them, and their backslidings reprove them; and it is found at last to be an *evil thing and bitter* to have forsaken the Lord. Such was the *noisome and grievous sore that fell upon the men which had the mark of the beast and upon the men which worshipped his image.* God dealt with papal Rome as with idolatrous Israel of old. Ephraim is joined to idols, let him alone—Israel and Ephraim shall fall in their iniquity. "The church of Rome had grown old," not in years only but in idolatry and crime. Long had it held supreme dominion over the minds of men, and the grossest corruption of morals was the effect of a kindred corruption of doctrine. If abominations were practised unblushingly in France, in the close of the eighteenth century, which heathens would have hid, they, at least, had *never* been instructed in the virtue of indulgences or the power of absolution, or the purchaseable and transferable merits of saints, or that money could be paid during life, or after death for the ransom of a soul from any place of trial or of torment. The moral taint remained after the cause that produced it was gone. The love of unrighteousness ceased not with the belief of a lie. Once men had been taught to think light of sin by its redemption at an easy price; conscience did not recover its power, when reason exposed the fooleries of superstition. Belief in the gospel ceased together with faith in the church; and even the belief of a God, "the birth-right of man," shared the fate of the profane dogmas with which it was associated, and freed from moral restraints as well as from superstitious fears, men sinned remorselessly, without the licence of a priest. Woes had come upon apostate Christendom, and wars had succeeded—but still men repented not of the works of their hands, nor of their idolatries, neither of their murders, nor of their sorceries, nor of their fornication, nor of their thefts. The Roman Catholic body-politic was morally corrupted to the core. The peccant and pestiferous humours spread throughout the frame. No ointment on the skin could touch the malady.—"Why," as unto backsliding Israel, it might be said, "why should ye be stricken any more? Ye will revolt more and more. The whole head is sick, and the whole heart faint. From the sole of the foot even to the head there is no soundness in it; but wounds, and bruises, and *putrifying sores;* they have not been closed nor bound up, neither mollified with ointment."

The church of Rome "could explain nothing, soften nothing, renounce nothing, consistently with her assertion of infallibility." It could not reform; the evil grew till it could grow no more; and *revolution* was both the natural consequence and the only remedy. In a diseased body, when inflammatory action runs high, and the malady approaches its crisis, gentle palliatives would have no efficacy, and external applications so strong as to touch the disease, might occasion a fatal revulsion; but, seizing on the most vitiated organ, a single grievous sore, bursting from the body itself, may, though threatening death, be the only cure. Such was the first of the seven last plagues. It came not from without, in the form of a foreign enemy, as, on the first of the trumpets, the hail and fire fell upon the earth; but this was the token of the vial being poured upon the earth, there fell a noisome and grievous sore upon the men which had the mark of the beast, and upon them which worshipped his image. It arose within the Roman Catholic kingdoms of Europe, and was seated and concentrated, at first, where the corruption was the rankest.

No power of reason could prevail against the rack, the gibbet, and the pile. Neither could any meekness of wisdom melt the heart of an inquisitor. Nor is the butchery-work of human slaughter the calling of Christians, the weapons of whose warfare are not carnal. Other agents were prepared for the execution of the judgment, so soon as it began to sit. "Religion cannot exist where immortality generally prevails. Infidelity was generated in the moral corruption, which was the issue of papal domination; the *blackness* of popery was turned into the *paleness* of death; and infidelity needed only to assume an active form, to fall *as a grievous and noisome sore upon the men that had the mark of the beast, and upon them that worshipped his image, and to kill with sword, and with hunger, and with death, and with the beasts of the earth.* The term *revolution* implies the *taking away of the dominion* from those who who possessed it. Till then the natural alliance had subsisted unchallenged in all Roman Catholic kingdoms, between despotic power and papal supremacy. But the revolutionary spirit of the times was specially and simultaneously directed against kings and priests. *Down* with both was the general rallying cry. Freedom of thought was the order of the day; liberty and equality were the doctrines of the revolution. No sentiments could be more abhorrent to the spirit of popery, or more completely subversive of all its principles. Neither was its *yoke* to be borne, nor its exaltation to subsist any *longer*. Ridicule was a weapon which superstition could not withstand. The thunders of the Vatican were the scoff of the sceptics. The rights of man supplanted the infallibility of the church. Men sinned openly against high heaven, and sought not absolution. The charm of purchased pardons was broken when men were hardened in unbelief through the deceitfulness of sin; a seared conscience spurned all palliatives, and sought no cure; and, when once the judgments of men, after long thraldom, were exercised again, the mummeries of Catholicism could not abide the light of reason, though it was otherwise misguided. Whenever the mental yoke was thus cast away, and no power of religion remained to restrain, vengeance was unsparingly executed on the priesthood, and on all the adherents of their falling cause. And the first vial of wrath was freely poured out.

Of the horrors of the French Revolution it were needless to write. It is enough to say, that the blood of the saints began to be avenged. France had for ages yielded the neck to the papal yoke, and lent its aid to bind it on other nations; but never, even under the dictation of the Abbot of Citeaux, did the counts, or knights, and soldiers of France exercise more atrocious cruelties against the saints of the Most High, than those of which churchmen and loyalists were then the victims. Tithes were abolished; monasteries suppressed; church lands confiscated; the priests despoiled and beggared;* and, at a time when every other form of faith was tolerated, and atheism itself esteemed rather a virtue than a vice, and religious liberty proclaimed, the clergy of France were required to abjure all allegiance to the see of Rome, and that church was

* Life of Nap. vol. i. p. 30.

"deprived of its earthly power," or, the dominion forcibly taken from its hands. Even the benefits which France derived from the Revolution, are associated with the record of the miseries of the priests.

"We might add," says Sir Walter Scott, "to the weight of benefits which France unquestionably owes to the Constituent Assembly, that they restored liberty of conscience by establishing universal toleration. But against this benefit must be set the violent imposition of the constitutional oath upon the catholic clergy, which led afterwards to such *horrible massacres* of innocent and revered victims, *murdered in defiance of those rules of toleration*, which, rather in scorn of religion of any kind than regard to mens' consciences, the Assembly had previously adopted.* The National Assembly was *victorious at once over altar and throne, mitre and coronet, kings, nobles, and clergy.* According to the sentiments which they had avowed, they were in their hands as clay in that of the potter, to be used or thrown away at pleasure.† The state of the expatriated French clergy, driven from their home, and deprived of their means of subsistence, because they refused an oath imposed contrary to their ecclesiastical vows, and to their conscience, added religious zeal to the general interest excited by the spectacle, yet NEW TO EUROPE, *of thousands of nobility and clergy compelled to forsake their country and take refuge among aliens.*"

A war of extermination had been waged in France, against the witnesses of Jesus; and there was no place of refuge within its boundaries, for those who had not the mark of the beast and disowned the spiritual supremacy of Rome, But the time was now come when the recognition, even by the priests, of the authority of the pope, was a crime which led to poverty and expatriation. An attempt to save the recusant priests from judicial banishment, was more than the worth of the crown or the life of the king of France.

"A decree was passed by the Assembly, that such priests as might be convicted of a refusal to subscribe the oath to the civil Constitution should be liable to deportation. This was a point of

* Life of Napoleon, vol. i. pp. 227, 254. † Ib. p. 289.

conscience with Louis. On the decree against the priests, his resolution continued unmoved and immoveable. Thus religion, which had for half a century been so slightly regarded in France, at length interposed her influence *in deciding the fate of the king and the kingdom.*"*

That a noisome and grievous sore fell upon the men that had the mark of the beast, and upon them that worshipped his image, is a fact too notorious to bear any question, and was too awfully demonstrated, as the fearful recollection of living millions may attest, to stand in need of illustration. Yet that we may not altogether leave a chasm in prophetic history, even where the most awful lessons were given to the world, of the death-like character of infidelity, of the righteous avenging of the blood of the saints, and of the ruin which the papacy brought upon itself, by fostering a serpent while crushing a lamb, a few notes may be taken of that evil time, to show how grievous was the sore, and how bitter a thing it proved, that men had departed from the living God, whenever an apostate church began at last to reap the ripened fruit of its doings, and of its doctrines. It was not for infidelity to replace the barrier which Catholicism had taken away between men and blood. And the revolutionists unsparingly multiplied their victims among those who had the mark of the beast, and worshipped his image, as if they had been reckoning up against them the million that in an antichristian crusade had been slain in France for the testimony of Jesus.

"From being one of the most light-hearted and kind-tempered of nations, the French seemed upon the Revolution to have been animated not merely with the courage, but with the rabid fury of unchained wild beasts.† While the *ancient institutions* of France were crumbling to pieces of themselves, or were forcibly pulled

---

* Life of Napoleon, vol. i. pp. 320, 321. †Ibid. p. 157.

down by state innovators,—that fine country was ravaged by a civil war of aggravated horrors, waged betwixt the rich and the poor, and marked by every species of brutal violence."*

In La Vendee the inhabitants supported the cause of the clergy and nobles, and revolted against the revolutionary government. "Upwards of two hundred battles and skirmishes were fought in this devoted country. The revolutionary fever was in its access; the shedding of blood seemed to have become positive pleasure to the perpetrators of slaughter, and was varied by each invention which cruelty could invent to give it new zest. The habitations of the Vendeans were destroyed, their families subjected to violence and massacre, their cattle houghed and slaughtered, and their crops burned and wasted. One republican column assumed and merited the name of infernal, by the horrid atrocities which they committed. At Pillau, they roasted the women and children in a heated oven. Many similar horrors could be added, did not the heart and hand recoil from the task."†—"The murders committed at Lyons, though hundreds were swept away by vollies of musket-shot, fell short of the horrors perpetrated by Carrier at Nantes, who, in avenging the republic on the obstinate resistance of La Vendee, might have summoned hell to match his cruelty, without a demon venturing to answer his challenge. Hundreds, men, women, and children, were forced on board of vessels which were scuttled and sunk in the Loire, and this was called republican baptism. Men and women were stripped, bound together, and thus thrown into the river, and this was called republican marriage. But we have said enough to show that men's blood seems to have been converted into poison, and their hearts into

* Life of Napoleon, vol. i. p. 175. † Ibid. vol. ii. p. 236.

stone, by the practices in which they were daily engaged.* France, during the years 1793 and 1794, exhibited instances of extreme cruelty, in principle and practice, which make the human blood curdle. The cruelties of the laws denounced the highest penalties against those who relieved proscribed fugitives. They were executed with the most merciless rigour. The interdiction of fire and water to outlawed persons, of whatever description, was enforced with the heaviest penalty. The recusant and *exiled priests* often found among their former flock the means of *concealment and existence, when it was death to administer them.* Nothing short of such heroic actions could have prevented France, during *this horrible period, from becoming an universal charnel-house, and her history an unvaried calendar of murder.*"†

"The progress of civil war," to adopt the words of Lavallette, "and the secret exertions of the royalists, could scarcely justify the massacres and the horrible tyranny under which the country groaned for so long a period. The rulers of the Assembly will remain for ever loaded with the odium which their *barbarous government (of which history does not present another instance)* will excite among future generations. Surely, if a few years before so many crimes were committed, they could have been pictured before the eyes of the most barbarous among their perpetrators, I fear not to say that all, even Robespierre himself, would have recoiled with horror. Men begin by caressing theories; a heated imagination presents them as useful and easy of execution; they toil, they advance unconsciously from errors to faults, and from faults to crimes, till

---

* Life of Napoleon, vol. ii. p. 296.
† Ibid. vol. ii. pp. 298—300.

the contaminated mind corrupts sensibility, and adorns by the name of state policy *the most horrible outrages*."*

Whatever may be the variety or discordance of political opinions respecting the French Revolution, there cannot be a question or a doubt that it began to *take the dominion* with irresistible violence *out of* the hands of the papacy, and that it fell *as a noisome and grievous sore npon the men which had the mark of the beast, and upon them which worshipped his image.* The authority of the pope was *judicially* disannulled; the church-lands were sold; the images were destroyed; "the churches were plundered of their gold and silver; even their bells were melted and cast into cannon;"† thousands of nobility and clergy were compelled to forsake their country, a thing new to Europe, and take refuge among aliens; and in a land where the saints of the Most High had been exterminated or expelled, it was death to administer the means of concealment or existence to the recusant and exiled priests; and while the men were marked on whom it fell, never was any fact on earth more clear, than that the French Revolution was to them *a noisome and grievous sore.* It maintained in all its progress the same unvaried character, till other vials of wrath were poured forth in other forms.

---

* Lavalette's Memoirs, vol. i. pp. 177, 178

† Brewster's Encyclop. vol. ix. p. 635.

CHAPTER XXV.

SECOND VIAL.

There is an obvious analogy between the second trumpet and the second vial; *the sea*, though, in regard to the former, in a more limited degree or restricted sense, being alike the scene of both. And in comparing things spiritual with spiritual, or one portion of scripture with another, in which the same words have the same signification, and looking to history in its order, the judgments of God may be seen as *manifestly* in the fulfilment of the second vial as of the second trumpet, the historical exposition of which was left exclusively to Gibbon.

Of the second trumpet it is said, "*And the second angel sounded, and,* AS IT WERE, *a great mountain, burning* with fire, was cast into *the sea*; and *the third part of the sea became blood;* and the third part of the creatures which were in *the sea*, and had life, died; and the third part *of the ships were destroyed.*" Under the second vial no symbol or *similitude* of the form in which the wrath was to come are given, but the scene and similar effect of it are told.

And the second angel poured out his vial upon the sea, and it became as the blood of a dead man; and every living soul died in the sea. In a more enlarged sense, we have to look once again, as in the days of Genseric, but after the lapse of nearly fourteen hundred years, *to the sea*, to witness the similar but still deadlier effect of the latter vision.

No prophecy of scripture is of any private interpretation; the *event* finally unfolds it. At the end it will speak and not lie. And if the time be indeed past, and the judgment be *manifest*, the proof of it may be obvious, and the most patent of all authorities may be appealed to in illustration. We have seen, from Gibbon, how the different events predicted in the Revelation of Jesus Christ followed in their due order and course, and were often intimately connected. And now, come down to modern times, we need but to open an almanac,* to see the close succession and connexion between the first and second vial, copying the words in their exact order.

1792 France became a republic.
1793 King of France guillotined, January 21.
—— Queen of France guillotined, October 1.
1794† French fleet defeated by Earl Howe, June 1.
1795 Again by Lord Bridport.
1797 Spanish fleet defeated by Earl St. Vincent, Feb. 14.
—— Dutch fleet defeated by Lord Duncan, October 11.
1798 French fleet defeated by Lord Nelson, August 1.

In February 1793, war was declared by France against Great Britain. The British sought in vain

---

* *Chronology of remarkable occurrences*, in the Edinburgh Almanac, for any year of the present century.

† Truth may sometimes be easily found in a common footpath, while it may be painfully searched for in vain in the most intricate mazes. It is here, we think, patent to the world. And it is but to show a token of its simplicity, to state that the inspection of the almanac, as above, first confirmed, if it did not suggest, the interpretation here given of the second vial. History, in these reforming days, has been called an old almanac. Though it were nothing more, it has still its facts and its dates; and these are enough for the elucidation of prophecy. And though it abounds with beacons rather than finger-posts, there are still marks and mile-stones to which the Christian can point in triumph, and claim as his own, as they show that, whether on the sea or the land, no conqueror ever strayed from the path which the scriptures predicted as the way he would take, or the work he would do.

to combat with the French on the continent; and an army, headed by the duke of York, speedily retreated before the republican troops, and left its artillery in their hands. It was on *the sea* that the vial was to be poured; on her own element Britain was triumphant, and there her thunder was poured with tremendous and irresistible efficacy. The preceding evidence, so *manifest* as to be supplied by any almanac, though it shows the succession of the first and second vials, is not complete; and the words of the prophecy require a *minute specification* of facts, to show how, as denoting the wrath of God, the sea became as the blood of a dead man; and how it might be said of that season as of no other, every living thing died in the sea.

The effect of the pouring out of the vial may be seen from the record not only of great naval victories, but of the incessant and continued destruction of which, from the time it began to be poured out, the sea was everywhere the scene.

A List of Ships of the line, Frigates, &c. late belonging to the French Navy, captured, destroyed, wrecked, foundered, or accidentally burnt, during the year 1793.*

Gun	Ships.	How, when, and where lost.
120	Commerce-de-Marseille	Captured, August 29, by the British fleet at Toulon.
80	Triomphant	Destroyed, December 18, at the evacuation of Toulon.
74	Centaure	
	Destin	
	Duguay-Trouin	
	Héros	
	Liberté	
	Suffisant	
	Thémistoclé	
	Tricolor	
	Leopard	Foundered, February 5, in the Bay of Cagliari.
	Name unknown	Wrecked near Ajaccio, in Corsica. Some accounts name her the Vengeur.

* James' Naval History, vol. i. page 546.

Gun Ships.		How, when, and where lost.
Gun. Frigs.	Pompée Puisant Scipion Arethuse Perte	Captured with the Commerce-de-Marseille.
38	Impérieuse	Captured, October 11, by the Captain, 74, near Genoa.
36	Cléopâtre	Captured, June 18, by the British Frigate Nymph, off the Start.
	Réunion	Captured, October 20, by the British Frigate Crescent, off Cape Barfleur.
	Modeste	Captured, October 20, by the the Beford and Captain, 74's, at Genoa.
	Alceste Topaze Lutine Aurore. Prosélyte	Captured along with Commerce-de-Marseille. Alceste was delivered up to the Sardinians.
	Inconstante	Captured, October 20, by the British Frigates Penelope and Iphigenia, off St. Domingo.
	Name unknown	Destroyed, May 21, by the Spanish fleet under Admiral Borga at St. Bietro.
	Victorieuse	Destroyed along with Triomphant, &c.
32	Montréal Iris	
28	Blonde	Captured, November 27, by the British Frigates Latona and Phæton, off Ushant.
	Belette	Captured along with Commerce-de-Marseille.

Of smaller French ships, the following were lost, taken, or destroyed in 1793: Ariel, 20 guns; Gordan, 14; Prompte, 20; Curieux, 14; Vanneau, 6; L'Ectair, 22; Lutin, 12; Convention Nationale, 10; L'Espiegle, 16; Auguste, 24; Mulette, 18; Poulette, 26; Sincere, 18; Meselle, 20; Tarleston, 14. One British ship of the line was burnt, and nine under the line were captured, destroyed, or wrecked, during the same year.

A new era was thus *commenced* in naval warfare; and the *second* vial began to be poured *upon the sea.* Referring the reader, who may be desirous of fuller illustration, to James' *Naval History of Great Brit-*

ain, and to Duncan's *British Trident*, or *Register of Naval Actions*, a brief and general summary may suffice to shew that the vial of the wrath of God continued to be poured out upon *the sea*; till far more than ever, at any time in the history of the world, it might well be said, in the same manner as previously, but only partially, illustrated under the *second trumpet, that the sea became as the blood of a dead man, and every living soul died in the sea.*

Number of ships captured, destroyed, wrecked, foundered, or burnt, from the year 1793 to 1801, inclusive.

	Ships of the line.	Frigates.	Smaller war ships.
1793	16	19	23
1794	11	16	39
1795	15	13	38
1796	7	33	56
1797	16	17	146
1798	15	26	Not
1799	9	37	stat-
1800	7	11	ed.
1801	9	19	
	105	191	

In addition to these, from the commencement of the renewed war in May 1803, to its termination in July 1815, eighty-four ships of the line, and one hundred and fifty-seven frigates, besides a vast and indefinite number of inferior vessels, both of war and commerce, were, as in the former war, captured or destroyed.

The whole history of the world presents not such a scene and period of naval warfare, as that which took its rise from the French revolution, immediately after that noisome and grievous sore fell upon them that had the mark of the beast, and upon them that worshipped his image. Nor, perhaps, was any war on earth ever carried on at such an expense of treasure; the total supplies granted by the British parliament, for the SEA-SERVICE, having amounted, during the period of its continuance, to three hundred and thirty-eight millions sterling.* Yet, the whole naval glory of Britain is emphatically written in a verse—*The sea became as the blood of a dead man.* That murderous warfare on the sea was not overmatched by any on the land. The ferocity of a British tar in the hour of battle, was not surpassed by that of the most savage Turk; and might even be compared, as well as the fanatical fury of atheistic Frenchmen, "to the rabid fury of wild beasts." A vial of wrath was indeed poured *upon the sea.* Never had such a warfare been heard of, since the days of Genseric; and even then the trumpet sounded only over a third part of the sea. But the war-ships of Britain covered the ocean. The Mediterranean and the Baltic, the Atlantic and the Indian Ocean, the North and the South Sea, were all stained with the blood of the enemies of Britain; and British men-of-war were launched from harbours in America and India. The continental nations of Europe had colonies in every quarter of the globe, and thither the ravages of war were carried. Wherever the ships or the fleet of an enemy were to be found, "a close and decisive battle"† was the order of warfare that Britain maintained on the ocean, which she held as her dominion, and from

* See Tables for each year, in James' Naval History.

† James' Naval History, vol. iii. p. 527. Lord Nelson's plan of attack,—"The *business of an English commander-in-chief,*" says his Lordship, "being to bring an enemy's fleet to battle on the most advantageous terms to himself,—I mean, that of laying his ships *close on board those of the enemy* as expeditiously as possible; and secondly, to *continue them there* without separating, until the business is decided. I am sensible, beyond this object it is not necessary that I should say a word, being fully assured that the admirals and captains of the fleet I have the honour to command, will, knowing my precise object, that of a close and decisive battle, supply any deficiency in my not making signals," &c.

which she finally swept, for a time, all the navies of the world. In achieving this conquest, and sustaining the empire of the sea, the blood of thousands, and of tens of thousands, was poured out like water, and their bleeding bodies cast into the deep. The tonnage, the rate, the calibre, the shot, the expenditure, may be reckoned; but who can tell the amount of *the blood* that was shed? The floor of a slaughter-house, and even the shambles, are not unsightly objects, compared to the deck and cockpit of a ship of war in the midst of battle, though the victims were human. The breasts of men were close before the muzzles of cannons, ranged in triple decks, and side by side. And what havock is involved in the one word *boarding!* Never on earth —the sites of guillotines excepted—were there such circumscribed spots so deeply defiled with human gore, or where it was poured so fast, or fell so thickly, as on the decks of the floating masses that were formed and fitted for destruction, the narrow death-fields of the sea, than which even Roman gladiators, though condemned malefactors, had more room for the work of slaughter. There the gunshot wounds, the cutlass slashes, the trunks from which limbs had been shot away, gushed freely. And even if we turn disgustingly from the sight of the manner in which *the sea* was dyed with *blood*, it would be enough to test the quality of *such* blood-bought glory, could but the eyes be unveiled of the magic of a name, to look on the scene when the battle was over, the spot on which a portion of that vial of wrath was poured out. Every reader has heard of the Bay of Aboukir, which may here supply a mournful illustration. In the battle of the Nile, "the British loss in killed and wounded amounted to eight hundred and ninety-five. Three thousand one hundred and five of the French, including the wounded, were sent ashore by cartel;

and *five thousand two hundred and twenty-five perished.* Long after the battle, innumerable *bodies were seen floating about the bay,* in spite of all the exertions which were made to sink them, as well from fear of pestilence, as *from loathing and horror which the sight occasioned."** "Of thirteen sail of the line, nine were taken, and two burnt; of the four frigates, one burnt, another sunk."—How small a proportion, even after such a scene, of the hundred and eighty-nine sail of the line, and the three hundred and forty-eight frigates, besides an innumerable multitude of smaller vessels, which were taken and destroyed in the course of the war. *The vial was poured upon the sea, and it became as the blood of the dead.*

And every living thing died in the sea. Numerous and vast as were the national engines of naval warfare, and terrible as was the destruction which they wrought, other agents were called in to enter in the strife and to do the work of seizure and of slaughter, besides the navies of Britain and France, Spain, Portugal, Holland, and Denmark. A system of *privateering* was established. A naval war became the trade of individuals as well as of nations. Letters of marque were issued; and the merchant could sit calmly at his desk, and under the sanction of *human* laws, fit out a privateer. The quarrel of nations was converted into the privilege of *private* plunder, or of *sharing* in the spoil. From being the high-way of the commerce of the world, which God had left open from shore to shore, the sea, whether for large fleets of ships of the line, or for the single two-gun privateer, became a field for the 'chace,' or the scene of battle, where warriors decided the controversy of kingdoms, and the licensed pirate went

* Southey's Life of Nelson, vol. i. pages 337, 338.

forth to capture or to slay: and hence, after the first few years of the war, the number of the smaller vessels that were taken or destroyed, cannot, from their multiplicity, be accurately ascertained. The ocean was never so polluted with blood. And interdicts and edicts, affecting commerce, or whatever pertained *to the sea,* were passed, such as had never before been heard of in the world; and such as, either on the earth or on the sea, there never was a power to enforce till then. On principles of reciprocal ruin, added to those of vengeance and plunder, the famous Berlin and Milan decrees, in the north and in the south of Europe, which shut all its harbours against Britain, were answered by Orders in Council; and the retaliation was seconded and enforced by more than a hundred thousand British seamen. France, during the war, lost every one of its colonies. But Europe was armed against Britain, or in alliance with her foe. And not a ship of Continental Europe could ride in safety on any part of the sea; an embargo was virtually laid along every coast and on every port, from the straits of the Dardanelles to the Gulf of Bothnia. And as if the open sea had been the bare desert, which the wild beasts claim as their own and where not a living man could encroach without danger or death on their domain, the British lion trode unchallenged over it, and many a jackal watched for the prey. As pertaining to all the dominions in league with France, or in subjection to its power, it might well be said, as of no time beside, when the vial was fully poured out, *every living thing died in the sea.*

They that are of God, said he who came from God, hear God's words; and the cause why men do not hear them is, that they are not of God. The cares of this world, said he also who knew what was in man, the deceitfulness of riches, the pleasures of this life, and the care of other things, choke the word and render it unfruitful. While busy thus in the service of the god of this world, and loading themselves with thick clay, or dead while they live in pleasure, how lightly, nay, contemptuously, from the blindness that is in them, do men treat the word of God, not counting it worth the reading or the hearing. Yet if not blinded by the god of this world, clearly might they see, as if by actual experiment, that all the treasures of the world, if weighed against a single word of the living oracles of God, are lighter than dust in the balance. Not only were ships without number destroyed, and colonies taken, and the sea dyed with blood, but to reckon by Mammon's only rule, more than three hundred millions were, from first to last, expended by Britain alone in illustration of a single verse, with as little thought or purpose of thereby fulfilling that word, as Saracens invaded the Roman empire and overspread great part of Asia, Africa, and Europe in fulfilment of another.

The prayers of saints, are golden vials full of odours; but the works of fanatical atheists and daring blasphemers were vials of wrath. Boldly as the British seamen rushed to the battle, it is a matter of bitter sorrow and lamentation, that, too generally, they rushed as fearlessly against the thick bosses of the buckler of the Almighty; and were guilty of doing, with the most reckless levity, what, *above all things*, men are commanded, in God's holy word, not to do—above all things, swear not. But yet the wrath of men, blasphemers though they were, *was made to praise* the Lord. And, if possible, more marvellously still, and not less manifestly, we have only, in the next place, to come and see, how avowed unbelievers, utterly controverting their own infidel principles, farther accomplished the same end; and how the Directory of France, in issuing their mandates to one of the greatest generals who ever filled the world with his fame, by the counsels which they devised, and the great task which they put into his hands, vied with the British Board of Admiralty in doing, in its appointed order, the express work that was written in those scriptures which they denied.

Judgments were not suspended, so soon as they began to sit, upon the earth, although the second vial of wrath had begun to be poured upon *the sea.* But the third vial, coming in its course, was poured out on its appointed place.

CHAPTER XXVI.

THIRD VIAL.

The reader may, perhaps, have already seen, how prophetic terms may derive their most intelligible exposition from historical facts. And it is not now, when we have reached the period of *manifest* judgments, that the word of God anywise needs that man should come in with his terms of explanation. But comparing things spiritual with spiritual, the meaning may be plain. And, looking unto events that fill their place in history, and that startled the world with their magnitude, no less than the foremost of naval wars, the proof may be as clear. The sea was the scene of the second trumpet as well as of the second vial. And, in like manner, the third *trumpet* determines the *site* of the third vial.

And the third angel sounded, and there fell a great star from heaven, burning as it were a lamp, and it fell upon *the third part of the rivers and upon the fountains of waters.* And the name of the star is called wormwood; and the third part of the *waters* became wormwood; and many men died of the *waters* because they were made bitter, Rev. viii. 10, 11.

And the third angel poured out his vial upon the RIVERS AND FOUNTAINS OF WATERS; *and they became blood. And I heard the angel of the waters say: Thou art righteous, O Lord, which art, and wast, and shalt be, because thou hast judged thus. For they have shed the blood of saints and prophets, and thou hast given them blood to drink; for they are worthy. And I heard another out of the altar say, even so, Lord God Almighty, true and righteous are thy judgments.*

The first trumpet sounded over the Roman empire. The second re-echoed from the coast of Africa to the shores of Italy and Spain, and spread over the Mediterranean sea. The scene of the third was *the rivers and fountains of waters,* the fountains that rise and the rivers that flow from the Alps and Appenines, and which render northern Italy a land of streams. There Attila, the great star, fell. Reducing, in his course, the cities of Acquileia, Altinum, Concordia, and Padua, to heaps of stones and ashes, and, burning as it were a lamp, the inland towns of Vicenza, Verona, and Bergamo having also been exposed to the rapacious cruelty of the Huns, he spread his ravages "over the rich plains of modern Lombardy, which are divided by the Po, and bounded by the Alps and Appenines." The *waters,* or the same region under the same name, continued to be *wormwood* to the empire of Rome, after the ravages and death of Attila. "Many thousands of his subjects assembled on *the plains of*

Piedmont." And subsequently, at *Tortona*, at the foot of the Alps, an impetuous sedition broke out in the Roman camp, the final result of which was the extinction of the western empire. The chief of the confederates of Italy fixed his residence at Milan (situated in the midst of waters) which Attila had previously possessed, and it was from Milan that "Ricimer marched to the gates of Rome."

The locality of the *rivers and fountains of waters*, as a specific region in the Roman territory, abridged as then it was, and in reference to the downfall of imperial Rome, may thus be held as determined. And without attaching any diversity of meaning, or adopting any other significancy, to the *same words* —which would throw the subject loose to every imagination as to the winds—we have to look again to the same *rivers and fountains of waters*—but to the whole and not merely a *part*—to the cities of Padua, Vicenza, Verona, Bergamo, Pavia, Tortona; to the spot where the Mincio flows from Lake Benacus; to the palace of Milan, which Attila possessed, and to the plains of Piedmont and Lombardy which he ravaged, and which were afterwards wormwood to Rome,—in order to see what accordance is to be found, in this express particular, between the decline, or the events which broke the power, both of imperial and papal Rome, and to witness thus, if indeed such witness be yet *manifestly* borne by history, the exact coincidence and precise affinity, in point of *place*, however different in time, between the completion of the third vial and of the third trumpet, corresponding to the description, in the identical terms, the *rivers and fountains of waters*, on which the great star fell, on the sounding of the third trumpet, and *the third vial of the wrath of God*, one of the *last plagues*, *was also to be poured out.*

In point of *time* the case is also as clear, and the

order of the judgment as manifest. The date of the pouring out of the third vial is necessarily subsequent to the period when the second vial began to be poured out. But as the great mountain burning with fire, that was cast into the sea, though it first rose, before the great star fell upon the rivers and upon the fountains of waters, continued to burn, after the sudden meteor had burned like a lamp and had fallen; so, in strict analogy, the pouring out of the third vial, though necessarily consequent to the time of the pouring out of the second, does not imply that the last drops of the previous vial were first to be dried up, or even that the festering sore, too grievous and noisome to admit of instantaneous cure, which marked the first, was wholly healed. All were the *last vials of the wrath of God;* and though, like the trumpets, they might follow in quick succession, the very nature and purpose of them tend to show that the first pouring out of the vial was not the last of the judgment. All are necessarily consecutive in their origin; but as the vials of wrath, they may continue to flow, till each has perfected its own special purpose; and the pouring out of a new vial upon any specified spot *on the earth,* interrupted not the farther progress or action of that which had previously been poured *upon the sea.*

Three years elapsed from the taking of Carthage by Genseric to the invasion of Egypt by Attila. And the *same period* elapsed from the siege of Toulon and the commencement of the greatest of naval wars since the days of Genseric, and unequalled either before or after, or even at that period, till every eye in Europe was fixed on the spot where Bonaparte had his station; but, looking more to earthly revolutions than to the word of God, men did not remember that it was the very region where Attila had been, amidst *the rivers and fountains of waters*. In the philosophy of the day, men thought of ruling the world without a Deity; and any appeal to his word would have been scouted by the warriors who, succeeding to the office of barbarous Saracens and ferocious Turks, were instrumental in fulfilling it.

The fool hath said in his heart, there is no God. But there is no wisdom, nor understanding, nor counsel against the Lord. The heathen are sunk down in the pit they have made; in the net which they hid is their own foot taken. The first successor of Mahomet issued his instructions to the Saracen invaders of the Roman empire, in exact conformity with the prophetic announcement "it *was commanded them* that they should not hurt the grass of the earth, neither any green thing, neither any tree; but only those men which had not the seal of God in their foreheads." Whether they be occupied in narrating, devising, or acting, God turns the counsels or labours of the adversaries of the faith into credentials of his word: and they may be raised up for the execution of a purpose, of which it is not in their heart to think. And as Volney and Gibbon wrote as if they had contended in emulous strife which of them would best illustrate the prophecies, so as soon as infidels presided over one of the finest countries in Europe, and, invested with unchallenged authority, wielded at their will the energies of a great nation, they shewed that, in the execution of their appointed work, they were not to be outdone, at the close of the eighteenth century, by the armed fanatics who, in the seventh, issued from the desert. The apostles of infidelity were not to be restrained, any more than the apostles of Mahomet, though both were fanatics alike, from yielding their testimony to the truth of the Revelation of Jesus Christ. It was not alone enough that infidelity had fallen a noisome and grievous sore upon the men which had the mark of the beast, and upon them which worshipped his image; but, after three years from the time that the vial began to be poured upon the sea, the Directory of France, no less than the Caliph in a remote age, gave the command that the very thing should be done, which was written in the word of God as the note and character of that evil time. In "*the Instructions for the* GENERAL-IN-CHIEF *of the army of Italy,*" "the *Piedmontese*" are the first people that are mentioned, almost in the very first line. From that precious document we extract a few sentences, by way of illustrating the *power* of infidelity—but whether against or for the truth as it is in Jesus, looking to his Revelation also, the reader, were he a sceptic, might tell.

"The principal enemies with whom the French republic has to contend on the Italian side, are two—*the Piedmontese* and the Austrians. The latter are formidable—from the sway which their possessions in Italy enable them to exercise over the Court of Turin" (the capital of *Piedmont*).—"It is the most immediate interest of the French republic to direct its principal efforts against the Austrian army and possessions in Lombardy.—The mere attack of Piedmont would not fulfil the object which the Executive Directory ought to have in view, that of expelling the Austrians from Italy.* Every thing urges us to endeavour, by every means in our power, to force the enemy to repass the Po, and to make our greatest exertion in the direction of the Milanese. It appears that this essential operation cannot take place, unless the French army be previously in possession of Ceva.

"The Directory leave the General-in-Chief at liberty to commence operations by the attack of the enemy at this point; and whether he obtain a complete victory over them, or whether they retreat towards Turin, the Directory authorise him to pursue them, to encounter them again, and even to bombard that capital, if circumstances should render it necessary.

"After having made himself master of Ceva, and placed the left of the army of Italy near Coni, in order to menace and keep in awe the garrison of that place, the General-in-chief *will supply*

* "To attack Piedmont, is to attack the Austrian army which covers it."—*Note by Bonaparte.*

the wants of the army, as speedily as possible, by means of the resources which Piedmont will afford. He will then direct his forces against the Milanese, and principally against the Austrians; he *will drive the enemy beyond the Po,* ascertain the means of passing that *river,* and endeavour to secure the fortresses of Asti and Valenza—to intimidate Italy by advancing as much as possible on the right and towards *Tortona,* &c. The army ought to make as short a stay as possible in Piedmont, and to advance briskly to engage the Austrians, &c.

"Although it be the interest of France to direct her principal efforts against the Austrians, and to lead the Piedmontese, by our victories over the former, into an alliance with ourselves, *the Piedmontese must not be spared so long as they are our enemies* &c. &c. (Signed)

Letourneur, Carnot, L. M. Reveillere, Lepaux, Rewbell."*
15th March, 1796.

In entering on the prophetic history of the achievements of Bonaparte, we deal only in such plain matters as every newspaper in Europe has recorded, and as every almanac might tell; and for the confirmation of which the remembrance of millions would not be appealed to in vain. Though renewing the risk of superfluous illustration, we still designedly adhere to the words of the historian, in order to exclude even the suspicion of any adaptation of terms, or any forced construction of facts, and to obviate the doubts and distrust which may have been generated in the minds of some inquirers,

* "Memoirs of the Hist. of France during the reign of Napoleon, dictated by the Emperor at Saint Helena, &c. vol. iv. pp. 372—383.

"Last of the ANOINTED FIVE behold, and least,
The Directorial Lama, sovereign priest,—
Lepaux: whom athiests worship; at whose nod
Bow their meek heads *the men without a God.*"

CANNING.

How poor is the keenest satire, in refutation and contempt of their principles, compared with their own signatures to such a document—the command given by these very men, to Bonaparte to pour out the vial upon the predicted spot.

by too incautious an acquiesence in imaginary theories, of which time may have brought a speedy refutation.

"Bonaparte at the age of twenty-six assumed the command of the army of Italy. He found the army in numbers about fifty thousand; but wretchedly deficient in cavalry, in clothing, and even in food; and watched by an enemy vastly more numerous. It was under such circumstances that he at once avowed the daring scheme of *forcing a passage to Italy*, and converting the richest territory of the enemy himself into *the theatre of war*. 'Soldiers,' said he, 'you are hungry and naked; the republic owes you much, but she has not the means to pay her debts. I am come to lead you into the most fertile plains that the sun beholds. Rich provinces, opulent towns, *all shall be at your disposal*. Soldiers! with such a prospect before you, can you fail in courage and constancy?' This was his first address to his army at this period." "This," in the words of Sir Walter Scott, "was showing the deer to the hound when the leash is about to be slipped."*

"He perceived that *the time was come for turning a new leaf in the history of war*. With such numbers of troops as the infant republic could afford him, he saw that no considerable advantages could be obtained against the vast and highly disciplined armies of Austria and her allies, unless the established rules and etiquettes of war were abandoned. It was only by such rapidity of motion as should utterly transcend the suspicion of his adversaries, that he could hope *to concentrate the whole pith and energy of a small force upon some one point* of a much greater force opposed to it, and thus *rob* them (according to his own favourite phrase) of the victory. To effect such rapid marches, it was necessary that the soldiery should make up their mind to consider tents and baggage as idle luxuries; and that, instead of a long and complicated chain of reserves and stores, they should dare to *rely wholly for the means of subsistence on the resources of the country into which their leader might conduct them*. They must be contented to conquer at whatever hazard; to consider no sacrifices or hardships as worthy of a thought. The risk of destroying the character of the men by accustoming them to pillage, was obvious. Against the enemies of the republic, its success (of the scheme) was splendid even beyond his hopes.

"The objects of the approaching expedition were three: First, to compel the king of Sardinia, who had already lost Savoy and Nice, but still maintained a powerful army on the *frontiers of*

---

* History of Napoleon Bonaparte, No. 1. Family Library, Murray, London. Vol. i. pp. 35, 36. Sir Walter Scott's Life of Napoleon, vol. iiii p. 98.

Piedmont, to abandon the alliance of Austria. Secondly, to compel the emperor, by a *bold invasion of Lombardy*, to make such exertions in that quarter as to weaken those armies which had so long hovered on the Rhine; and if possible to stir up the Italian subjects of that crown to adopt the revolutionary system and emancipate them for ever from its yoke. The third object, though more distant, was not less important. THE INFLUENCE OF THE ROMISH CHURCH was considered by the Directory as the chief though secret cause of the support of royalty within their own territory, and TO REDUCE THE VATICAN INTO INSIGNIFICANCE, or at least to force it into submission and quiescence, appeared indispensable to the internal tranquillity of France. The revolutionary government, besides this general cause of hatred and suspicion, had a distinct injury to avenge. Their agent Basseville had, three years before, been assassinated in a popular tumult at Rome; the papal troops had not interfered to protect him, nor the pope to punish his murderers; and the haughty republic considered this as an insult, which could only be washed out with A SEA OF BLOOD."*

"The *original idea* entertained by the French government for prosecuting their resentment, had been by a proposed landing at Civita Vecchia with an army of ten thousand men, marching to Rome and exacting complete atonement for the murder of Basseville. But, as the *English fleet rode unopposed* in the Mediterranean, it became a matter of very doubtful success to transport such a body of troops to Civita Vecchia *by sea*, not to mention the chance that even if safely landed, they would have found themselves in the centre of Italy, cut off from supplies and succours, assaulted on all hands, and most probably blockaded by the British fleet. Bonaparte, who was consulted, recommended that the *north of Italy* should be first conquered, that Rome might be with safety approached and chastised."†

"Napoleon's plan for gaining access to the fair regions of Italy differed from that of all former conquerors: they had uniformly penetrated the Alps at some point or other of that mighty range of mountains; he judged that the same end might be accomplished more easily by advancing along the narrow strip of comparatively level country, which intervenes between these barriers and the Mediterranean sea, and forcing a passage WHERE THE LAST OF THE ALPS MELT, AS IT WERE, INTO THE FIRST AND LOWEST OF THE APPENINE RANGE."‡

"In penetrating into Italy *by the* SOURCES *of the Bormida*, some hopes might be entertained of separating and intersecting the Sardinian and Austrian armies, because from that position *Lombardy and Piedmont* were both menaced."§

---

* Hist. of Napoleon, vol. i. pp. 36, 38.
† Scott's Napoleon, ib. p. 96. ‡ Hist. of Napoleon, p. 38.
§ Las Casas' Journal, vol. i. part 2. p. 184.

"The battle of Monte Notte was the first of Bonaparte's victories. In consequence of the success of Monte Notte, and the close pursuit of the defeated Austrians, the French obtained possession of Cairo, *which placed them on that side of the Alps,* which slopes towards Lombardy, and where the STREAMS *from the mountains run to join the Po.*"*

"Beaulieu (general of the Austrians) had now to retreat northward in all haste to Dego, *in the valley of the river Bormida.*—Determined upon a general attack on all points of the Austrian position, the French army advanced in three bodies upon a space of four leagues in extent. Augereau advanced on the left against Millesimo; the centre under Massena, directed themselves upon Dego, *by the vale of the Bormida;* the right wing, commanded by La Harpe, manœuvered on the right of all, for the purpose of turning Beaulieu's left flank.—La Harpe having crossed the Bormida, where the STREAM *came up to the soldiers' middle,* attacked in front and in flank the village of Dego, where the Austrian commander-in-chief was stationed. The first attack was completely successful,—the heights of Biastro were carried, and the Piedmontese routed. The assault of Dego was not less so, although after a harder struggle. Beaulieu was compelled to retreat; and was entirely separated from the Sardinians, who had hitherto acted in combination with him.—Leaving sufficient force on the Bormida to keep in check Beaulieu, Bonaparte now turned his strength against Colli, who, overpowered, and without hopes of succour, *abandoned his line of defence near* Ceva, and *retreated to the line of the* (*river*) *Tanaro.*"†

"Napoleon, in the meantime, fixed his head-quarters at Ceva, and enjoyed from the heights of Monte-zemoto, the splendid view of the fertile fields of *Piedmont,* stretching in boundless perspective beneath his feet, WATERED *by the Po, the Tanaro, and* A THOUSAND OTHER STREAMS *which descend from the Alps.*"‡

"'In *less than a month,*' to quote from another history of the same events, 'did Napoleon lay the gates of Italy open before him. He had defeated in three battles forces much superior to his own; inflicted on them, in killed, wounded, and prisoners, a loss of 25,000 men; taken eighty guns and twenty-one standards; reduced the Austrians to inaction; utterly destroyed the Sardinian king's army; and lastly, wrested from his hands CONI and TORTONA, the two great fortresses called 'the keys of the Alps;' and, indeed, except Turin itself, *every place* of any consequence in his dominions," &c.§

"Bonaparte, meanwhile, had paused for a moment to consolidate his columns on the heights, from which the vast *plain of Lombardy,* rich and cultivated like a garden, and WATERED *with*

---

* Scott's Life of Napoleon, vol. iii. pp. 102, 103.
† Ibid, pp. 104—107. ‡ Ibid. pp. 107, 108.
§ Hist. of Napoleon, ibid.

innumerable fertilizing STREAMS, lay at length within the full view of his victorious soldiery. '*Hannibal forced the Alps*,' said he gaily, as he now looked back on those stupendous barriers, '*and we have turned them*;'—'a happy idea, says Las Casas, '*which conveyed in two words, the idea and results of the campaign*.' The army *passed the Tanaro*; for the first time, it was now absolutely in the plains. General Staingel *passed the Cursaglia* and secured the plain. The head-quarters were fixed at the castle of Lezegno, on the right of the Cursaglia, near the *point at which it falls into the Tanaro*. Massena passed the Tanaro *to attack the Piedmontese*. Three columns, on the 25th April, entered at the same time Cherasco, Tossano, and Alba. On the 28th, the armistice of Cherasco was concluded, at the junction *of the Tanaro and Sturа*, and there 'Bonaparte thus addressed his army—'Soldiers! you have, in fifteen days, gained six victories, taken twenty-one stand of colours, fifty-five pieces of cannon, and several fortresses, and conquered the richest part of Piedmont. You have made 15,000 prisoners, and killed and wounded more than 10,000 men. You have gained battles without cannon, *and passed rivers without bridges*. But you have done nothing, since there remains ought to do. *Neither Turin, nor Milan* are in your power. The ashes of the conquerors of Tarquin are still trodden under foot by the murderers of Basseville. You have still battles to fight, towns to take, *rivers to cross*. People of Italy, we aim only at the tyrants who enslave you.'"*

---

*Las Casas, vol. i. part ii. pp. 195, 203.

"The great northern plains of Italy comprised between the Alps, which divide them from France, Switzerland, and Germany, the Appenines, which divide them from Genoa and Tuscany, and the Adriatic compose the valley of the Po, the valleys which extend to the Adriatic north of the Po, and the valleys which extend to the Adriatic south of the Po. These valleys are not subdivided by any hills, so that communications might be opened between all the rivers if necessary. This immense plain comprises *Piedmont*, *Lombardy*, Parma, Placentia, Modena, Bologna, Ferrara, Romania, and the Venetian countries. The Po rises in Mount Viso, and receives, successively, on its left at Turin, the *Doire*, which descends from Mount Genevre; a little lower at Chivasso, the *Dorea-Baltea*, which comes from the Great Saint-Bernard; between Casal and Valenza, the *Sesia*; at Pavia, the *Ticino*, which descends from *Lake Maggiore*, and the heights of the Simplon; near Borgo-Forte, the *Oglio*, from the *lake Iseo*; near Governolo, the *Mincio*, from the lake of Garda. The Po receives on its right bank all the streams which rise in the Appenines; the *Tanaro* below Valenza and Alexandria; the *Scrivia* below Tortona and Castel-Nuova; the *Trebbia* above Placentia; the *Taro* above Casal Maggiore; the *Crostollo* near Gaustalla; the *Secchia* near Saint Benedetto; the *Panaro* and the *Reno* in the vicinity of Ferrara; and finally falls into the

"The consummate genius of this brief campaign could not be disputed—*the eyes of all Europe were fixed in admiration on his career.*"*

"The *shattered relics of the Sardinian army* had fallen back, or rather fled to within two leagues of *Turin*, without hope of being able to make an effectual stand. The *Sovereign of Sardinia, Savoy, and Piedmont*, had no means of preserving his *capital*, nay, his *existence*, on the continent, excepting by an *almost total submission to the will of the victor*. Victor Amadeus the Third was the descendant of a race of heroes; and now, so born, so connected, and with such principles, he was condemned to sue for peace, on any terms which might be dictated, from a general of France, aged twenty-six years, who, a few months before, was desirous of an appointment in the artillery service of the Grand Seignor!†—*The surrender was absolute.*"‡

"The ardent disposition of Bonaparte did not long permit him to rest, after the advantages which he had secured. He had gazed on Italy with an eagle's eye; but it was only for a moment, ere stooping on her with the wing, and pouncing on her with the talons of the king of birds."§

"It was asked, where are we to stop? Should we pass the Ticino, the Adda, the Oglio, the Mincio, the Adige, the Brenta, the Piave, the Tagliamento?"‖

"He determined to give the republic of Venice, the Grand Duke of Tuscany, and the other states in Italy, no time to muster forces, and take a decided part, as they were likely to do, to oppose a French invasion. Their terror and surprise could not fail to be increased by a *sudden irruption*, &c. A speedy resolution was the more necessary, as *Austria*, alarmed for her Italian possessions, was about to *make every effort for their defence.*"¶

"All thoughts were therefore turned to Italy. The fortress of TORTONA was surrendered to the French by the king of Sardinia; *Bonaparte's head-quarters were fixed there.* Massena concentrated another part of the army at Alexandria, menacing *Milan*, and threatening by the *passage of the Po*, to invade the territories belonging to Austria on the northern bank of *that river*. As Bonaparte himself observed, the passage of a *great river* is one of

---

Adriatic, thirty miles beyond Ferrara, by several mouths. *This river may be almost considered as a sort of sea*, on account of THE GREAT NUMBER OF STREAMS *it receives in all directions.* It is raised above the soil, and embanked with dikes, so that the finest countries of Italy are, like Holland, gained by art from the dominion of the WATERS," &c.—*Las Casas' Journal*, vol. i. part ii. pp. 213, 214.

* Hist of Napoleon, vol. i. pp. 41, 42.

† Life of Napoleon, vol. iii. pp. 110, 111. ‡ Ib. 112.

§ Ibid. p. 115. ‖ Las Casas' Journal, vol. i. p. 210.

¶ Life of Napoleon, vol. iii. pp. 116, 117.

the most critical operations in modern war; and Beaulieu had collected his forces to cover Milan, and prevent the French, if possible, *from crossing the Po*."* "The Austrian general *concentrated his army behind the Po.* Napoleon employed every device to make Beaulieu believe that he designed to attempt the passage of the Po at Valenza. Meanwhile, he executed a march of incredible celerity upon Placenza, fifty miles lower down the river, and appeared there on the 7th of May, to the utter consternation of a couple of Austrian squadrons, who happened to be reconnoitering in that quarter. He had to convey his men across that great stream in the common ferry boats, and could never have succeeded had there been any thing like an army to oppose him. The skill of his arrangements enabled him to pass *one of the greatest rivers in the world* without the loss of a single man."†

"The advanced divisions of the hostile armies met (at the village of Fombia, not far from Casal) on the 8th of May. The Austrians occupied the steeples and houses, and hoped to hold out until Beaulieu could bring up his main body. But the French charged so impetuously with the bayonet, that the Austrian, after seeing one-third of his men fall, was obliged to retreat in great confusion, leaving all his cannon behind him, across the Adda, a *large* river, which, descending from the Tyrolese mountains, joins the Po, at Pizzighitone, and thus forms the immediate defence of the better part of the Milanese against an enemy advancing from Piedmont. *Behind this river* Beaulieu now concentrated his army, establishing strong guards at every ford and bridge, and especially at Lodi, where as he guessed (for once rightly) the French general designed to force his passage."‡

"Beaulieu was again concentrating his scattered forces upon Lodi, for the purpose of covering Milan, *by protecting the line of the Adda.*

"'The passage of the Po,' said Bounaparte to the Directory, 'had been expected to prove the most bold and difficult manœuvre of the campaign, nor did we expect to have an action of more vivacity than that of Dego. But we have now to recount the battle of Lodi."§

In the face of the Austrian army, across a bridge "swept by twenty or thirty Austrian pieces of artillery, whose thunders menaced death to any one who should attempt that pass of peril," in the midst of "a storm of grape-shot," and in despite of "the tempest of fire," Bonaparte accomplished "the ter-

* Scott's Life of Napoleon, ibid. p. 119.
† Hist. of Napoleon, vol. i. pp. 44, 45. ‡ Ibid. pp. 45, 46.
§ Scott's Life of Nap. vol. iii. p. 124.

rible passage," as he himself called it, "of the bridge of Lodi."

"'It was, indeed, terrible to the enemy.' 'The Austrian artillery were bayonetted at their guns. Napoleon's infantry forming rapidly as they passed the bridge, and charging on the instant, the Austrian line became involved in inextricable confusion, broke up, and fled. The *slaughter* on their side was great.'* In their retreat they lost perhaps two thousand wounded and slain.' "†

"The passage of the bridge of Lodi 'deprived the Austrians of *another excellent line of defence.* Beaulieu gathered the scattered fragments of his force together, and soon threw the line of the Mincio, *another tributary of the Po,* between himself and the enemy. No obstacle remained between the victorious invader and the rich and noble capital of Lombardy. The French cavalry pursued Beaulieu as far as Cremona, which town they seized; and Buonaparte himself prepared to march at once upon Milan.' "‡

"The movements which had taken place since the king of Sardinia's defeat, had struck terror into the government of Milan, and the Archduke Ferdinand, by whom Austrian Lombardy was governed. But while Beaulieu did his best to cover the capital by force of arms, the measures resorted to by the government were rather of a devotional (!) than warlike character. Processions were made, relics exposed, and rites resorted to, which the Catholic religion prescribes as an appeal to heaven in great national calamities. But the saints they invoked were deaf or impotent; for the passage of the bridge of Lodi, and Beaulieu's subsequent retreat to Mantua, left no possibility of defending Milan."§

"'On the 14th of May, four days after Lodi, Napoleon entered, in all the splendour of a military triumph, the venerable and opulent city of the old Lombard kings.' 'He took up his residence in the archiepiscopal palace; and *church plate* was seized as part of the requisition.' "‖

"The Austrian had now planted the remains of his army behind the Mincio, having his left on the great and strong city of Mantua, which has been termed the citidel of Italy, and his right at Peschieria, a Venetian fortress. PESCHIERIA STANDS WHERE THE MINCIO FLOWS OUT OF ITS PARENT LAKE, THE LAGO DI GUARDA. That great body of WATERS, stretching many miles backwards towards the Tyrolese Alps, at once extended the line of defence, and kept the communication open with Vienna. The Austrian veteran *occupied one of the strongest positions that is possible to imagine.* The invader hastened once more to dislodge him."¶

"The heavy exactions of the French, and even more perhaps

---

* Hist. of Napoleon, p. 47. † Scott's Life of Nap. ib. p. 130.
‡ Hist. p. 48. § Life of Nap. ib. p. 135.
‖ Ibid. p. 137. *Hist.* p. 49. ¶ Hist. of Nap. vol. i. pp. 51, 52.

the wanton contempt with which they treated the churches and clergy, had produced or fostered the indignation of a large part of the population throughout Lombardy. Reports of new Austrian levies being *poured down* the passes of the Tyrol, were spread and believed. Popular insurrections against the conqueror took place in various districts; at least 30,000 men were in arms. At Pavia the insurgents were entirely triumphant; they had seized the town, and compelled the French garrison to surrender.

"This flame, had it been suffered to spread, threatened immeasurable evil to the French cause. Lannes instantly marched to *Benasco,* stormed the place, plundered and burnt it, and *put the inhabitants to the sword without mercy.* The general in person appeared before *Pavia;* blew the gates open; easily scattered the townspeople; and caused the leaders to be executed, as if they had committed a crime in endeavouring to rescue their country from the arms of a foreign invader. *Every where* the same *ferocious system* was acted on. The insurgent commanders were tried by court-martial, and shot without ceremony. At Lugo, where a French squadron of horse had been gallantly and disastrously defeated, *the whole of the male inhabitants were massacred.* These BLOODY examples quelled the insurrections; but they fixed the first dark and indelible stain on the name of Napoleon Buonaparte.

"The spirit of *the Austrian and Catholic parties in Lombardy thus crushed,* the French advanced on the MINCIO. The Austrian army at Borghetto (situated on the Mincio) in vain destroyed one arch of the bridge. Buonaparte supplied the breach with planks; and his men, flushed with so many victories, charged with *a fury not to be resisted.* Beaulieu *was obliged to abandon the Mincio, as he had before the Adda and the Po, and to take up the new line of the Addige.** Beaulieu, evacuating *Peschieria,* marched his dismayed forces *behind the Addige.* Ere Augereau had time to approach Peschieria, it was evacuated by the Austrians."†

"The Austrian had in effect abandoned for the time the open country of Italy. He now lay on the frontier, between the vast tract of rich provinces which Napoleon had conquered and the Tyrol. Beaulieu anxiously waited the approach of new troops from Germany, to attempt the relief of the great city of Mantua; and his antagonist, eager to anticipate the efforts of the imperial government, sat down immediately before it. *Mantua lies on an island* being cut off on all sides from the mainland *by the branches of the Mincio,* and approachable only by five narrow causeways, of which three were defended by strong and regular fortresses or intrenched camps, the other two by gates, drawbridges, and batteries. *Situated amidst stagnant waters and morasses,* its air is pestilential, especially to strangers. The garrison were prepared to maintain the position with their usual bravery; and it remained to

* Hist. of Napoleon, vol. i. pp. 52—54.
† Scott's Life of Napoleon, ibid. p. 162.

be seen whether the French general possessed any new system of attack, capable of abridging the usual operations of the siege, as effectually as he had already done those of the march and battle. His commencement was alarming; of the five causeways, by sudden and overwhelming assaults, he obtained four; and the garrison were cut off from the mainland, except only by a fifth causeway, the strongest of them all, named, from a palace near it, *La Favorita.* It seemed necessary, however, in order that this blockade might be complete, that the Venetian territory, lying immediately beyond Mantua, should be occupied by the French. The imperial general had neglected the reclamations of the Doge, when it suited his purpose to occupy Peschiera. 'You are too weak,' said Buonaparte when the Venetian envoy reached his head quarters, 'to enforce neutrality on hostile nations such as France and Austria. Beaulieu did not respect your territory when his interest bade him violate it; nor shall I hesitate to occupy *whatever falls within the line of the Adige.*' In effect, garrisons were placed in *Verona, and all the strong places of that domain.* The tri-colour flag now waved at *the mouth of the Tyrolese passes;* and Napoleon, leaving Serrurier to blockade Mantua, returned to Milan, where he had important business to arrange."*

"With no friend behind him, *the pope saw himself at the mercy of the invader;* and in terror prepared to submit. Buonaparte occupied immediately his legations *of Bologna and Ferrara,* making prisoners, in the latter of these towns, four hundred of the papal troops, and a cardinal under whose orders they were. The churchman militant was dismissed on parole; but being recalled to head-quarters, answered that his master the pope had given him a dispensation to break his promise. This exercise of the *old* dispensing power excited *the merriment of the conquerors.* The nation meanwhile perceived that no time was to be lost. The Spanish resident at the Roman court was despatched to *Milan;* and the terms on which the holy father was to obtain a *brief respite* were at length arranged. Buonaparte demanded and obtained a million sterling, a hundred of the finest *pictures and* STATUES *in the papal gallery,* a large supply of military stores, and the cession of Ancona, Ferrara, and Bologna, with their respective domains."†

It formed a part of the generalship of Bonaparte to conquer kingdoms, as well as armies, in detail. He entered into treaty with the pope and with the king of Naples, after he held as his vassal the subject king of Sardinia. But he thereby prepared to meet a more formidable foe, who soon brought

---

* Hist. of Napoleon. Ibid. p. 57. † Ibib. p. 58.

into requisition all the energies of his active mind and all the undivided strength of his intrepid army. The strong but sluggish Austria was roused, by a succession of defeats, to put forth its power. The empire, venerable in years, was soon taught not to despise the infant republic. And aged generals, long versant in the art of war, were sent forth with veteran and well appointed armies, to check the career of an "inexperienced youth, who conquered by the breach of all its rules!"

We have seen how the analogy which runs in right order from age to age, between the most momentous events that have ever been transacted on the theatre of the world, and the words of inspiration which declared the things that were to be, does not fail in the first campaign of Napoleon, as recorded by his historians. He was the Nelson of the land. Of all men it was he who had in his hand *a vial of wrath to pour out upon the earth.* And of all places on earth, he chose that very spot which was defined in explicit language, and long before determined by actions not, as yet, second to his own. It were superfluous to specify so minutely the events of succeeding campaigns, for the *scene* was the same, except in so far as he trode still more closely on the steps of Attila, along the *rivers and fountains of waters*—till the Corsican outrivalled the Hun, and poured his vial over them *all,* while the trumpet of the barbarian reached only to a *part.* And, interweaving the words of the historian, without discolouring a fact, a succinct narrative may be attempted, to show, how the great captain of infidel France still farther illustrated a text by his deeds, before he became the head of the empire, and illustrated another.

It was the plan of the French directory, the scheme of Carnot, that the armies of the Rhine and of Italy, subduing the forces of Austria in their course, should open a communication through the passes of the Tyrol, and meeting in the heart of Austria, dictate peace at Vienna. Bonaparte's portion of the task was promptly and fully executed: and after the repeated defeats of the Austrians, he was ready to open up his way to the capital of Germany. But the defeat of Jourdan and the retreat of Moreau, (the most memorable event of the Rhenish warfare,) left him to struggle single-handed with all the strength of Austria. Holding Lombardy as his own, and declaring in all his proclamations that his war was with the government and not with the people, he prepared to withstand the armies of Germany, and, on the same spot, like another Attila, he broke again the power of "the empire."

"The thunder-cloud which had been so long blackening on the mountains of the Tyrol, seemed now about to discharge its fury." Wurmser, the most celebrated of the Austrian generals, with an army of 80,000 men, marched from Trent against the French in northern Italy, whose armies he had already driven from Germany to France. One division directed its march on Breschia *along the valley of the Chiese;* another *descended the Adige* and manœuvered on *Verona,* while the other passed along the left *bank of Lake of Garda.* Bonaparte rushed at the head of an army, "which his combinations had rendered superior," upon the right wing of the Austrians, and defeated them in separate detachments at Salo, which touches its *waters,* and at Lonato, which is situated at the bottom of the lake; where also the second division of the Austrian army was speedily routed. The third was defeated at Castiliogne, upon the banks and near the source of a stream that flows into the Mincio,—and the last portion of their army was broken at *Peschiera.*

They fled in all directions upon the *Mincio.* "After their defeat," says sir Walter Scott, "there can be nothing imagined more confused or calamitous than the condition of the Austrian divisions, who found themselves opposed and finally overwhelmed by an enemy who appeared to possess ubiquity. They could hardly be brought to do their duty, in circumstances where *it seemed that destiny itself was fighting against them.* The splenid army was destroyed in detail. The Austrians are supposed to have lost 40,000 men in these disastrous battles." The sprinklings of the vial fell as suddenly as before on the rivers and fountains of waters. Bonaparte toiled like a slave at his task; he flew from battle to battle, and from *river to river,* "nor slept except by starts" during "seven days, the brief period of the campaign."

Twenty thousand fresh troops were added to the discomfitted army of Wurmser: and "he marched from Trent towards Mantua, through the defiles of *the Brenta,* at the head of 30,000 men; leaving 20,000 or 25,000 under Davidowich at Roveredo, to cover the Tyrol." Bonaparte, says one historian, darted on Roveredo.* It was upon Davidowich, says another, that Bonaparte first meant to POUR his thunder. The battle of Roveredo, (4th September 1796,) was one of that great general's splendid days. *The action took place on both sides of the River.*† The wrecks of Davidowich's army fled deeper into the Tyrol, and took up a position at Lavissa, a small village on a *river* of a similar name, about three leagues to the northward of Trent. Bonaparte instantly pursued them—*passed the Lavissa*—drove them from their position, secured and occupied it

* Hist. of Napoleon, vol. i. p. 69.
† Scott's Life of Napoleon, vol. iii. pp. 200, 201.

—*being the entrance of one of the chief defiles of the Tyrol.* Wurmser "doubted not that Napoleon would march onward to Germany;" but the scene of warfare was not yet to be changed, and the victor rapidly returned from the defiles of the Tyrol, or the fountains of the Adige, to the banks of the Brenta. "Wurmser was his mark. After a forced march of not less than sixty miles, performed in two days—the Austrian van was destroyed in a twinkling." Next day Napoleon reached Bassano, the head-quarters of Wurmser. The French descended the defiles of the Brenta. "Augerau and Massena penetrated into both sides of the town; bore down all opposition; seized the cannon by which the *bridge* was defended, and Wurmser and his staff were in absolute flight." Joining a previously detached portion of his army, and having collected with difficulty the remnant of his discomfited troops, "the aged Marshall had still the command of about *sixteen* thousand men, out of *sixty thousand*," with whom he had, scarce a week before, commenced the campaign—and after repeated contests, unable any longer to keep the field, he threw himself into Mantua, with the shattered fragment of his army.

In those terrible campaigns, *three imperial armies had already been annihilated.* A formidable army of 60,000, under Alvinzi, again advanced from Germany. The French retreated. Bonaparte fixed his head-quarters at *Verona.* The whole territory between the Brenta and the Adige was again in the hands of the enemy, and had to be reconquered anew. Unable to combat the more wary general and his combined host on the plain, Bonaparte, by occupying a station in their rear, drew them "among *vast morasses,* where numbers could no longer avail." "*Arcola is situated upon a small stream which finds its way into the Adige,* through a *wilderness of marshes*, intersected with ditches and traversed by dikes in various directions." Such was the scene of "the three battles of Arcola," which decided the fate of the fourth imperial army.

"It was at the *point* where he wished to *cross the Alpon*, that Buonaparte *chiefly desired* to attain a decided superiority; and, in order to win it, he added stratagem to audacity. Observing one of his columns repulsed, and retreating along the causeway, he placed the 32d regiment in ambuscade in a thicket of willows which bordered *the rivulet*, and saluting the pursuing enemy with a close, heavy, and unexpected fire, instantly rushed to close with the bayonet, and attacking the flank of a column of nearly three thousand Croats, forced them into the *marsh, where most of them perished*."* "In these three days Buonaparte lost 8000 men: *the slaughter among his opponents must have been terrible*."† "It is calculated," says Las Casas, "that out of Alvinzi's 60,000 or 70,000 men, he lost from 30,000 to 35,000."‡ "Thus ended the fourth campaign, undertaken for the Austrian possessions in Italy."

"Austria, who seemed to cling to Italy with the tenacity of a dying grasp, again, and now for the fifth time, recruited her armies on the frontier, and placing Alvinzi once more at the head of sixty thousand men, commanded him to resume the offensive against the French in Italy."§ The Austrians, still holding by the fatal *rivers of waters* made the fifth descent on Northern Italy, with the same infatuation as before, in two different lines and divisions along the *Upper Adige* and the *Brenta*. "Bonaparte, uncertain which of these attacks was considered as the main one, concentrated his army at *Verona*, which had been so important a place during all these campaigns as a central point, from which he might at pleasure *march either up the Adige* against Alvinzi, or *descend the river* to resist the attempts of Provera."‖

---

* Scott's Life of Napoleon, p. 231. † Hist. of Nap. vol. i. p. 89.
‡ Journal, vol. ii. part 3d, p. 172.
§ Scott's Life of Nap. ib. p. 236. ‖ Ib, p. 239.

In the clear and beautiful moonlight, where the passions in the breasts of men ill accorded with the calm of nature, "Napoleon ascended several heights, (on the night before the famous battle of Rivoli,) and observed the different lines of the enemy's fires. *They filled the country between the Adige and the lake of Garda;* the atmosphere was reddened by them."* They lay between the *river* and the *fountains of waters;* and there a vial would be poured on the morrow that would quench them. The 14th of January 1797, was one of the brightest days in the military chronicles of Napoleon. The discomfiture of the Austrians was as complete as ever. Massena, afterwards duke of *Rivoli*, "swept every thing before him." "The French batteries thundered on the broken columns of the enemy—their cavalry made repeated charges, and the whole Austrians who had been engaged fell into inextricable disorder. The columns which had advanced were irretrievably defeated; those which remained were in such a condition, that to attack would have been madness."† Entrusting to Massena, Murat, and Joubert the pursuit of the flying columns of Alvinzi; Bonaparte, resting neither after victory nor before it, having heard during the battle that Provera, the general of the second Austrian army, had forced his way to *the lake of Garda*, and was already, by *means of boats*, in communication with *Mantua*, hastened with all speed from the *Adige* to the *Mincio*, "surrounded and attacked with *fury* the troops of Provera, while the blockading army compelled the garrison, at the bayonet's points, to re-enter the besieged city of Mantua."‡ The troops of Provera were "*taken or killed.*" "The

---

* Las Casas, ib. p. 182. † Scott's Life of Napoleon, p. 242.
‡ Ibid. p. 246.

larger army of Alvinzi, were close pursued from the *bloody* field of Rivoli, and never were permitted to draw breath or to recover their disorder." "The ground which the French had lost in Italy was speedily resumed. Trent and Bassano were again occupied by the French. They regained all the positions and strong-holds which they had possessed on the frontiers of Italy before Alvinzi's first descent, and might perhaps have penetrated deeper into the mountainous frontier of Germany, but *for the snow which choked up the passes*."* "One crowning consequence of these victories was the *surrender of Mantua* itself, which had cost so much *blood*," and which was *surrounded with waters*. The siege of that city had continued for six months, during which the garrison is said by Napoleon to have lost 27,000 men by disease, and in the various, numerous, and bloody assaults that took place. This decisive event put an end to the war in Italy. "The contest with Austria was hereafter to be waged on the hereditary dominions of that haughty power;" and the scene of it reached to the fountains of waters.

The power of Austria, the great stay of Rome, and the right arm of popery, having been broken in Italy, and Lombardy being wholly in possession of Napoleon, "he found leisure to *avenge himself on the pope* for those hostile demonstrations which, as yet, he had been contented to hold in check. The terror with which the priestly court of the Vatican received the tidings of the utter destruction of the Austrian army, and of the irresistible conqueror's march southwards, did not prevent the papal troops from making some efforts to defend the territories of the Holy See. General Victor, with 400 French and as many

---

* Scott's Life of Napoleon, p. 242.

Lombards, advanced upon the route of Imola. A Papal force, in numbers about equal, lay encamped on the *river Senio*, in front of that town. Monks, with crucifixes in their hands, ran through the lines, exciting them to fight bravely for their country and their faith. The French general, by a rapid movement, threw his horse across the *stream* a league or two higher up, and then charged *through the Senio* in their front. The resistance was brief. The Pope's army, composed mostly of new recruits, retreated in confusion. Faenza was carried by the bayonet. Cotti and 3000 men laid down their arms; and the strong town of Ancona was occupied. On the tenth of February the French entered Loretto,* and *rifled that celebrated seat of superstition of whatever treasures it still retained:* the most valuable articles had already been packed up and sent to Rome for safety.† Victor then turned westward from Ancona, with the design to unite with another French column, which had advanced into the Papal dominions by Perugia.

---

* "The priests had an image of the Virgin Mary at this place, which they exhibited to the people in the act of shedding tears, the more to stimulate them against the impious republicans. On entering the place, the French were amused with discovering the machinery by which this trick had been performed; the Madonna's tears were a string of glass beads, flowing by clock-work within a shrine which the *worshippers* were too respectful to approach very nearly. Little a-molu fountains, which stream on the same principle, are now common ornaments for the chimney-piece in Paris." Note, ibid. See also Scott's Life of Napoleon, Las Casas' Journal.—Such was the divinity and miraculous power of our Lady of Loretto—who has yet her place in the Roman breviary, and her worship and honour in the Roman catholic churches.

† "The *sancta casa* or *holy house* of Loretto, is a little brick building, round which a magnificent church has been reared, and which the Romish calendar states to have been the original dwelling-house of the Virgin Mary in Nazareth, transported through the air to Italy by miracles. This was for ages the chief resort of Romish pilgrims; and the riches of the place were *once* enormous."—Compare with p. 132, &c.

"The panic which the French advance had by this time spread, was such, that the Pope had no hope but in submission. The alarm in Rome itself *recalled the days of Alaric the Goth.* The treaty of Tollentino (12th Feb. 1797) followed. By this the Pope conceded formally (for the first time) his ancient territory of Avignon; he resigned the legations of Ferrara, Bologna, and Romagna, and the port of Ancona; agreed to pay about a million and a half sterling, and to execute to the utmost the provisions of Bologna with respect to the works of art. On these terms Pius was to remain nominal master of some shreds of the patrimony of St. Peter. Bonaparte was satisfied, on the whole, that he should best secure his ultimate purposes by suffering the Vatican to prolong, *for some time further* the shadow of that sovereignty, which had *in former ages trampled on kings and emperors.*"*

"In nine days the war with the Pope had reached its close; and having left some garrisons in the towns on the Adige to watch the neutrality of Venice, Napoleon hastened to carry the war into the hereditary dominions of Austria. He proceeded to the *frontier* of the Frioul. The Austrian army had once more on a double basis—one great division on the Tyrolese frontier, and the greater under the Archduke Charles himself on the Triulese.† To give the details of the sixth campaign would be to repeat the story which has been already five times told. Bonaparte found the Archduke posted behind the river Tagliamento, in front of the rugged Carinthian mountains, which guard *the passage in that quarter from Italy to Germany.* Detaching Massena to the (river) Piave, *where* the Austrian division of Lusignan were in observation, he himself determined to charge the Archduke in front. Massena was successful in driving Lusignan before him as far as Belluno, and thus turned the Austrian flank. Bonaparte then attempted and effected the passage of the Tagliamento. After a great and formal display of his forces, which was met by similar demonstrations on the Austrian *side of the river,* he suddenly broke up his line and retreated. The archduke, knowing that French had been marching all the night before, concluded that the general wished to defer the battle till another day; and, in like manner withdrew to his camp. About two hours after, Napoleon *rushed with his whole army,* who had merely lain down in ranks, upon *the margin of the Tagliamento,* no longer adequately guarded, and had forded *the stream,* ere the Austrian line of battle could be formed. In the action which followed (12th March, 1797) the troops of the Archduke displayed great gallantry, but every effort to dislodge Napoleon failed; at length retreat was judged necessary. The French followed hard behind. They stormed Gradisca, where they made 5,000 prisoners, and occupied, in the course of a few days, Trieste, Fiume, *and every stronghold in Carinthia.* In the course of a campaign of twenty days, the

* Hist. of Napoleon, vol. i. pp. 90—93. † Ibid. p. 95.

Austrians fought Bonaparte ten times, but the *overthrow of the Tagliamento* was never recovered; and the Archduke, after defending *Styria inch by inch as he had the Fiume and Carinthia*, at length adopted the resolution of reaching Vienna by forced marches, there to gather round him whatever force the royalty of his nation could muster, and make a last stand beneath the walls of the capital."* Vienna was panic-struck on hearing that Bonaparte had stormed the passes of the Julian Alps.† The war with Austria was at an end. "The provisional treaty of Leoben was signed, April 18, 1797."

The commentary is clear as full; the prophecy is not of any private interpretation, not a word of which is needed; and the *judgment* is so *manifest*, that, on reading this record of blood, as of all that have preceded them, it may be said, "he that hath ears to hear let him hear."

But as yet the illustration is not complete; nor the full measure of the vial poured out. There was a spot, a portion of the waters, on which Attila had been, which Bonaparte had not touched; and instead as he had purposed, of leaving the streams of Italy, and dictating peace under the walls of Vienna, he had injuries and treacheries to avenge against Venice. And in fulfilling, for the time, the appointed task, prescribed in the word of that God whom his directorial masters denied, Bonaparte, by his *words*, as well as by his actions, becomes the expositor of the sacred oracle, the first act of the fulfilment of which had already placed his name among the first of blood-stained heroes.

"No sooner was the negotiation in a fair train, than Napoleon, abandoning for a moment the details of its management to inferior diplomatists, hastened to retrace his steps, and to POUR the full storm of his WRATH upon the Venetians. The Doge and his Senate, whose only hopes had rested on the successes of Austria on the *Adige*, heard with utter despair that the Archduke had shared the fate of Beaulieu, of Wurmser, and of Alvinzi, and that

* Hist. of Napoleon, vol. i. pp. 96, 97. † Ibid. p. 98.

the preliminaries of peace were actually signed. The rapidity of Bonaparte's return gave them no breathing-time."*

The senate despatched agents to deprecate his wrath. "Are the prisoners at liberty?" he said, with a stern voice, and without replying to the humble greetings of the terrified envoys. They answered with hesitation, that they had liberated the French, the Polish, and the Brescians, who had been made captive in the *insurrectionary war*. "I will have them all—all!" exclaimed Bonaparte, "all who are in prison on account of their political sentiments. I will go myself to destroy your dungeons on the Bridge of Tears—*opinions shall be free*—I will have *no Inquisition*—I will hear of no Inquisition, and no Senate either—*I will dictate the law to you*—I WILL PROVE AN ATTILA TO VENICE."†

The tidings of the massacre of Verona, and of the batteries of a Venetian fort on the Lido having fired upon a French vessel, added new fuel to the wrath of Bonaparte. "The news of these fresh aggressions did not fail to aggravate his indignation to the highest pitch. The terrified deputies ventured to touch with delicacy on the subject of pecuniary atonement. Bonaparte's answer was worthy of a Roman. 'If you could proffer me,' he said, 'the treasures of Peru—if you could strew the whole district with gold, it could not atone for the French blood that has been treacherously spilt. The lion of St. Mark must lick the dust.'"‡ War was declared against Venice.

---

* Hist. of Napoleon, vol. i. p. 100.

† Sir Walter Scott's Life of Napoleon, vol. iii. pp. 316, 317. Bonaparte was not unused to this title, or designation—and complained that he had been "stigmatised—as the MODERN ATTILA, ROBESPIERRE ON HORSEBACK," &c. both of whom, in different ways, as the reader will be at no loss to see, were, prophetically, his predecessors.—*Las Casas' Journal*, vol. i. part ii. p. 307.

‡ Ibid. p. 317.

The French were commanded to advance, and to destroy in their progress, wherever they found it displayed, the winged lion of St. Mark, the ancient emblem of Venetian sovereignty. Venice fell. Bonaparte, as he had threatened, did, like another *Attila*, dictate the law to that proud city. "The Senate submitted wholly, 31st May 1797. He exacted severe revenge. A democratical government was established in the stead of the ancient oligarchy, and besides the exaction of a heavy tribute, a large portion of the Venetian territories was ceded to the conquerors."*

Bonaparte thus completed his victorious career in northern Italy, and had passed over the *rivers and fountains of waters*, from the *sources* of the Bormida to the city of Venice; and from the banks of the Reno to the streamlets that issue from the farthest mountains of Tyrol. But though sprinkled from one extremity to the other of this extensive and defined region, the *vial of wrath* was yet only half poured out upon *the rivers and fountains of waters*.

Peace was concluded between France and Austria on the 3d October, 1797. The Ligurian or Piedmontese republic was established; and such were the effects of French fraternization, that in a brief space the inhabitants of the north of Italy were ripe for revolt. The battle of the Nile gave new hope to the enemies of France. A new confederation of kingdoms was formed against it. A Russian army approached towards Germany; the French republic declared that its entrance into that country would be held tantamount to a declaration of war: and before the close of the year 1798, while the flower of the French army was withering in the deserts of Egypt,

* Hist. vol. iii. p. 100.

or on the coast of Palestine, (where, thus early, preparation had to be made for the pouring out of the sixth vial,) the war between Austria and France was renewed. In the former war, Austria was, in the first instance, the aggressor, had provoked the vengeance of the fierce republic, and brought down *judgment* on its own head. But now France was the first to declare war, as before it had done, in calling down the vial that was poured out upon *the sea.* And the French were vanquished, where none before could withstand them.

While the genius of Bonaparte was contending with the desert, and his attention was divided between a portion of Africa and Asia, and while even he was beat back, at *Acre*, where he contended with British Seamen, as he touched on the borders of *the sea*, the war was renewed in Northern Italy, under different auspices and with a very different issue than before. There was another man in Europe who was fitted, no less than Buonaparte, for holding the *vial of wrath* in his hand, and for sprinkling it anew over the *rivers and fountains of waters;* and the French, who had once been joint agents in the work of *shedding the blood of the saints of the Most High*, were made the victims of the *wrath* of which they had so recently been the instruments. In savage cruelty no name could overmatch Suwarrow's. The siege of Ishmail is a black spot, even on a bloated world. The "merciless victor," who had presided over it, and who, without uttering one word of mercy, had calmly looked on the massacre of thirty thousand vanquished enemies, was, upon the first tidings of war, on the march to Italy to retrace the steps of Bonaparte. Like a demon of destruction, he lighted on the *rivers*, and stopped not till he reached the *fountains of waters.* Suwarrow who shrunk not from blood, at the head of a Russian army, that shewed no mercy and knew no fear, combined with Austrians bent on revenging their country's wrongs, reversed and redeemed the conquests which Bonaparte had won; and with activity and desperate resolution scarcely second to his own, and acting on his system of *concentrating* his forces on a single point, as if *pouring out a vial of wrath* on one spot after another, repelled the French, with immense slaughter, from *river to river*, till they lost every inch of ground which they had formerly gained, and not one republican corps was to be found in Lombardy or Piedmont. The career of Suwarrow along the *rivers*, and till he reached the *fountains of waters*, was not less bloody, along them all, from the lake of Garda and the banks of Mincio, to the sources, or *fountains*, of the Po, than that of Bonaparte. And the evidence that his course also was marked by *a vial of wrath*, is too abundant to be effectually condensed in a brief narrative.

The fifteenth chapter of the Annual Register for 1799, contains an interesting account of the Italian campaign of Suwarrow, the locality of which was precisely that of Bonaparte's campaigns. The whole chapter is one continued illustration; and even the *contents* of it may convey to the reader some faint impression of the severity of the judgment, as well as of its perfect appositeness, in place, as well as in character and time, to the third vial.

"Situation and force of the French and Austrian armies in Italy, at the beginning of 1799. The French driven with great loss from the *left bank of the Adige*. Operations of the Austrians on the flanks of the French army The French on the fifth of April *defeated with great loss.—Retire to the Mincio.*—And *afterwards to the Chiese.* The Austrian General, Melas, *passes the Mincio with all his army.*—23,000 Russian auxiliaries arrive with Marshal Suwarrow, who takes the chief command of the troops of the two emperors. *Peschiera and Mantua invested. Brescia* taken by the allies, who march to the *Aglio*, which the *French abandon.* Moreau succeeds in the command of the French army to Schaerer, who was become the object of public animadversion.

The *allied army* encamps on the *Adda.* *Distribution of the French army on that* RIVER.—*Dislodged therefrom* on the twenty-seventh by Marshal Suwarrow. Battle of *Cassano.* *The French compelled to fly* TOWARDS MILAN, *which is entered by the Austrians* on the twenty-eighth. Embarrassing situation of Moreau. The plan he determines to pursue. Reduction of the fortresses of *Peschiera and Pizzighitone.* Plan of operations pursued by Marshal Suwarrow. Capture of the cities *of* TORTONA *and Turin.* Moreau *passes the Bormida,* and retreats towards *Coni.* Reduction of the citadels of MILAN *and Ferrara.* *The French driven from Ravenna.* General Macdonald with all his army evacuates the kingdom of Naples. —*Crosses the Appennines.*—Makes himself master of *Modena, Reggio, Parma, and Placentia, but is defeated in a* SERIES OF BATTLES ON BOTH SIDES OF *the* TREBBIA, by Marshal Suwarrow. Moreau, who had crossed the *Appenines,* with a view of drawing near to Macdonald, and gained several advantages, on the approach of the Russian commander, retires to Genoa. *Reduction of the citadel of Turin.* Insurrection of the inhabitants of Tuscany. Macdonald accomplishes his *retreat,* and junction with Moreau. *Alexandria and Mantua surrender* by capitulation. Military measures taken by the new French directory. The command of the army of Italy restored to Joubert, who puts his troops in motion on the eleventh of August. *Battle of Novi.* Victory long doubtful; at last decided in favour of *the allies.* *Enormous loss on both sides.* Conditional capitulation of *Tortona,* which *falls* on the eleventh of September. General Suwarrow sets off for Switzerland. Coni becomes the sole object of the campaign. Capture of Ancona, and of Coni. Other places taken by the Austrians. *Genoa and its small territory, the* ONLY POSSESSION *remaining to the French in Italy at the close of* 1799."

Suwarrow's campaign in the north of Italy, though a notable event which rivetted the attention of Europe at the time, has sunk into comparative oblivion, before the subsequent achievements of Napoleon. A brief abstract of the bloody tale may not therefore be superfluous, in order to set before the general reader a renewed illustration of the manner in which the *vial of wrath* was still poured upon the *rivers, and* lastly *on the fountains of waters.* The place is the same, and the *wrath* was not less than before; and the order is more definitely marked, as the full effect of the vision is told. The natural features of that singular region, which formed the field of blood, towards the close of that murderous warfare, are set most vividly before our eyes, by a Marshal of

France, in a manner which no verbal description could emulate. Bonaparte speedily passed along the *fountains;* and his battles were fought along the *rivers*, till he reached the farthest streams of Italy, and the passes of the Julian Alps, where these have their sources. But, reversing his course, the Russian closed his victories, where those of the Corsican began; and the chart for illustrating the campaign of 1799, sets before our sight, in their due order, *the fountains of waters.* While war for a time, gave to France the sovereignty of Europe, military engineering attained, in that country, a nicety and perfection previously unknown. Military maps of the seat of war, require the utmost attainable accuracy; for so essential are the exact knowledge of the ground, and the means of calculating distances, that the fate of armies or of empires might possibly depend upon the accurate position, in a chart, of a single stream. The map of Lombardy was the study of Napoleon, before that country had been surveyed by engineers equal to his own. But the Atlas from which the maps are taken, was published in Paris in the year 1831,* after the long-continued possession of the country, together with every possible facility for accomplishing the task, had enabled the French engineers to define and depict the scene of so many battles, from which too the boasted glory of France took its rise. And as Bonaparte, in lording over subjugated foes, laid his exactions on Piedmont, and supported his army with the spoils of the vanquished, so even military engineering, a beautiful art for a bloody purpose, must pay its tribute, and yield the best of its fruits to sus-

---

* *Atlas des Mémoires pour servir a l'Histoire Militaire sous les Directoire, le Consulat, et l'Empire, par le Marechal Gouvion Saint-Cyr. Paris,* 1831.

tain the cause of the gospel of Jesus, under the influence of which men shall learn no more. For, next to the view from the summit of Montezemoto, from whence *the rivers and fountains of waters* are seen in actual vision, and where, from the snow-clad Alps and the opposite Appenines, such multitudes of streams glitter on each side, while the intermediate plain lies in broad perspective, thronged with new rivers, stretching forth to the farthest reach of sight, is the inspection of the military map, constructed by Marshal St. Cyr, for exemplifying the campaign of 1799, and which may be said to set us down among the *fountains of waters*, where, *after* having again passed over the *rivers*, the vial of wrath was that year poured out. The chart itself thus possesses an interest infinitely superior to that of a perishing memorial of glories that have perished, and which themselves were but the dream of a day. The warrior presents the believer in Jesus with a gift that will retain its value, beyond all that the sword could conquer, a visible illustration of that word which abideth for ever.

While the whole valley of the Po may be aptly designated the region of *rivers*, Piedmont may specially be denominated the *fountains of waters*. And the map, in like manner, specially illustrative of the campaign of 1799, is that of Piedmont. After an enumeration of the rivers which the Po receives on the right bank, it is stated in the memoirs of Napoleon, "THE SOURCES OF ALL WHICH RIVERS *are in the Ligurian Alps*,"* or Piedmont, the country of the *fountains of waters*. There the combined Austrian and Russian armies closed their career of conquests, in 1799; and on the plains of Piedmont, Bonaparte afterwards, in one battle, restored the lost

* Memoirs of Napoleon, vol. i. part 1, p. 106.

laurels of France, and *poured out* the last of the *vial* which was first given into his hand. The map may serve for illustrating the prediction as well as the campaign. The history of the war will farther shew that it was indeed the spot on which the *vial of wrath* was finally *poured out.*

In the beginning of 1799, eighty thousand French troops, and fifty thousand auxiliaries, held Italy and Naples in subjection. The army of Italy chiefly occupied its northern frontier, including Piedmont, Milan, and the countries of Bergamo and Mantua; and fifty thousand, ready for active service, "were in cantonments on the banks of the lake of Garda, of the Mincio, and of the Po." The Austrians occupied the parrallel line of the Adige. It was the allotted task of the army of Italy, "to pierce through the line of the Adige, and to drive the Austrians beyond the Brenta." The republican forces assaulted the entrenchments of the imperial army, (26th February,) and the battle was very obstinate the whole day. A Polish legion was exterminated "with the bayonets of the Austrians and the butt ends of their muskets." So numerous were the slain, that within three days "the air began to be infected;" and the only suspension of arms was for the burial of the dead (February 29). On the succeeding day, ten thousand men, commanded by Moreau, having passed the Adige, and advanced within half a league of Verona, were attacked by the Austrians with such resistless fury, and yet fought with such determined resolution, that "their retreat was nothing but a continued engagement;" but on approaching the bridge, they were driven from it by two battalions of Austrian grenadiers, who, "without firing, and using only the bayonet, overcame all resistance, seized the bridge, and thus all who had not already passed were cut off."

"On the first of April, General Sheerer, abandoning all his posts which he occupied between the *Adige and the lake of Garda*, and placing a strong garrison in *Peschiera*, took a position with his left and centre, *beyond the Tartaro*, at Magnan, between Villa Franca and Ysola-della-Scala, his right wing being before Lignano. On the following day the Austrians encamped on the *right bank of the Adige*, before Verona, and on the road to Villa Franca. These first days of the campaign cost the French the immense loss of ten thousand men in killed, wounded, taken, or deserted; and that of the Austrians amounted to half the number."*

Fearing the rapid advance of other Austrian forces and of the Russian army, Sheerer resolved to make a new effort to drive the Austrians over the *Adige;* and stimulated by their great and unwonted, but dear-bought success, the general of the Austrians "formed on his side the project of driving the French from their grand camp of Magnan, and beyond the Tanaro, or, if possible, behind the Mincio. It was on the same day, 5th April, that the two generals resolved to attack each other." The hostile armies met, and the battle was soon general along "the whole front of the line." The French got possession of Villa Franca, and, maintaining that position, were pressing on towards Verona, when they were assailed and broken by a column of the Austrian reserve, and their brief triumph converted into flight. Sheerer and Moreau, with all their remaining forces, "rushed so vigorously on the centre of the Austrians, that they compelled it to give way." Three battalions of grenadiers, of the imperial army, the last to mingle in the contest, checked anew the victorious French, and "the battle was renewed with redoubled fury, and long maintained with equal success. The obstinacy of the Austrians at last prevailed, and the French on this point likewise were broken, routed, and pursued with the bayonet at their backs." The

* Annual Register, Lond. 1799, vol. xli. pp. 277—280.

victors lost "in killed and wounded 2500 men. The loss of the French in killed and wounded was at least 3500 men. The revolt of Italy was the result of the victory." "The long suppressed detestation of the Italians for the French now broke forth, and the inhabitants of the *two banks of the Po* took up arms against them." On the extremity of the Austrian line, their arms were equally successful, and they drove their enemies *from the valley of Chiesa, and the two shores of the lake of Idro.* Sheerer *passed the Mincio,* quitted *the line of that river, and retired behind the Chiesa, leaving Peschiera and Mantua to their fate.*

The barbarities of war were not mitigated, nor was the slaughter diminished by the arrival of Suwarrow. The whole Austrian army having pass-the Mincio, and being joined by the Russians at Vallegio, the supreme command of both armies devolved on Suwarrow. "The marshall immediately took measures for pushing forwards, and made the necessary arrangements for the double blockade of Mantua and Peschiera. Sheerer, with his army reduced to less than 20,000 men, pursued his retrograde movements. The allied armies followed close on his footsteps, reduced the town and citadel of Brescia, and forced the French to *abandon the Oglio.* On the 20th General Kaim severely beat the rear-guard of the enemy's right, at Cremona, where the Russians were engaged, for the first time, with the French." But insurrectionary bands were around them on every side, as well as imperial armies in their rear. "They had scarcely suffered a first defeat, when the hatred felt, and the revenge reserved for them, broke forth with Italian heat. In a moment the insurrection spread itself on the *two banks of the Po.* The French dispersed about the country, fell under the blows of those Italians, who were a few days before so obedient. Even some towns, and among others Mirandola, were taken from them by the armed peasants, supported by some light imperial troops. The sparks of this fire passed, as it were, over the heads of the French, and lighted up the Brescian, the Bergamese, and Piedmont. The people assembled in several places, and where it did not burst it threatened. The fear of seeing a numerous population arriving behind him, and the impossibility of making head at once against this and the Austrians, contributed not a little to determine Sheerer to retire, that he might concentrate his force, secure the fortified places of Piedmont, and receive those reinforcements sooner, which were on their way from France and from Switzerland." But his repeated reverses, and continued retreat induced the Directory of France to supersede their favourite general, and to nominate Moreau in his stead, who was invested with the supreme command *on the banks of the Adda:* and, under a new commander-in-chief, the French army, reinforced by troops from Piedmont, Genoa, and France, prepared to make a stand against their victorious enemies, and the war was carried on with renewed obstinacy, vigour, and barbarity. Mantua, Peschiera, Brescia, and Pizzighitone had already been garrisoned, as if they had been left as spots upon the waters, on which the vial of wrath had still to be poured out.

The French had retired as rapidly from the scene of Bonaparte's repeated contest and desperate battles with a succession of Austrian armies, as that general had advanced over Piedmont and Lombardy; and they were now again returning to that portion of the *rivers*, and especially of the *fountains of waters*, over which his triumphant course had been as rapid as their retreat from the lake of Garda to the banks of Adda. It remained to be seen, whether more than before, and last in order, the vial had to be poured out *upon the fountains of waters*, even as it had previously been poured out upon the rivers.

"The positions taken by the French army were these; the left wing of the French army, commanded by Serurier, defended the upper Adda from Lecco, on the lake of Como, to Frezzo, where it joined to the centre, where Moreau took his station, composed of the divisions of Generals Victor and Grenier. All the place comprised between Trezzo and Cassano, was occupied by these two divisions. At their right and behind Cassano, was placed the main body of their cavalry. The bridge head of Cassano was strongly entrenched and protected by the artillery of the castle. It was protected likewise by the canal between the Adda and Milan, lined with riflemen, and defended by a great number of batteries raised *along the banks of the river*. The right of the French army, guarded by General Delmas, had its principal force at Lodi and Pizzighitone.

"On the 23d the allies continued their march without impediment, and encamped on the *banks of the Adda*, taking their positions *along that river*, and leaving those occupied by the French. Their head-quarters were at Treviglio. General Kaim's division held Pizzighitone in check, observed the Lower Adda, and advance parties beyond the Po, to Placentia and Parma. One of these parties was sent into the latter place to carry off the Pope, whom the French were conducting into France. But the Austrians, who were not informed of this circumstance before it was too late, did not arrive at Parma till twenty-four hours after the unfortunate Pius the Sixth had been torn from thence."*

The seven last plagues are the vials of the wrath of God, poured out upon the earth, while the *judgment sits* upon the papacy; and, although the Austrians conquered, and Italy was freed, the Pope was a prisoner in the hands of republicans. The French did tear the Pope from his kingdom and country, but they could not defend the frontiers of Lombardy or Piedmont; nor, though they led him into captivity, was their own *blood* the less freely *shed* in the place where French armies had mercilessly persecuted to the death the *witnesses of Jesus*.

* Annual Register, ibid. pp. 282, 283.

Suwarrow, unable to turn the line of the Adda, which was occupied by the French, resolved to force it at two points at once. One bridge, imperfectly destroyed by the enemy, was repaired: and another was thrown over the Adda in a night, where "its banks were steep and its course rapid and sinuous." On the 27th, after accomplishing "a passage which could be effected only by a concurrence of boldness, activity, and good fortune," the allied army assaulted the French, drove them from Frizzo, defeated them in a battle between Pozzo and Brivio, where, "by surprising the passage of the Adda, they battered them in every direction with cannon, and charged with cavalry," and pursued the vanquished enemy towares *Milan*, which Suwarrow entered the next day.

"The battle of the twenty-seventh, and the actions to which it led on the Upper Adda, cost the republicans five thousand men made prisoners, besides four thousand wounded or killed. The loss of the allies, on these different heads, amounted at least to two thousand five hundred men. Thus it appears that the imperialists fought for the safety of Verona under its walls, on the 26th and 30th March, and that eight and twenty days after they were established in Milan, having in the interval invested two fortresses, forced the passage of a river lined with entrenchments, obtained two brilliant victories, killed or wounded more than fifteen thousand men, made a like number of prisoners, and taken more than one hundred pieces of cannon."*

After "the battle of the Adda," Moreau, compelled to yield the Milanese to the conquerors, chose a position (7th May), by which his right rested on Alexandria, and the Tanaro, and his left

* Annual Register, ibid. p. 264.

on Valentia and the Po. By this position, on one side, he supported *Tortona*, and on the other, by the course of the Po, gave some protection to Turin.—He hoped to oblige the allies to waste the campaign in a *war of posts and sieges*, and give the republic time to collect *new armies*.

"The imperialists, taking possession of the whole of the left bank of the Upper Po, abandoned by the French, pushed their advanced posts as far as Chiavasso. A strong detachment entered the valley of Aasti, and took possession of Jarea. The centre of the Russian army entered the Lummeline, presenting a front against the French army. The left wing traversed the duchy of Parma, and occupied Bobbio. The right pushed its advanced posts as far as Vaghera. Morbegno and Como were taken, and a corps, sent from Milan, proceeded as far as Arona, on the lake Maggionne. *Such is the condensed picture of the multiplied operations which the allied army undertook at the beginning of May: operations which divided it into a great number of corps, and thus, very much reducing the principal body of the army, afforded Moreau the hope to be able to maintain his ground.* THE ALLIES WERE ACTING ON A LINE ALMOST CIRCULAR ROUND THE BASON FORMED BY THE ALPS AND APPENINES, *and intersected by the Po.* Of the great variety of objects which this campaign embraced, and the MULTIPLICITY OF ACTIONS *going on at the same time in different places*, it is utterly impossible, in any other than a history professedly and solely military, to give a detailed account."*

Moreau, induced by the movements of the Austrian camp, suddenly passed the Bormida, by a bridge of boats, at the head of ten thousand troops, but was

---

* Annual Register, ibid. pp. 284—286.

repulsed with the loss of twelve hundred men. The allied army, more than 30,000 strong, encamped in the vicinity of Turin. And the fortified cities, garrisoned by the French, on their previous retreat, having been rapidly reduced, immense magazines, the spoils of Italy, were transferred from the republicans to the imperialists, on the surrender of Mantua, Peschiera, Ancona, Ferrara, and Ravenna. "The Austrians, confined and threatened as they had been at the end of March, on the line of the Adige, had in two months carried their right to the frontiers of France, and their left to the Adriatic sea."

The wide and watered expanse of northern Italy was again clear of the invader, except on a single region "where so many rivers have their sources," the *fountains of waters*. But the contest was the fiercer, as the territory became circumscribed. Armies rushed towards Piedmont. Not only were the forces, that had invested the cities and fortresses, again free to act in the field; but, exclusive of these and of the multitude of armed peasants that voluntarily rose to resist the French, a new accession of twenty-five thousand Russians and Austrians swelled the ranks of the imperialists. The French army in Piedmont, bordering on France, lay close to its supplies. And Macdonald, the commander of the French "army of Naples," in retreating from Italy, "had resolved to advance between the Appenines and the Po." To form a junction of their forces, Moreau advanced to meet Macdonald, and occupied the upper valley of the Tanaro, the defile of Bochetta, and other passes of the Appenines. Suwarrow hastened to intercept and to attack the foe, and, like Bonaparte, to cut off armies by detail. "A dreadful battle ensued, which was interrupted only by night, on the 17th, 18th, and 19th, *on both sides of the Trebbia*." In the battle, or series of battles, the French lost above ten thousand men, or more than a third part of their army. So sanguinary was the conflict, that "the loss of the allies was little less than that of the enemy." On the surrender of Turin, which, after a terrible bombardment, was simultaneous with the victories of the Trebbia, ninety thousand Russians and Austrians contended in Piedmont as their field of blood, with seventy thousand French in garrisons and the field. And on the subsequent union of his army with that of Macdonald, Moreau had a disposable force of forty or fifty thousand men, who were spread from the eastern extremity of the state of Genoa, as far as Coni, and occupied in that line "*all the defiles of the Appenines*."*

Twenty thousand troops being on the point of joining the forces of Suwarrow, and many more rapidly advancing, Joubert, who had been newly nominated commander-in-chief of the republican army, "determined to act on the offensive, and to hazard a battle, in order to relieve *Tortona*. The French advanced from Milesimo, crossed the Bormida, and took a position at Orba, in the plain of Alexandria. Suwarrow *concentrated his forces* and (August 13th) marched towards the enemy, who had then penetrated to Novi. The French were attacked with Russian ferocity. After a desperate and long-contested battle, the republicans were defeated, "pursued by the whole line, and eight thousand were slain. Of the imperialists seven thousand were killed, wounded or lost of whom the lost did not exceed six hundred. *The Russians gave no quarter*." "As soon as the republicans had recovered from their consternation, they took their positions nearly in *the line* they had before occupied. Suwarrow pursued a plan for dispossessing them of their situation, and forcing the passages to Genoa." But having accomplished his object in the discomfit-

* Annual Register, ibid; pp. 286—291.

ure of the republicans, till they could no longer keep the field, Suwarrow, (Sept. 11,) leaving to the Austrians the task of expelling them from Italy, withdrew to Switzerland, only to suffer disappointments and disasters, and speedily re-conducted his army into Russia. Whenever his work was accomplished his laurels faded, and retained nothing but the deep shade of blood.

The Austrians closed the campaign with no less energy amidst the *fountains of waters* in Piedmont, than that with which they had commenced it on the banks of the Adige. One division drove the enemy from the vale of Domo Dossola, and forced them to re-ascend the mountains; another, in like manner, repulsed them at Aosta, and drove the enemy into the higher valley; a third dislodged them again and took Pignerol. Twelve thousand were defeated on the plains of Sturo, and compelled to retire to Coni. The republicans fought with no better success in the neighbourhood of Alexandria, and were discomfited in all their attempts to raise the siege of Coni: but blood was still so profusely shed that in these battles the victors lost two thousand killed and wounded. Coni, Mondovi, Ceva, and Seravalle, and all the important posts of the valley of Sturo, were finally surrendered to the Austrians; and "*there remained in all Italy, only Genoa and its small territory*," (situated beyond the bounds of Piedmont, or its fountains of waters,) "*in the possession of the French, at the close of the year* 1799."*

"The loss of the allies, *in killed and wounded*, has been stated by most competent judges, at *thirty thousand*,—that of the French at *forty-five thousand*,"†—or, *seventy-five thousand killed and wounded* in the course of one campaign, all slain, as before,

* Annual Register, pp. 291—307. † Ibid.

where the *vial was poured out upon the rivers and fountains of waters, and they became blood.*

But the dregs of the vial of wrath had still to be poured along other fountains yet untouched, and were exhausted at last on the plains of Piedmont.

In 1800 the armies of France in Europe, were again under the command of Bonaparte: and Piedmont, which he formerly had conquered, was again his mark. In no part of Europe did he lead on an army to battle, from the time that he was first invested with the command till he was crowned as emperor, but solely amidst the *rivers and fountains of waters.* And when the directory fell, and the consulate was established in France, the new form of government was not less faithful to its task than the former; and Bonaparte, as consul, freely completed that which he first had begun at the dictation of the Directory.

"Bonaparte left Paris on the 6th of May 1800." —During the interval between the 15th and 18th of May, all the columns of the French army (60,000) were put in motion to cross the Alps:—one column by Mount Cenis, on Exilles and Susa; another by the route of the Little St. Bernard." On the 15th Bonaparte himself, at the head of the main body of the army, passed the Great St. Bernard, an immense and apparently inaccessible mountain,"*—"and the next morning, 16th May, the vanguard took possession of Aosta, a village, of Piedmont, from which extends the valley of the same name, *watered* by the *river* Doria."† "They advanced down the valley to Ivrea, carried the town by storm, combated and defeated an Austrian division at Romano. The roads to *Turin* and *Milan* were now alike open to Bonaparte." "Marches, man-

* Sir Walter Scott's Life of Napoleon, vol. iv. pp. 250—256.
† Ibid. pp. 262—268.

œuvres, and *bloody battles,*" between the Austrian army and the other columns of the French, followed each other in detail; and Suchet took up a line on Borghetta.—Bonaparte formed the resolution to pass the *rivers* Sesia and Tesino, to push straight for Milan, to join 20,000 men who had crossed the mountains by the route of St. Gothard's. Bonaparte entered *Milan.* *Pavia* fell into the hands of the French; *Lodi* and *Cremona* were occupied, and Pizzighitone was invested; and Bonaparte again occupying the place of Attila, fixed his residence in the ducal palace of Milan. The French occupied the best and fairest share of northern Italy, while the Austrian general found himself confined to Piedmont. Bonaparte, on his part, was anxious to relieve Genoa. With this view he resolved to force his passage over the Po, and move against the Austrians, who were found to occupy in strength the villages of Casteggio and Montebello. These troops proved to be the greater part of the very army which he expected to find before Genoa. The battle of Montebello was a most obstinate one. The tall crops of rye hid the hostile battalions from each other's sight till they found themselves at the bayonet's point, a circumstance which led to much close fighting, and necessarily to much slaughter. It was a conflict of man against man, and determined at a dear cost of blood. The Austrians retreated, leaving the field of battle covered with their dead. The remains of their defeated army were rallied under the walls of *Tortona.*

But the battle of Marengo decied the fate of Italy. The plain, on which it was fought, "seemed lists formed by nature for such an encounter, when the fate of kingdoms was at issue." The French occupied the plain. The Austrians concentrated their forces in front of Alexandria, divided by the *river Bormida* from the purposed field of fight. It was the last, long the most doubtful, and finally the most decisive battle of all the Italian campaigns, which had introduced a new era in war: nor was it less desperate and bloody than any of its predecessors: for it was only after the Austrians "had been wearied with fighting the whole day and disordered with their hasty pursuit," and after "the plain had been filled with flying soldiers, and Bonaparte himhimself was seen in full retreat," that, on the advance of fresh troops from a distance to the field, the exhausted Austrian column was charged with new vigour, its ranks were penetrated, their army divided, and the whole French line, rallying at the voice of Napoleon, forced back their enemies at all points, who were pursued along the plain, suffering immense loss, and were not again able to make a stand till driven over *the Bormida.** The confusion at passing the river was inextricable,—"*the river rolled red* amidst the corpses of horse and men."† *It became blood.*

Such was the effect of the last of the many battles fought in this single region, so full of rivers and numberless fountains of waters, that, in the words of Sir Walter Scott, "even Pitt himself, upon whose declining health the misfortune made a most unfavourable impression, had considered the defeat of Marengo as a conclusion to the hopes of success against France for a considerable period,—'Fold up the map,' he said, pointing to that of Europe; 'it need not be again opened for these twenty years.'"‡

"Almost all the loss sustained by the French in the disastrous campaigns of 1799, was regained by the battles of Montebello and Marengo." "Bonaparte set out for Switzerland on the 6th of May. Two months had not elapsed, and in that brief

* Sir Walter Scott's Life of Napoleon, vol. iv. pp. 268—282.
† Hist. of Napoleon, vol. i. p. 223. ‡ Vol. iv. p. 289.

space what wonders had been accomplished?" "Enough," says Sir Walter Scott, "had been done to shew, that as the fortunes of France appeared to wane and dwindle after Bonaparte's departure, so they revived with even more than their original brilliancy as soon as this *Child of Destiny* had returned to preside over them."* And enough has been said to shew, how hitherto that destiny was accomplished, as it was written in the Revelation of Jesus Christ. Napoleon became the avenger of the blood of the saints, against the king of Sardinia, the emperor of Germany, and the pope of Rome. And the like retribution was exacted of the French by the hands of Suwarrow. And enough may have been said to shew how *the third angel poured out his vial upon the rivers and upon the fountains of waters and they became blood. And I heard the angel of the waters say, Thou art righteous, O Lord, which art, wast, and shalt be, because thou hast judged thus. For they shed the blood of saints and prophets, and thou hast given them blood to drink, for they are worthy. And I heard another out of the altar say, Even so, Lord God Almighty, true and righteous are thy judgments.*

Events in history follow in their natural course, or maintain their due consecutive order. And one *vial*, like the judgments that preceded them, leads on to another. The connexion is too conspicuous to pass unnoticed by the historian. But it is not easy to see how more can reasonably be asked, than the unconscious adoption of the identical symbol. The concluding paragraphs of Gibbon's History of the Decline and Fall of the Roman Empire, have, in this respect, more than once served us in good stead; and the concluding paragraph of the ninth chapter of Sir W. Scott's Life of Napoleon

* Vol. iv. p. 283.

Bonaparte, which closes the narrative of his Italian campaigns, has these words, which may form an appropriate conclusion to the third, or introduction to the fourth vial. "It appeared as if Bonaparte was the sun of France; when he was hid from her all was gloom, when he appeared, light and serenity were restored."* That sun, indeed, then began to arise, which not only dazzled France with its glory, but scorched Europe with its heat, and which, as speedily as it arose, has been blotted from the political horizon.

CHAPTER XXVII.

THE FOURTH VIAL.

And the fourth angel poured out his vial upon the sun, and power was given unto him to scorch men with fire. And men were scorched with great heat, and blasphemed the name of God, which hath power over these plagues; and they repented not to give him glory, ver. 8, 9.

If we look to the political horizon, after the Italian campaigns of the close of last century, a sun is seen arising, which, *manifest* as the sun in the firmament, soon shone with unparalleled brilliancy over Europe, scorched the nations in its course, and of which the

---

* Sir Walter Scott's Life of Napoleon, vol. iv. p. 285.

setting or the smiting was scarcely less marvellous than the great heat of its scorching blaze.

But it is not by one symbol alone, however apt its significancy, and however suited to the time, nor by a general description that might be indefinite in its application, but by the scriptural exposition of the symbol, (in reference to the imperial power,) derived from history long past, and by a discrimination which vividly marks all the strongest features of that eventful era, as well as by the rise to supreme earthly dominion and the contrasted doom of this "child of destiny," that, *at the end*, after the events have been accomplished and the facts may be retrospectively seen, this *prophecy*, like all whose fulfilment has preceded it, does *speak*, and calls on the whole reign of Napoleon to bear witness that it does *not lie*.

Divested of hypothesis—the scriptural warrant for the appropriation of the emblem, the *sun*, to Napoleon I.; the *power that was given him*; the *scorching* of *men* with *great heat*, or the grievous effect of his ascendancy, in chastisement of the nations, over the kingdoms of Europe; the blasphemy which prevailed and abounded throughout his reign; the impenitence which succeeded it; his fall, like the smiting of the sun; and the power of God over these plagues;—all *speak* in such a manner as to shew, that this *judgment* too has been *made manifest*.

The import of the symbol has first to be regarded, as a joint view of scripture and history expound it.

The rivers and fountains of waters formed the scene, limited to a specified region, and strongly marked by local peculiarities, over which the third trumpet sounded and the third vial was finally poured out. The order is still progressive; and there is a like accordance between the fourth trumpet and the fourth vial, but, as in the former, without restriction to the *third part*. The third and fourth trumpets may be viewed conjointly with the third and fourth vials, that the order may be more distinctly seen, and that the similarity of meaning attached to the very same terms may be obvious in the one case as in the other.

"*And the* THIRD *angel sounded, and there fell a great star from heaven, burning as it were a lamp, and it fell upon the third part of the* RIVERS AND UPON THE FOUNTAINS OF WATERS. *And the name of the star is called wormwood, and the third part of the* WATERS *became wormwood, and many men died of the waters, because they were made bitter. And the* FOURTH *angel sounded, and the third part of the* SUN *was smitten, and the third part of the moon, and the third part of the stars, so as the third part of them was darkened, and the day shone not for a third part of it, and the night likewise.*" Rev. viii. 10, 12.

And the THIRD *angel poured out his vial upon the* RIVERS AND FOUNTAINS OF WATERS, *and they became blood. And I heard the angel of the* WATERS *say, Thou art righteous, O Lord, which art, wast, and shalt be, because thou hast* JUDGED *thus. For they have shed the blood of saints and prophets, and thou hast given them blood to drink, for they are worthy. And I heard another out of the altar say, Even so, Lord God Almighty, true and righteous are thy* JUDGMENTS. *And the* FOURTH *angel poured out his vial upon the* SUN, *and power was given unto him to scorch men with fire. And men were scorched with great heat, and blasphemed the name of God, which hath power over these plagues, and they repented not to give him glory.*

After Attila had partially ravaged Northern Italy, or had fallen upon the *third part of the rivers and fountains of waters,* and after these had become *wormwood* to Rome by the rebellion of the confederates of Italy at *Tortona,* not only was the emperor taken out of the way, but the IMPERIAL POWER in

Italy was speedily extinguished, and the third part of the SUN was smitten. Yet it was *darkened* only for a season, *for the third part of the day and of the night likewise.* He that previously *letted*, had indeed been *taken out of the way*, and Rome became the seat of papal supremacy to lord over the minds of men. But *popery* gave renewed life to the *empire.* The *second-beast* not only exercised *all the power of the first-beast before him*, but he also *caused the earth and them that dwell therein to worship the* FIRST BEAST *whose deadly wound was healed.* The time *passed away* during which the *sun* of Rome, or the emperorship, as exercising temporal jurisdiction over Italy and the once imperial city was to be smitten with darkness, or cease to *shine.* And CHARLEMAGNE WAS BY THE POPE CROWNED EMPEROR OF THE ROMANS. He restored the western empire. And after the kingdom of Italy was subdued by Otho, the king of Germany, he appropriated the *western empire*, and, says Gibbon, "*for ever* fixed the *imperial crown* in the name and *nation of Germany.*" But from that memorable era this maxim of public jurisprudence was introduced by force and ratified by time, "*that he might not legally assume the titles of emperor and Augustus till he had received the crown* FROM THE HANDS OF THE ROMAN PONTIFF." "The successors of Charlemagne and Otho were content with the humble names of kings of Germany and Italy, till they had passed the Alps and the Appenines, to seek their *imperial crown* on the banks of the Tiber." Such was the institution of the power superior to that of kings, which formed the restoration of the imperial authority of ancient Rome, and which was established by the prescription of ages. But Gibbon, who thus describes it, and who could paint so well the image of things that were past, was not a prophet, nor the son of a prophet, nor a believer in the prophets, and the time is come in which the word *for ever*, as he has written it, must be blotted out. The imperial power, in an early age of its renovated existence, was transferred from France to Germany, and, but as yesterday, for the sake of regaining that power anew, we have seen the contest between France and Germany carried on again and again from side to side of the region where the supremacy of Rome has been repeatedly contested, along the rivers and fountains of waters. And we have now simply to look to the next word that is written in prophecy, which abideth for ever, and to the next event in history, which, like all the former, has left its memorial to ages. But it is meet that history, in respect to events so prominent that it cannot there err, should do its own office, in order that no hand of man need here be raised to touch the ark of the testimony, at this spot of its far progress, or at any other; but that prophecy itself should *speak*, by facts, to expose the impotency and refute the fallacy, while it utterly and entirely disclaims the aid, of any private interpretation.

Looking then, in due course, and in its stated order and time, for the exaltation of the emperorship, as it was seen in the days of Cæsar or of Charlemagne, or for the rising of the *sun*, as it was once seen in the heavens, may we not, in full assurance of the truth of God's holy word, and in speaking of manifest judgments, open the almanac again, or read from history its next most remarkable event, to see whether the next vial has been poured out, or the next judgments have been made *manifest*, and whether Bonaparte's imperial glory, like that of Britain on the sea, bears not its true character and eternal mark, when all else pertaining to it shall pass into oblivion, that of one of *the least plagues, or of the vials of the wrath of God poured upon the earth.*

1800. The Austrians defeated at Marengo, June 14.
1801. Treaty of Peace between Austria and France.
1802. Peace of Amiens, March 27.
1803. War with Britain and France.
1804. Bonaparte EMPEROR, May 18.
—— War with Spain begun, &c. &c.

"The motion was carried in the tribunate with one dissenting voice, that the supreme power should be rendered hereditary in the person and family of Napoleon. The legislative body, without hesitation, adopted it, and a *senatus consultum* forthwith appeared, by which Napoleon Bonaparte was declared emperor of the French. He openly assumed the imperial title and dignity. In assuming the title of emperor, not of king, it escaped not observation, that Napoleon's object was to carry back the minds of the French to a period antecedent to the rules of the recently dethroned dynasty, to the days of CHARLEMAGNE, *who with the monarchy of France combined both a wider dominion and a loftier style.* As that great conqueror had caused himself to be crowned by Pope Leo, so *Napoleon* now determined that his own INAUGURATION should take place under the auspices of Pius VII., nay that the more to illustrate his *power*, the head of the Catholic church should repair to Paris for this purpose."*

"The title of king most obviously presented itself. That of emperor implied a yet higher power of sovereignty, and there existed no competitor who could challenge a claim to it. To Napoleon's own ear the word king might sound as if it restricted his power within the limits of an ancient kingdom; *while that of emperor might comprise dominions equal to the wide sweep of ancient Rome herself, and the bounds of the habitable earth alone could be considered as circumscribing their extent.*"†

---

* Hist. of Napoleon, vol. i. pp. 300, 302.
† Sir Walter Scott's Life of Napoleon, vol. v. pp. 147, 148.

"The emperor and empress received the congratulations of all the powers of Europe, excepting England, Russia, and Sweden, upon their new exaltation."*

"But the most splendid and *public recognition of his new rank* was yet to be made by the *formal act of coronation*, which, therefore, Napoleon determined should take place with circumstances of *solemnity which had been beyond the reach of any temporal prince for many ages.* His policy was often marked by a wish to *revive, imitate, and connect his own titles and interest, with some ancient observance of former days;* as if the novelty of his claims could have been rendered more venerable by investing them with antiquated forms, or as men of low birth, when raised to wealth and rank, are sometimes desirous to conceal the obscurity of their origin under the *blaze* of heraldic honours. *Pope Leo*, he remembered, *had placed a golden crown on the head of Charlemagne, and proclaimed him emperor of the Romans.* Pius VII., he determined, should *do the same* for a successor to much more than the actual power of Charlemagne. But though Charlemagne had repaired to Rome to receive inauguration from the hands of the pontiff of that day, Napoleon resolved, that he who now owned the proud, and in protestant eyes profane, title of Vicar of Christ, should travel to France to perform the coronation of the successful chief, by whom the See of Rome had been more than once humbled, pillaged, and impoverished, but by whom also her power had been recreated and restored, not only in Italy, but in France itself. On the 25th November, the pope met Bonaparte at Fontainbleau; and the conduct of the Emperor Napoleon was as stu-

* Sir Walter Scott's Life of Napoleon, vol. v. p. 156.

diously respectful toward him, *as that of Charlemagne, whom he was pleased to call his predecessor, could have been towards Leo.*—On the 2d December, the ceremony of the coronation took place in the ancient cathedral of Notre Dame, with the addition of every ceremony which could be devised to add to its solemnity."*

"The emperor took his coronation oath as usual on such occasions, with his hand upon the Scripture, and in the form in which it was repeated to him by the pope. But in the act of coronation itself, there was a marked deviation from the universal custom, characteristic of the man, the age, and the conjuncture. In all other similar solemnities, the crown had been placed on the sovereign's head by the presiding spiritual person, as representing the Deity, by whom princes rule. But not from the head of the Catholic church would Bonaparte consent to receive as a boon the golden symbol of sovereignty, which he was sensible he owed solely to his own unparalled train of military success. The crown having been blessed by the pope, Napoleon took it from the altar with his own hands, and placed it on his brows."†

"The northern states of Italy had followed the example of France through all her change of models. They had become republican in a directorial form, when Napoleon's sword conquered them from the Austrians; had changed to an establishment similar to the consular, when that was instituted in Paris by the 18th Brumaire; and were now destined to receive *as a king* him who had lately accepted and exercised with legal authority the office of their president. On the 17th March, a deputation ob-

* Sir Walter Scott's Life of Napoleon, vol. v. pp. 158, 159.
† Ibid.

tained an audience of the emperor, to whom they intimated the unanimous desire of their countrymen that Napoleon, founder of the Italian republic should be *the monarch of the Italian kingdom.* He was to have power to name his successor."*

"The senators of the Italian republic sent in their humble petition that their president might be pleased to do them also the favour to be crowned as their king at Milan. The emperor proceeded to that city accordingly, and in like fashion, on the 26th May 1805, placed on his own head the old *iron* crown, said to have been worn by the Lombard kings, uttering the words which according to tradition they were accustomed to use on such occasions, "*God hath given it me. Beware who touches it.*"† *In every thing it was the plan of Napoleon* to sink the memory of the Bourbon monarchy, and *revive the image of Charlemagne, emperor of the West.*"‡

On the conquest of Italy by Theodoric, the imperial power was no longer dominant over Rome, and the authority of the emperor at Constantinople ceased in Italy. The *sun* shone not for a third part of the day, and the night likewise. But Charlemagne was the restorer of the western empire; and "in every thing it was the plan of Bonaparte to revive the image of Charlemagne emperor of the West." The pope, whose toe the successors of Charlemagne had kissed, and the bridle of whose horse they had led, stood at the steps of Napoleon's throne, travelled, like a vassal at the command of his lord, and officiated at his coronation, that the form of imperial inauguration might be observed; but no hand except his own put the golden crown

---

* Sir Walter Scott's Life of Napoleon, vol. v. p. 170.
† Hist. of Napoleon, vol. i. p. 303. ‡ Ibid.

upon the head of the emperor. He was next installed as king of Italy—and thither he went, to be crowned its monarch. And as formerly he had threatened to be a second Attila, while the region of waters was, like Attila's, his allotted sphere of action—so in the act of placing the crown of Italy on his head, as soon as the symbol of the *sun* was there his badge, he took up in his lips the very *word* of the Revelation of Jesus Christ concerning him; and out of his own mouth, whenever the crown of Italy was on his head, he supplied an illustration, that he who is higher than the highest regarded him, and that power was given him to execute still farther the just judgment of God. While he placed on his head the old *iron* crown, he uttered the words, "God *hath given it me.*"* The first thing that is said of the *sun* on which the vial was poured, is *power was given unto him.*

On this important point it may not be superfluous to adduce more direct and repeated testimony—that of the school-fellow, the secretary, and the companion of the more solitary hours of Bonaparte.

"Setting aside the means, it must be acknowledged that it is impossible not to admire the genius of Bonaparte, his tenacity in advancing towards *his object*, and that adroit employment of suppleness and audacity, which made him sometimes dare fortune, sometimes avoid difficulties which he found insurmountable, to arrive, not merely at the throne of Louis XVI., but *at the re-constructed throne of Charlemagne.*"† "Bonaparte had *a long time be-*

---

* It has been stated, but I do not recollect on what evidence or on what occasion, that Bonaparte, after his exile in St. Helena, having been presented with a Bible, pushed it carelessly aside, saying, that he "knew all about it." How differently would he have regarded it, if he had known, that all his glory and his fall were written in one verse, of which too his first words, as king of Italy, were a literal illustration.

† Bourrienne's Memoirs of Bonaparte, vol. iii. pp. 37, 38, 8vo. ed.

fore spoken to me of the title of *emperor*, as being the most appropriate for the *new sovereignty*, which he wished to found in France. This, he observed, was not restoring the old system entirely, and *he dwelt much on its being the title which Cæsar had borne*."*

"The year 1804 teemed with great events, and it would be difficult to find in history so many circumstances exercising so great an influence *on the destinies of Europe*, crowded together within the short space of twelve months."†—"Bonaparte was crowned king of Italy, May 1805. The old iron crown of the kings of Lombardy was brought from the dust in which it had been buried; and the new coronation took place in the cathedral of Milan, the largest in Italy, with the exception of St. Peter's at Rome. Napoleon received the crown from the archbishop of Milan, and placed it on his head, exclaiming, 'Dieu me l'a donnée, gare à qui la touche.' This became *the motto of the iron crown*, which the emperor founded in commemoration of his being crowned king of Italy. *By this measure Bonaparte completed the assimilation between himself and Charlemagne*."‡

Power, in the words of the prophecy and in his own WAS GIVEN *unto him*. Twelve years before he was seated on the imperial throne, his name was unknown in Europe; eleven years only had elapsed since his first military service in Corsica; within a still shorter period he had sought to transfer his services to the sultan; and now he was possessed of *power* unequalled in Europe, and before which almost all its kingdoms successively fell, till scarcely any career of conquest ever equalled his own. The

* Bourrienne's Mem. pp. 70, 71. † Ibid. p. 173
‡ Ibid. p. 192.

myriads of Xerxes and Darius, of Alaric and Attila, would have been as flocks of sheep to wolves, compared to the masses of Napoleon; and, contrasted with his, their motions would have been those of a sloth, compared to the eagle flight of Napoleon. The naval war of Britain mocked all comparison on the ocean; and it may perhaps be said, that, as to intrinsic power, none on earth, under the command of one man, equalled that of Napoleon. As his conquests spread, he drew forth armies under his banners from conquered kingdoms. And war for a long season became the occupation of Europe. France was a military school: scarcely was a man to be seen in the fields; they were left to be cultivated by the women. The vast annual conscription was often anticipated, till men, far from the prime of life, were called forth by thousands. Military glory was, in France, the rage of the day. And they who but shortly before had beheaded their king, and drenched their country with blood in the cause of liberty, were little else than the worshippers of a Corsican despot, who a little time before, would have been proud of the charge of a single cannon, but who speedily exercised an authority and *power* over France and Europe, which passed the wildest dream of the most ambitious of their kings. But the *power* that *was given him* was neither inactive, nor wasted in vain. The first vial which he poured out was local; and he flew only from river to river, where these were closely crowded. But when he had reached a throne, and held an empire as his own, like the scorching sun that shines at once on half the world, his power was felt over Europe, whose kingdom became his prey.

All *power* of government cenetred in himself. He had no divided empire over France or Italy, as he strove to have none throughout the world. "In reading the history of this period we find," says Bourrienne, "that in whatever place Napoleon happened to be, there was the *central point* of action. The affairs of Europe were arranged at his head quarters, in the same manner as if he had been in Paris.* One *very remarkable* feature of the *imperial wars* was, that with the exception of the *interior* police, the *whole government* of France was at the *head-quarters of the emperor.* In fact, during his reign the government of France was always at his head-quarters."† That was the centre of his power; and from thence he shone, like the sun, and scorched the world.

And power was given unto him to scorch men with fire and men were scorched with great heat. Though symbolised by the sun, he is spoken of as a person; yet, in conformity to the symbol, the destruction which he wrought, no longer confined to a single region, is described as his *scorching men with fire*, and *with great heat*, denoting the severity of the *judgment*, and the withering influence of his power, while dominant, against all on whom it fell. Within the space of eight years, he scorched every kingdom in Europe, from Naples to Berlin, and from Lisbon to Moscow. Ancient kingdoms withered before the intense blaze of his power. Plagues accompanied his progress. In the wars which he waged, the conquest of kingdoms was the work of a day. Decrees were issued; supplies, the most exorbitant, were levied; kingdoms were unsparingly reft like garments. He parcelled out continental Europe, as a heritage; and a system of spoliation, extortion and oppression was established, that the subjected nations might be enslaved to the will of one man. Like the sun, there was nothing hid from his great heat;

* Bourrienne's Memoirs, vol. iii. p. 228.

† Ibid. p. 409.

and the exercise of his power was the misery of millions.

The *contents of chapters* of history have heretofore borne palpable evidence of manifest judgments fulfilled in ancient times, and of the close order of their succession; and the same obvious illustration of events within our own remembrance is still open to our sight. The conclusion of the contents of the eighteenth chapter, and the whole of the nineteenth, of the able and interesting *History of Napoleon Bonaparte*,* already so frequently quoted, thus follow in exact order.

"Napoleon emperor of France—King of Italy—Genoa united to the empire—New coalition against France—Sweden, Russia, Austria join the alliance—Napoleon heads the army in Germany—Ulm surrendered by Mack—Vienna taken—(Naval operations—Battte of Trafalgar)—Battle of Austerlitz—Treaty of Presburg—Joseph Bonaparte king of Naples—Louis Bonaparte king of Holland—Confederation of the Rhine—New nobility in France."

The triumphs in the northern Italy along *the rivers and fountains of waters* raised Bonaparte to the throne, and prepared the way for the destruction of the *empire* of Germany. On the 26th May 1805, Bonaparte was crowned king of Italy. The battle of Ulm, after a previous defeat of the Austrians, was fought on the 19th October; and Ulm was surrendered, with 30,000 men. In November, the Austrians were five times defeated by the French; and Vienna was taken. And on the 2d December, the battle of Austerlitz was fought. The emperors of Russia and Germany saw their armies defeated by the newly-created emperor of France, and no sun

* Nos. I. and II. Family Library, published by Murray.

was henceforth to shine, for a season, like himself in the political horizon. Napoleon, who came *to pour out* the first portion of a new *vial of the wrath* of God, observing an opening in the hostile line, the result of a snare which he had laid for the enemy, and seizing the opportunity, "*forthwith poured a force* upon that space, which *entirely destroyed* the communication between the Russian centre and left." "They resisted sternly, but were finally broken, and fled. The French centre advanced, and the charges of its cavalry under Murat were decisive. The emperors of Austria and Germany beheld, from the heights of Austerlitz, the *total ruin of their centre*, as they had already of their left. Their right wing had hitherto contested well against all the impetuosity of Lannes; But Napoleon could now *gather round them on all sides*, and HIS ARTILLERY PLUNGING INCESSANT FIRE on them from the heights, they at length found it impossible to hold their ground. They were forced down into a hollow, where some small frozen lakes offered the only means of escape from the *closing cannonade*. The French broke the ice about them by a storm of shot, and nearly 20,000 *men died on the spot*, some swept by the artillery, the greater part drowned. Bonaparte, in his bulletin, compares *the horrible spectacle of this ruin* to the catastrophe of the Turks at Aboukir, when the sea was covered with turbans. It was with great difficulty that the two emperors rallied some fragments of their armies around them, and effected their retreat. Twenty thousand prisoners, forty pieces of artillery, and all the standards of the imperial guard of Russia remained with the conquerors. Such was the battle of Austerlitz, or as the French soldiery delighted to call it, "the battle of the emperors."*

* Hist. of Napoleon, vol. i. pp. 323, 324.

On the morning of the battle, the sun rose with uncommon brilliancy: on many an after-day, the French soldiery hailed a similar dawn with exultation, as the sure omen of victory, and "*the sun of Austerlitz" has passed into a proverb.* It was the battle of the emperors; and on that day the *sun* of Bonaparte not only arose with brilliancy, and eclipsed at once the two great rival luminaries of continental Europe, but men *were scorched with great heat* before it. Power was given unto him to *scorch* men WITH FIRE. He poured his ever-firing troops between the ranks of the enemy, and his artillery plunged incessant *fire* on them, till the spectacle of ruin was horrible, even in the sight, and according to the word, of the great destroyer. Such is the first of manifold illustrations of the *power* that was *given* to the *Emperor* Napoleon to scorch men with *fire.* Such was the effect of the first burning rays which it emitted. But it shone with like intensity over continental Europe, which that day witnessed the power it was destined to feel. Marengo was the last of the vial of wrath poured upon *the rivers and fountains of waters.* Austerlitz was the first portion of the fourth vial—of which, not the north of Italy alone, but wide Europe was the scene, even as the sun shines over it all.

Not only does the *power* of *scorching men with fire,* and of their being *scorched with great heat,* preserve the symmetry of the symbol, as descriptive of the destruction and the misery of which Bonaparte was the instrument; but, as the tale of Austerlitz declares, such might even be said to be the direct effect of his power, as evidenced also in all his subsequent battles. It was the "incessant *fire*" that caused "the horrible spectacle of ruin." The artillery was the peculiar province of Bonaparte, in which he was trained from his boyhood.

Instead of hundreds of men transporting a single cannon a short distance in many days, "flying artillery," as aptly denominated, cannons mounted on wheel carriages, kept pace with the celerity of Bonaparte's march. On his elevation to imperial power, he chose other fields of battle than circumscribed spots on the borders of lakes, or the banks of rivers, or amidst mountain torrents, where, with a few troops, he could outmanœuvre and successively discomfit, in detail, the armies of a mighty empire. For, when that empire and another had felt in one field the might of his power, he followed out the art of war on a higher scale, and chose the plains of Europe to decide its fate, where he could fully bring his favourite science into tremendous practical effect, and plant, to an extent before unparalleled, parks of artillery, where hundreds of cannon were ranged in a spot; and while the bayonet is the weapon of the British, Russian, and Austrian soldiers, the active French excelled in the extreme rapidity of their *fire;* and as Constantinople fell before the *fire,* and the smoke, and the brimstone which issued out of the mouth of the artillery and musketry which volumed forth destruction and death around it, so might it well be said of Bonaparte, that *power was given him to scorch men with fire.*

But the power of destroying was given to Napoleon, not for one day only, but for successive years, in such a manner as fully to bear out another resemblance to Attila, that of "the Scourge of God." Many volumes could not describe the miseries which were caused by his wars. But their succession and the chief of his batttles may be briefly noted, to show how excessively and intensely the *sun* which first burst forth with scorching rays at Austerlitz, still *scorched men with fire.*

After the battle of Austerlitz, Napoleon created

a new order of nobility, conferred principalities, and sought in every thing "to revive the image of Charlemagne, emperor of the West." "The establishment of the Confederation of the Rhine rendered Napoleon in effect sovereign of a large part of Germany, and seemed to have so totally revolutionized central Europe, that Francis of Austria declared the imperial constitution at an end. He retained the title of emperor as sovereign of his own hereditatry dominions, but 'THE HOLY ROMAN EMPIRE,' having lasted full one thousand years, was declared *to be* NO MORE, and of its ancient influence the *representative* was to be sought for not at *Vienna* but at *Paris*."*

The fate of the German empire was decided in one battle, and that of the kingdom of Prussia in another. The successor of Frederick the Great saw unpitied the fall of the empire, and being then without a master or a rival among the German princes, he cherished the proud hope that the house of Brandenburg would rise to imperial authority on the ruin of the house of Austria. But after 'the battle of the emperors,' there was but one *sun* in Europe, and every satellite in the political horizon, that had previously shone in the once papal kingdoms of Europe, was, with the exception of a bright star on the *sea*, eclipsed and darkened before it. Prussia, like Germany, was scorched before it in a day, and *great heat* continued to wither it for years. Instead of obtaining an empire, a kingdom was lost by the man who stood at the head of armies, and brought not forth his own power to the aid of a brother in the day of need.

Bonaparte, when his time was come and his armies waiting for the word, provoked Prussia to a

* Hist. of Napoleon, vol. i. p. 330.

declaration of war on the 1st October, 1806. And he stood ready with a vial of wrath in his hand. The Prussian troops which had broken into Saxony were discomfitted before the French. The explosion of the magazines of Naumburg first announced to the king of Prussia that the emperor "was in his rear." The Prussians were isolated, and the battle of Jena sealed at once the doom of Prussia. After a severe contest on a single point, "the French centre advanced to a general charge, before which the Prussians were forced to retire. They moved for some space in good order, but Murat now POURED his masses of cavalry on them, storm after storm, with such rapidity and vehemence that their route became miserable. It ended in the complete breaking up of the army, horse and foot all flying together, in the confusion of panic, upon the road to Weimar. At that point the fugitives met and mingled with their brethren flying as confusedly as themselves, from Averstadt. In the course of this disastrous day *twenty thousand* Prussians were killed or taken, three hundred guns, twenty generals, and sixty standards. The loss of superior officers on the Prussian side was so great, that of an army which on the 13th of October mustered not less than 150,000, but a few regiments were able to act in concert for some time after the 14th. The various routed divisions roamed about the country, seeking separately the means of escape; they were in consequence destined to fall an easy prey."*— Thus, in the course of a few short weeks was the proud and vigorous fabric of the Prussian monarchy levelled with the ground,"† and that kingdom, like others, was reduced to become one of the agents of his tyranny or instruments of his power.

The overthrow of Prussia was the campaign of a

* Hist. of Napoleon, vol. i. pp. 340, 341. † Ibid. p. 343.

week, the work of a day. The *sun* shone to *scorch with fire.* The emperor Napoleon entered Berlin, issued his *decrees,* and speedily advanced to meet more stubborn foes. The rashness of Prussia in rushing into the war before the advance of the Russian armies, gave freer scope to the genius and activity of Napoleon to cut off his enemies in separate and successive combats. The Russians, heretofore used to triumph over their republican foes, tried all his strength. He took Warsaw, and roused the enthusiasm of the Poles. But the conflicts were obstinate and terrible. In the battle of Pultusk, 13,000 were killed or wounded. The battle of Preuss Eylau was the longest and by far the severest battle in which Bonaparte had as yet been engaged. The field was covered with 50,000 corpses. At Heilberg "the carnage was fearful." But Napoleon's extraordinary exertions enabled him to take the field again at the head of not less than 280,000 men. In the decisive battle of Friedland, "the Russians sustained numberless charges of foot and horse, and were exposed for six hours to a *murderous cannonade.* At length *Napoleon put himself at the head of the French line,* and commanded a general assault of all arms, which was executed *with overpowering effect.* Having lost full 12,000 men, General Benningsen was at last compelled to attempt a retreat, and the French *poured* after him into the town." The results of the battle of Friedland were as great as could have been expected from any victory. The treaty of Tilsit terminated the war. The king of Prussia agreed to adopt "the continental system," in other words, to be henceforth the vassal of the conqueror. The Grand Duchy of Warsaw was conferred on the submissive elector of Saxony, henceforth a king. The kingdom of Westphalia was created for a portion to Jerome Bonaparte. Joseph Bonaparte was recognised as king of Naples, and Louis of Holland. The *sun* of Bonaparte increasing in the intensity of its heat, began to approach its zenith.

After the treaty of Tilsit, the authority of the emperor appeared to be consolidated over the whole continent of Europe. The imperial power was finally organized. "His favourite saying during the continuance of his power was, 'I am the State,' and in the exile of St. Helena he constantly talked of himself as having been, from necessity, the Dictator of France. In effect, *no despotism within many degrees so complete and rigid was ever before established in a civilized and Christian country.* The whole territory was divided into prefectures—each prefect being appointed by Napoleon—carefully selected for a province with which he had no domestic relations—largely paid—and intrusted with such a *complete delegation of* POWER, that, in Napoleon's own language, each was in his department an *empereur à petit pied.* Each of these officers had under his *entire control* inferior local magistrates, holding *power* from him as he did from the *emperor; each had his instructions direct from Paris;* each was bound by every motive to serve, to the utmost of his ability, the government from which all things were derived, to be hoped for, or to be dreaded. *Wherever the emperor was,* in the midst of his HOTTEST CAMPAIGNS," (scorching men with *fire,*) "he examined the details of his administration at home, more closely than perhaps any other sovereign of half so great an empire did during the profoundest peace."* All *power* was exercised not only as delegated, but as directed, by him. Whether in peace or in war, he shone and scorched like the sun. In war he scorched men, as with *fire;* and even in peace, under the

* History of Napoleon, vol. ii. pp. 1, 4, 5.

reign of the emperor Napoleon, men were thus *scorched with great heat.*

France itself, in the vast extent of taxation, and in the "unsparing rigour" with which the "conscription" was enforced, was the victim, no less than the instrument, of the *power that was given* to Napoleon. "He *drained the very life-blood* of the people intrusted to his charge, not for the defence of their own country, but to *extend the ravages of war* to distant and unoffending regions. No distinction was made between the married man, whose absence might be the ruin of his family, and the single member of a numerous lineage, who could be easily spared. The son of the widow, the child of the decrepid and helpless, had no right to claim an exemption. Three sons might be carried off in three successive years from the same desolated parents; there was no allowance made for having already supplied a recruit. The difficulty of obtaining exemption by substitution was so great, that very many young men, well educated, and of respectable families, were torn from all their more propitious prospects, to bear the life, discharge the duties, and die the death, of common soldiers in a marching regiment. *The brand, the pillory, or the galleys, awaited the magistrate himself*, if he was found to favour *any* individual on whom the law of conscription had claims. Refractory conscripts were *treated like convicts of the most infamous description.* Clothed in a dress of infamy, *loaded with chains, and dragging weights which were attached to them, they were condemned like galley slaves to work upon the public fortifications.* But the *most horrible* part of the fate of the conscript was, that it was determined for life. But whatever distress was inflicted on the country by this mode of compulsory levy, it was a weapon particularly qualified to serve Bonaparte's purposes. He succeeded to the POWER which it gave the government, amongst other spoils of the revolution, and he used it to the greatest possible extent."* *Power was given him*, &c.

While France, in its temporary military glory, was thus exposed, throughout all its families, to the arbitrary and despotic *power* of Bonaparte, which often withered all the charities of domestic life, the conscripts of the empire became the pillagers of Europe, and, subduing its kingdoms, spread over them like a *plague*. "The French Revolution *first* introduced into Europe a mode of conducting hostilities, which transferred almost the whole burden of the war to the country which had the ill fortune to be the seat of its operations. At the commencement of a campaign, nothing could be so complete as the arrangement of a French army. It was formed into large bodies called *corps d'armée*, each commanded by a king, viceroy, mareschal, or general officer of high pretensions, founded on former services. Each *corps d'armée* formed a complete army within itself, and had its allotted portion of cavalry, infantry, artillery, and troops of every description—which might vary in number from fifty to eighty thousand men and upwards. This system of dividing his collected forces into separate and nearly independent armies, gave great celerity and efficacy to the French movements; and, superintended as it was by the master-spirit which planned the campaign, often contributed to the most brilliant results. But whenever it became necessary to combine two *corps d'armée* in *one operation*, it required the *personal presence of Napoleon himself*."† "Thus organized, the French army was POURED into some foreign country by forced marches, without any previous

---

* Sir Walter Scott's Life of Napoleon, vol. vi. pp. 104, 105.
† Ibid. pp. 108, 109.

arrangement of stores or magazines for their maintenance, and with the purpose of maintaining them solely at the expense of the inhabitants. *Bonaparte was exercised in this system; and the combination of great masses*, by means of forced marches, was *one great principle of his tactics.* This species of war was carried on at the least possible expense of money to his treasury; but it was necessarily at the *greatest possible expenditure of human life, and the incalculable increase of human misery.* Napoleon's usual object was to surprise the enemy by the rapidity of his marches, defeat him in some great battle, and then seize upon his capital, levy contributions, make a peace with such advantages as he could obtain, and finally return to Paris."*

"In these *dazzling campaigns*, the army usually began their march with provisions, that is, bread and biscuit, for a certain number of days, on the soldiers' backs. In a very short time the soldiers became impatient of their burdens, and either wasted them by prodigal consumption, or actually threw them away. The officers gave them authority to secure supplies by what was called *la maraude*, or plunder. The most hideous features of this system were shown when the army marched through a thinly peopled country, or when the national character, and perhaps local facilities, encouraged the natives and peasants to offer resistance. Then the soldiers became animated alike by the scarcity of provisions, and irritated at the danger which they sometimes incurred in collecting them. As their hardships increased, their temper became relentless and reckless, and besides indulging in every species of violence, they increased their own distresses by *destroying what they could not use.* FAMINE and sickness were not long of visiting an army, which

* Scott's Life of Napoleon, ib. pp. 109, 110.

traversed by forced marches a country exhausted of provisions. These stern attendants followed the French columns as they struggled on. Without hospitals and without magazines, every straggler who could not regain his ranks fell a victim to *hunger*, to weather, to weariness, to the vengeance of an incensed peasantry. In this manner the French army sufferred *woes*, which, *till these tremendous wars, had never been the lot of troops in hostilities carried on between civilized nations.* Still Bonaparte's object was gained; he attained amidst these losses and sacrifices, and at the expense of them, the point which he had desired; displayed his masses to the terrified eyes of a surprised enemy, and reaped the reward of his despatch in a general victory."*

But while the whole world witnessed the *power that was given* to Napoleon, and the whole continent of Europe felt the degrading oppression and bitter miseries attendant on his reign, we need not appeal to any doubtful or distant testimony; and no other picture need here be looked on, than that which has been drawn by his own secretary, who, perhaps above all others, knew the mind of the man, was intimately versant with the most secret principles of his government, and who afterwards acted as one of the many agents of his *power*, as prefect at Hamburgh.

"A rapid and immense impulse," says Bourrienne, "given to great masses of men by the will of a single individual, may *produce transient lustre and dazzle the eyes of men*," (shining like the *sun*,) "but when at a distance from the theatre of glory, we see only the melancholy results which have been produced, the genius of conquest can only be regarded as the *genius of destruction*" (*scorching*

---

* Scott's Life of Napoleon, vol. vi. pp. 112, 113.

men with great heat). "What a sad picture was often presented to my eyes! I was continually doomed to hear the *general distress*, and to execute orders which *augmented the immense sacrifices* already made by the city of Hamburgh. Thus, for example, the *emperor* desired me to furnish him with 50,000 cloaks, which I immediately did. I also received orders to seize at the town of Lubec 400,000 lasts of corn. The whole government was at the head-quarters of the emperor."*

"*To tyrannise over the human species*, and to exact uniform admiration and submission, is to require an impossibility. It would seem that *fate*, which had still some splendid triumphs in store for Bonaparte, intended to deprive him of all his triumphs at once, and plunge him into reverses even greater than the good fortune which had favoured his elevation.† The Berlin decree could not fail to cause a reaction against the emperor's fortune, by raising up whole nations against him. The hurling of twenty kings from their thrones would have excited less hatred than this contempt of the wants of nations. This profound ignorance of the maxims of political economy caused *general privation and misery*, which in their turn occasioned general hostility. It is necessary to have witnessed, as I have, the *numberless vexations and miseries* occasioned by the unfortunate 'continetal system,' to understand the mischiefs its authors did in Europe, and how much that mischief contributed to Bonaparte's fall."‡

"Revolution," says Sir Walter Scot, "is like a *conflagration*. Bonaparte had destroyed the proper scale of government in France, and had assumed an almost unlimited authority over the fairest part of Europe. Over foreign countries, the military re-

---

* Bourrienne's Memoirs, vol. iii. pp. 397, 409.
† Ibid. vol. iii. p. 391. ‡ Ibid. pp. 339, 364.

nown of France *streamed like a comet*, inspiring *universal dread and distrust;* and, while it rendered indispensable similar preparations for resistance, it seemed *as if peace had departed from the earth for ever*, and that its destinies were hereafter to be disposed of according to the law of *brutal force* alone."* *Power was given unto him over the fourth part of the earth*, or over "continental Europe," one of the four quarters of the globe, *to kill with sword and with hunger, and with death, and with the beasts*, or kingdoms of the earth. He exercised his power in enforcing "the continental system." *Power was given unto him to scorch men with fire; and men were scorched with great heat.*

Towards the close of 1807, on the invasion of Portugal by the French, the House of Braganza ceased to reign in Europe, and sought a kingdom, of brief duration, beyond the Atlantic. The heaviest exactions were laid on Portugal. The court of Spain, in its horrible corruption, soon became the prey of the artifice and arms of Napoleon; and Ferdinand, the king of a day, on the abdication of his father, Charles IV., resigned his crown into the hands of Napoleon, and became, with his family, an exile from his kingdom. The spirit of loyalty, afterwards ill-requited, the power of the priesthood, and the prevalence of superstitution, and, as Saragossa testifies, the resolute bravery, in some instances, of the defenders of their country, only served, for a season, to infuriate Napoleon, and to aggravate the miseries of the Spaniards and Portuguese. "Soult *poured* down his columns on the plains of Burgos"† (November 1808); and defeated and dissipated the Spanish armies, headed by Blake, Belvedere, Palafox,

* Life of Nap. vol. vi. p. 116. † Hist. of Nap. vol. ii. p. 48.

and Castanos. In the beginning of December, Napoleon entered Madrid; and the metropolis of proud Spain received a Corsican as its conqueror. The British army retreated before him, and embarked from the Spanish shore; the armies of France held for a brief period the unchallenged supremacy of the Peninsula; and a brother of Napoleon was the king of Spain.

The insurrection of Spain gave hope to Austria, whose monarch, no longer the head of the empire, ill brooked the portion of being virtually a vassal. Napoleon, as, while the former vial was in his hand, he had previously passed from river to river, now, in his eagle flight, flew from kingdom to kingdom. On the 6th April 1809, Austria declared war. Her exertions were gigantic, and her armies unequalled in any former period of her history, having been computed, including the reserve, at 550,000. On the 9th of April, the Generalissimo, the archduke Charles, invaded Bavaria with 180,000 men. On the 20th and 21st, Napoleon defeated two Austrian divisions, at Abensberg and Landshut; the 22d was the day of the celebrated battle of Eckmuhl, in which 20,000 prisoners were left in the hands of Napoleon. "Thus within five days,—the space, and almost the very days of the month, which Bonaparte had assigned for settling the affairs of Germany,—the original aspect of the war was entirely changed; and Austria, which had engaged in it with the proud *hope of reviving her original influence in Europe*, was now to continue the struggle for the doubtful chance of securing her existence. At no period in his momentous career, did the genius of Napoleon appear more completely to prostrate all opposition; *at no time did the talents of a single individual exercise such an influence on the fate of the universe.* It is no wonder that others, nay, that he himself should have annexed to his person the degree of superstitious influence claimed for the CHOSEN INSTRUMENTS OF DESTINY, whose path cannot be crossed, and whose arms cannot be arrested."*

Vienna was besieged. "A *shower of bombs* first made the inhabitants sensible of the horrors to which they must necessarily be exposed by defensive war."† It speedily capitulated. The great battles of Asperne and Essling, were fought upon the 21st and 22d of May. "The carnage was terrible, and the pathways of the villages were literally choked with the dead."‡ "The loss of both armies was dreadful, and computed to exceed *twenty thousand* men on *each* side, killed and wounded."§ On the 5th and 6th July was fought the dreadful and decisive battle of Wagram. A hundred pieces of cannon and a chosen division broke through the Austrian ranks. "The archduke had extended his line over too wide a space, and this old error enabled Napoleon to ruin him by his *old* device of POURING the *full shock* of his strength on the centre."‖ "Napoleon himself was ever in the *hottest* of *the action*." The slaughter was terrible; the destruction was complete; and "at the close there remained 20,000 prisoners, besides all the artillery and baggage, in the hands of Napoleon."¶ The power of Austria was again broken.

In the midst of this career of hard-won conquests, Bonaparte, after the defeat of the Austrians, and while the ancient empire lay at his feet, and Vienna, the capital of Germany, was in his hands, issued the following remarkable decree, from the *imperial*

---

* Sir Walter Scott's Life of Napoleon, vol. vi. p. 300.
† Ibid. p. 306. ‡ Hist. of Napoleon, vol. ii. pp. 64, 65.
§ Scott's Life of Napoleon, vol. vi. p. 327.
‖ Hist. of Napoleon, vol. ii. p. 66. ¶ Ibid. p. 67.

palace of Schoenbrunn:—"Whereas the temporal sovereign of Rome has refused to make war against England, and the interests of the two kingdoms of Italy and Naples ought not to be interrupted by a hostile power; and whereas the *donation of Charlemagne*, OUR ILLUSTRIOUS PREDECESSOR, of the countries which form the holy see, was for the good of Christianity, and not for that of the enemies of our holy religion, we, therefore, decree that the duchies of Urbino, Ancona, Macrata, and Camarino, be for ever united to the kingdom of Italy."*

"On the 17th of May, Napoleon issued *from Vienna*, his final decree, declaring the temporal sovereignty of the pope to be wholly at an end, incorporating *Rome* with the French empire, and declaring it to be his second city; settling a pension on the holy father in his spiritual capacity,—and appointing a committee of administration for the civil government of Rome."†

Italy was wholly in his power; and the pope was a prisoner in his hands. Austria ceded large territories to France, with a population of nearly four millions. "Napoleon obtained the whole coasts of the Adriatic, and deprived Austria of her last seaport." Established in his empire, which was declared to be hereditary, Bonaparte made a sacrifice of duty and of honour, if not also of affection, on the shrine of ambition; and, adding the pride of alliance to the gifts of fortune, in hopes of giving an heir to his empire, divorced the plebeian wife of his youth, married a princess of the House of Austria, and, on the birth of a son, proclaimed him *king of* ROME.

"A population of forty-two millions of people, fitted in various ways to secure the prosperity of a

---

* Ibid. p. 72. Scott's Life of Napoleon, vol. vi. p. 366.
† Hist. of Napoleon, p. 73.

state, and inhabiting, for wealth, riches of soil, and felicity of climate, by far the finest portion of the civilized earth, formed the *immediate* liege subjects of this magnificent empire. Yet to stop here, were greatly to undervalue the extent of Napoleon's *power*." Italy, Carniola, and the Illyrian provinces were portions of "his personal empire." "As mediator of the Helvetian republic, the emperor exercised an almost absolute authority in Switzerland. The German confederation of the Rhine, though numbering kings among their league, were at the slightest hint bound to supply him each with his prescribed quota of forces." The king of Naples was one of his generals; and the resistance of the rebels in Spain and Portugal "seemed in the speedy prospect of being finally subdued. Thus *an* EMPIRE of 800,000 square miles, and containing a population of *eighty-five millions*, in territory one-fifth part, and in number of inhabitants one-half, of united Europe, was either in quiet subjection to Napoleon's sceptre, or on the point, as was supposed, of becoming so."*

Of the other kingdoms of Europe, that had once been subject to papal domination, "Denmark, so powerful was the voice which *France* had in her councils, might almost be accounted humbled to one of the *federative principalities*. Sweden had but a moderate and second degree of power. She felt, *as other German nations*, the WITHERING BLIGHT of the continental, or anti-social system" (*scorched with great heat*); "but, circumstanced as she was, with the possession of Swedish Pomerania, *dependent on French pleasure*, she had no other remedy than to wait her opportunity. Still more was this the case with Prussia, through all her provinces the mortal enemy of the French name, but whom the

* Scott's Life of Napoleon, vol. vii. pp. 119, 120.

large garrisons which France had planted in her dominions, and the numerous forces which she maintained there, compelled for the time to be as submissive as a hand-maiden. The general eye saw in Prussia, only a nation resigned to her bondage. Austria, besides the terrible losses which the last war had brought upon her, was now fettered to Napoleon by a link which gave the proud House of Hapsburg an apology for the submission, or at least the observance which she paid to the son-in-law of her emperor."*

Such was the supremacy of imperial *power* over wide Europe that *was given* to Napoleon; and such the "withering blight," as if *scorching with great heat,* which he cast over the Continent. As the *successor of Charlemagne,* he revoked, by express decree, the temporal sovereignty of the Roman Pontiff; and, "imitating his illustrious predecessors," he designated his infant son the king of Rome. But, after having seen his aggrandisement thus completed, his empire consolidated and doubly secured both by conquest and alliance, and the joint imperial lineage and succession of the ancient and modern *empire* combined in his son,—the son of one emperor, the first of his dynasty, and the grandson of another the last of a long race who had swayed the imperial sceptre for a thousand years,—to use the words of the historian, "we are now approaching the verge of that fated year, when Fortune, hitherto unwearied in her partiality towards Napoleon, turned first upon himself, personally, a *clouded* and stormy aspect."†

Power was given unto Napoleon, as emperor, to *scorch men with fire, and men were scorched with great heat,* yet the vial was poured *upon the sun* it-

* Scott's Life of Napoleon, vol. vii. pp. 121, 122. † Ibid. p. 144.

self, till it could neither scorch nor hurt any more, and every ray of its glory was extinguished.

From prophecy and from history we see the nations which Cyrus congregated around Babylon the great; the millions which Xerxes stirred up against Greece; the intrepid band of Greeks who, under Alexander the Great, breasted the river and broke through the centre of the Persian hosts; the legions of Rome which desolated Judea, and subjugated the world; the Gothic nation in arms, headed by Alaric; the fiery Huns, led on by the blazing Attila; the swarms of Saracens, that flew, like locusts, from the desert, and spread over Europe; the Turkish horsemen, rated by myriads, that issued from Turkomania; the crusading hosts, that poured, like a torrent, upon Asia, and also the multitudinous Moguls, that flocked from the borders of China, to bind the Turkish sultanies;—yet not the Persians glittering with silver, nor the Greeks clothed in brass, nor the iron Romans, neither the furred Goths, the sable Saracens, the turbaned Turks, nor the mailed knights of Europe, ever formed an effective force, or showed the perfection of the art of war, like the armies, from all the kingdoms of continental Europe, that were ranged under the banners of the Emperor Napoleon. Moral culture is ever apt to decay in the rugged and degenerate soil of human nature. But instruments of destruction are wont to be improved in a world lying in wickedness. And in modern times, in which athiesm has taken to itself the name of philosophy, science was not slack to devote its energies to the work of slaughter; and men, thus far wiser than their fathers, failed not to improve the evil art of war. The French revolution, which promised to *fraternize* the world, made war its trade. And having seen, and traced in his progress, "the little Corsican officer," who longed for a lieutenancy in the Turkish service, and who was called from the streets of Paris to clear them of an insurrectionary mob, till power was given him *over a fourth part of the earth*, to shine like the sun, and to scorch with fire, and till he scarcely found a compeer in Alexander, Attila, Tamerlane or Charlemagne, we may not only contemplate the splendour of his course and the scorching glare of his brilliancy, but we may look again on the mighty conqueror to see how soon his glory came to nought, or how the *vial of wrath* was *poured upon* that very *sun* to which such power of scorching was given.

The fated year approached when Fortune, hitherto unwearied in her partiality towards Napoleon, turned first upon *himself personally* a *clouded* and stormy aspect,—or, in other words, not less significative and expressive, *the vial of wrath was poured out upon the sun*, even upon him to whom *power was given to scorch men with fire*. And, as under the former vial, the French were in the same place the victims of the *wrath* of which they had been the executioners, so Bonaparte *himself*, or the *imperial power* identified with his person, though before "the child of destiny," whose path was not to be crossed, nor his arms to be arrested, while his work remained to be done, was fated to destruction, even as he himself had destroyed. The *fourth part of the earth* was his allotted sphere. The judgment as yet was sitting on the papacy, or the kingdoms where it once had prevailed. Whenever Russia came to the aid of other continental powers, within the range of Bonaparte's commission, its aid was ultimately ineffective. Italy, Austria, and Prussia fell in defiance of its helping hand; and though, the British excepted, by far the most stubborn of his foes, the soldiers of Russia were repulsed by Bonaparte, not only from Germany, but even from the Catholic kingdom of Poland. The "fated year" was that in which, passing his bounds, Napoleon invaded Russia, and quenched the scorching beams of his sun amidst its snows. Till that fatal moment it shone more brightly than ever.

The Emperor of Russia refused to acknowledge Joseph Bonaparte as king of Spain; and an edict issued by the emperor of Austria (no longer emperor of Germany, or head of *the empire*) for the free passage of the armies of Napoleon through his territories, gave token of an approaching war with Russia.

"Napoleon omitted nothing as to the preparation of the military forces of his own empire. Before yet all hopes of an accommodation with St. Petersburgh were at an end, he demanded, and obtained, two new conscriptions in France; and, moreover, established a law, by which he was enabled to call out 100,000 men at a time, or those whom the conscriptions had spared, for service at *home*. This limitation of their service he soon disregarded; and in effect—the new system—that of *the Ban*, as he affected to call it,—became a mere extension of the old scheme. The amount of the French army at the period in question (exclusive of *the Ban*) is calculated at 850,000 men; the army of the kingdom of Italy mustered 50,000; that of Naples 30,000; that of the Grand Duchy of Warsaw 60,000; the Bavarian 40,000; the Westphalian 30,000; the Saxon 30,000; Wirtemberg 15,000; Baden 9,000; Saxony 30,000; and the minor powers of the Rhenish league 23,000. *Of these armies Napoleon had the entire control.* In addition, Austria was bound to furnish him with 30,000, and Prussia with 20,000 auxiliaries. The total sum is 1,187,000. Deducting 387,000,—a large allowance for hospitals, furloughs, and incomplete regiments,—there remained 800,000 effective men at his immediate command. The Spanish peninsula might perhaps occupy, even now, 150,000; but still Napoleon could bring into the field, against Russia, in case all negotiation failed, an army of 650,000 men; numbers such as Alexander could have no chance of equalling; *numbers such as had never before followed an European banner.*"*

The armies of mortals are powerless before the word of God, as the host of Sennacherib before the breath of an angel. Bonaparte's fall was more rapid, and not less marvellous than his rise. He crossed the Niemen "at the head of at least 470,000 men." He passed the bounds of his conquests. The Russians, instead of advancing to meet him retired at his approach, burned their villages, and laid waste their country. Their continued retreat lured him on to destruction. A thrice repeated attack on Smolensko was thrice resisted and repelled. But the garrison abandoned the city they had defended; and left it in flames to the invaders. The conflagration, (the houses being chiefly of wood, and the season being dry,) according to the French bulletin, "resembled, in its fury, an eruption of Vesuvius." On the 7th September, the hostile armies, of nearly equal numbers, encountered each other at Borodino, where a thousand cannon were in the field. "In no contest, by many degrees so desperate, had Bonarate hitherto been engaged. Night found either army on the ground they had occupied at day-break. The number of guns and prisoners taken by the French and Russians was about equal; and of *either* host there had fallen *not less than forty thousand men.* Some accounts raise the gross number of the slain to *one hundred thousand.*"† The French entered the old capital of the Czars, and found it a deserted city. It was but for one day a prey to the enemy; on the next it was enveloped in flames. The conflagration of Smolensko was

* Hist. of Napoleon, vol. ii. p. 113. † Ibid. p. 131.

rekindled in Moscow: and the burning of Moscow would have been the saving of Europe if men, from judgments, would have learned righteousness. The high ambition of Napoleon had placed the Kremlin in proud vision before him: and when he looked from its battlements he saw nothing but "the raging sea of fire which swept the capital, east, west, north, and south. 'Palaces and temples,' says the Russian author, Karamsin, 'monuments of art and miracles of luxury, the remains of ages long since past, and the creations of yesterday, the tombs of ancestors and the cradles of children, were indiscriminately destroyed. Nothing was left of Moscow save the memory of her people, and their deep resolution to avenge her fall.' During two days Napoleon witnessed from the Kremlin this fearful devastation."* No triumphal arch awaited his entrance into the metropolis of Muscovy; but when the Kremlin itself, on the third night, took fire, "Napoleon at length rode out of Moscow, through streets in many parts arched over with flames." He who had *scorched men with fire*, felt, by more than an emblem, that he now was the victim rather than the scourge, that *wrath* was prepared for himself, and that the destruction of his *power* was begun. "He could not withdraw his eyes from the rueful spectacle which the burning city presented, and from time to time repeated the same words; 'this bodes great misfortune.'"†

The retreat of the French from Moscow, perhaps unparalleled in its miseries, of which the horrible details beggar description, is fresh in the recollection of Europe, and pertains to the history of the world. The reflection might have been repeated at each step, how are the mighty fallen! In the first encounter with the Russians, the French lost 4000

* Hist. of Napoleon, vol. ii. p. 136. † Ibid. p. 137.

men, and were compelled to retreat through the desolated country which they had passed through.

In strict accordance with the prophetic word, Bonaparte in his wrath threatened to be an Attila, and in his pride proclaimed himself a second Charlemagne; but when snow-heaps marked where his soldiers had ingloriously fallen, when he heard that his allies began to withdraw, when cities were taken by his enemies in his rear, and when he who had been a terror to kingdoms, and whose rapid movements and fierce assaults had often astounded the most cautious of his foes, was threatened on every side, "in the bitterness of his heart he exclaimed, 'Thus it befalls when we commit faults upon faults:'" And when doubting of his next movement, he heard that positions essential to his security were in possession of the Russians, "IS IT THEN WRITTEN," he said, looking upwards, and striking the earth with his cane, "Is it written that we shall commit nothing but errors!"* All, but one word, that was written concerning him had been fulfilled. He had acted the part of an Attila, and occupied the seat of Charlemagne. And it *was written* also that the vial of WRATH had to be *poured upon the sun*, although the power of scorching men with fire had been given him, and though men, by his instrumentality, had been scorched with great heat. Scarcely had he uttered the ominous words "is it written," looking up to heaven and striking the earth, when the fact, which excited the exclamation, decided the fate of his army. Napoleon had crossed the Beresina at Borigoff, with a portion of his troops, when that town was taken, and the bridge so necessary to him was lost. And "the passage of the Beresina was one of the most fearful scenes recorded in the annals of war." The Russians "engaged in fierce

* Sir Walter Scott's Life of Napoleon, vol. vii. pp. 368, 370.

combat with the rear-guard or defensive line; and their cannon began to open upon the mingled and disordered mass that thronged along the river." "It was then that the whole body of stragglers and fugitives rushed like distracted beings towards the bridges, every feeling of prudence or humanity swallowed up by the animal instinct of self-preservation. The horrible scene of disorder was augmented by the desperate violence of those, who, determined to make their own way at all risks, threw down and trampled whatever came in their road. The weak and helpless either shrunk back from the fray, and sat down to wait their fate at a distance, or, mixing in it, were thrust over the bridges, crushed under carriages, cut down perhaps with sabres, or trampled to death under the feet of their countrymen. All this while the action continued *with fury*, and, as if the *heavens meant to match their* WRATH with that of man, a hurricane arose, and added terror to a scene which was already of a character so dreadful."*

"About mid-day the French, still bravely resisting, began to lose ground. The Russians coming up gradually in strength, succeeded in forcing the ravine, and compelling them to assume a position nearer the bridges. About the same time the larger bridge, that constructed for artillery and heavy carriages, broke down, and multitudes were forced into the water. The scream of mortal agony, which arose from the despairing multitude, became at this crisis for a moment so universal, that it rose shrilly audible over the noise of the elements and the thunders of war, above the wild whistling of tempest, and redoubled hourras of the Cossacks. The witness from whom we have this information," continues Sir Walter Scott, "declares that the

* Sir Walter Scott's Life of Napoleon, vol. vii. p. 383.

sound was in his ears for many weeks. This dreadful scene continued till dark, many being forced into the icy river, some throwing themselves in, betwixt absolute despair and the faint hope of gaining the opposite bank by swimming, some getting across only to die of cold and exhaustion. All night the miscellaneous multitude continued to throng across the bridge under the fire of the Russian artillery, to whom, even in the darkness, the noise that accompanied their march made them a distinct mark. At day-break, the French engineer finally set fire to the bridge. All that remained on the other side, including many prisoners, and a great quantity of guns and baggage, became the prisoners and the prey of the Russians. The amount of the French loss was never exactly known; but the Russian report, concerning the bodies of the invaders which were collected and burnt as soon as the thaw permitted, states that upwards of 36,000 were found in the Beresina."*

The spoils, cannon, baggage, and provisions of the French army were left beyond the Beresina, or finally abandoned; and the grand army, dispirited and disorganized, was left in the desert to contend, in vain strife, with the elements of nature, while the enemy hovered around them, to witness and accelerate their destruction. Their bed was the frozen earth, their passage through the snow, horse flesh formed the best part of their food, and it even has been said of the soldiers of Napoleon, whose wont it was to snatch food unsparingly from others, that, sometimes their only contest at last was with the famished dogs for the flesh of an expired comrade. "To enhance misfortunes so dreadful, the cold, which had been for some time endurable, increased on the 6th December to the most bitter degree of

* Sir Walter Scott's Life of Napoleon, vol. vii, pp. 383, 384.

frost, being twenty-seven or twenty-eight degrees below zero. Many dropped down, and expired in silence; the blood of others was determined to the head by the want of circulation, it gushed at length from the eyes and mouth, and the wretches sunk down on the gory snow, and were relieved by death. At the night biveuacs, the soldiers approached their frozen limbs to the fire so closely, that falling asleep in that posture, their feet were scorched to the bone while their hair was frozen to the ground. In this condition they were often found by the Cossacks, and happy were those upon whom the pursuers bestowed a thrust with a lance to finish their misery. Other horrors there were which are better left in silence. Enough has been said to show, that *such a calamity, in such an extent, never before darkened the pages of history.*"*

Napoleon, on entering on the war with Russia, "was prepared to pass the Niemen at the head of at least 470,000 men"—"numbers such as had never before followed an European banner." "On the 24th June, 1812, the grand imperial army, consolidated into three masses, began their passage of the Niemen." Within the space of six months, "they passed the Niemen at Kowno; and the Russians did not pursue them into the Prussian territory. At the time when they escaped finally from Poland, there were about a thousand in arms, perhaps 20,000 more utterly broken, dispersed and disorganised"—even of these many were garrison troops or part of a detached corps which had not passed the Beresina.

"Thus ended the invasion of Russia. *There had been slain in battle, on the side of Napoleon,* 125,000 *men. Fatigue, hunger, and cold had caused the*

* Sir Walter Scott's Life of Napoleon, vol. vii. pp. 400, 401.

death of 132,000, *and the Russians had taken of prisoners* 193,000, *including forty eight generals, and three thousand regimental officers. The total loss was therefore* 450,000 *men. The eagles and standards left in the enemy's hands were seventy-five in number, and the pieces of cannon nearly one thousand.*"* As such numbers had never before followed an European *standard, so* "*such a calamity in such an extent never before* DARKENED *the pages of history.*" The sun was smitten in its zenith, and when its radiance was the brightest, it was darkened in a moment, whenever its rays were shot beyond its proper hemisphere. *Power was given unto* Bonaparte when he had none, and at the time when he possessed unrivalled authority and unequalled splendour, the withering wrath of heaven fell on his imperial power,—fortune, so to speak, "hitherto unwearied in her partiality towards Napoleon, turned first upon *himself* personally a clouded and stormy aspect;" the mighty host was dissipated like a vapour, and thousands and tens of thousands of the soldiers that formed his glory, his pride, and his strength, lay stiffened on the gory snow, or raised the whitened surface into graves, or were frozen in the ice, or were bleached in the blasts of heaven. The toil of the enemies they had gone to destroy was to gather and to burn them. And a thousand cannon, piled into a pyramid, left a monument unto future ages, that the fire that had scorched the nations began there to be quenched.

"They that wait upon the Lord shall renew their strength, they shall mount up with wings as eagles, they shall run and not be weary, they shall walk and not faint." But Bonaparte's power was not based in righteousness, and there was nothing stable

* Hist. of Napoleon, vol. ii. pp. 165, 166.

to uphold it. The imperial eagle, winged with ambition, and watching for the prey, fell benumbed upon the earth, and first screamed beneath the paw of the bear. The fate of Napoleon was an illustration of the saying most rife upon his lips, immediately after his flight from Smorgoni, that there is but one step from the sublime to the ridiculous. He passed the Niemén as the head of half a million; he recrossed the frontier of Russia slouching in a sledge, beside a single companion, whose name he adopted at Dresden. On his way to Russia he kept a court of kings, and assumed "a style of splendour and dignity becoming one who might, if any earthly sovereign ever could, have assumed the title of king of kings. The city was crowded with princes of the most ancient birth, as well as with others who claimed a higher rank, as belonging to the family of Napoleon. It was appointed as a mutual rendezvous for all the kings, dominations, princes, dukes, and dependant royalties of every description who were subordinate to Napoleon, or hoped for good or evil at his hands." The emperor of Austria and king of Prussia were among the number. "Amidst all these dignitaries no one interested the public so much as he for whom, and by whom the assembly was collected; the wonderful being who could have governed the world, but could not rule his own restless mind. Napoleon was the principal figure in the group."* It was the last but brightest glare of the dazzling sun, before it was clouded or darkened. While thus encircled by kings and princes, he commanded the attendance of the diplomatist, De Pradt, whom he appointed ambassador at Warsaw. But the gold soon became dim, the scene and the sight were soon changed, and the

* Sir Walter Scott's Life of Napoleon, vol. vii. p. 1.

sun was seen as smitten. "After narrowly escaping being taken by the Russians, Napoleon reached Warsaw upon the 10th December. Here the Abbe de Pradt, then minister of France to the diet of Poland, was in the act of endeavouring to reconcile the various rumours which poured in from every quarter, when a figure, like a spectre, wrapped in furs, which were stiffened by hoar frost, stalked into his apartments supported by a domestic, and was with difficulty recognised by the ambassador as the duke of Vicenza. 'You here, Caulincourt?' said the astonished prelate; 'and where is the emperor?' '*At the hotel d'Angleterre, waiting for you.*' 'Where is the army?' '*It no longer exists.*' The abbe hastened to the hôtel. In the yard stood three sledges in a dilapidated condition. One for the emperor and Caulincourt, the second for two officers of rank, the third for the Mameluke Rustan and another domestic. He was introduced with some mystery into a bad inn's bad room, where a poor female servant was blowing a fire made of green wood. Here was the emperor, whom the Abbe de Pradt had last seen when he played king of kings among the assembled sovereigns of Dresden. He was dressed in a green pelisse, covered with lace and lined with furs, and by walking briskly about the apartment was endeavouring to obtain the warmth which the chimney refused."* "He saluted 'Monsieur l'Ambassadeur,' as he termed him, with gaiety. The abbe felt a movement of sensibility to which he was disposed to give way, but as he says, '*The poor man* did not understand me.' He limited his expressions of devotion, therefore, to helping Napoleon off with his cloak." Such now was the great Napoleon,—a bad

* Sir Walter Scott's Life of Napoleon, vol. vii. pp. 390, 392.

ian's bad room his only council chamber, the humblest menial his only attendant—three shattered sledges his vehicles for flight; without any appurtenances of war,—seeking by quick motion to excite the warmth which the cheerless green wood, the only fuel, could not impart, and needing help to strip him of his cloak. From Smorgoni to Warsaw a few Cossacks might anywhere have staid and taken prisoner the captain of the age, who six months before held a million of soldiers at his command, and had invaded Russsia at the head of five hundred thousand. And now when he had reached again the capital of one of his dependant kingdoms, which he would not make free, he who had cast kings from their thrones and raised others in their places, who held Italy his own, Rome his second city, and the pope his prisoner, stood as "a poor man" before an abbe. Xerxes repassing the Hellespont in an open boat was not a more humiliating sight for human pride to profit by.

Though thou shouldst bray a fool in a mortar, says Solomon, yet will not his folly depart from him. And Bonaparte, though fallen, had still high thoughts of earthly glory. He hastened *incognito* to Paris, to rouse again the energies of his empire. "New conscriptions were called for and yielded. Regiments arrived from Spain and from Italy. Every arsenal resounded with the preparation of new artillery, thousands of horses were impressed in every province. Ere many weeks had elapsed, Napoleon found himself once more in a condition to take the field with not less than 350,000 soldiers."* The sun burst forth from the midst of clouds to dazzle the world with its lustre, once and again, before it should be

* Hist. of Nap., vol. i. p. 169.

blotted from the heavens, or rather, the *imperial power* of Bonaparte was renovated, that on it the *vial of wrath* might yet be more fully *poured out.* A brief glance at his downward course may suffice.

Among the nations which he had subdued the fancied charm of his irresistible power was broken, the magic of his terrible name was gone; but the memory of deep injuries remained, the wrathful nations were roused to vengeance, Europe was free to reckon with the tyrant, and Bonaparte at length had to fight for the existence of his empire.

The campaign of Saxony succeeded the invasion of Russia. The allies now stood the shock of Napoleon. After great carnage from the morning till seven in the evening, on the 2d May 1813, the allies kept the field of Lutzen. At the town of Bautzen the whole army of Napoleon bivouacked in presence of the allies; who, after a terrible battle, retired "with all the deliberate coolness of a parade, halting at every favourable spot and renewing their cannonade." The French lost 15,000 men; the allies 10,000—"What," exclaimed Napoleon, "no results after so much carnage! not a gun! not a prisoner?—these people will not leave me so much as a nail. Fortune has a *spite* at us this day." "It was not"—says Sir Walter Scott rightly—"it was not yet exhausted." The *empire* of Napoleon existed—his sun was not yet black, and the vial of wrath was not yet "exhausted." At Dresden, "fortune revisited her ancient favourite with a momentary gleam of sunshine;" but, after repeated defeats, the battle of Leipsic, in which he lost 50,000 men,* killed and wounded, or prisoners, decided the fate of Napoleon.

* By some accounts, 100,000.

Meanwhile the time had passed in which British troops retired before the French in the swamps of Flanders, or the fields of Spain, or sickened and died amidst the marshes of Walcheren, or were pent up in the lines of Torres Vedras on the coast of Portugal. From that spot the British army now advanced triumphantly to the eastern borders of Spain; and France, not Britain was invaded. On one side of that now fated kingdom the British descended the Pyrenees, and on the other the allies passed the Rhine. Within the space of eighteen months the French were in Moscow, and the Russians in Paris; the soldiers of the allies were quartered in the capital of France, and the Cossacks bivouacked in the *Camps Elysées*. Bonaparte abdicated, and, *with the title of emperor*, the island of Elba was assigned and occupied, as the portion of the man whose ambition before was not bounded by Europe.

But the hero of a hundred battles had yet reserved for him the reign of a hundred days. That reign terminated, and his empire ceased with the battle of Waterloo. And even in title, or in name, he was no longer an emperor. At first he came, a youth of unknown name, from an island in the Mediterranean; and, at last, transported like a felon, under the name of a general, common to thousands, "he died a prisoner on a rock in the Atlantic." His history, of itself, is instructive—and how should it teem with wisdom, while, looking from the sources of the Bormida, where the first steps of his conquests were taken, to the tomb in St. Helena, where his body was interred, there is seen in all his history a palpable illustration of the word of God, who ruleth over the kingdoms of the earth, and giveth them to whomsoever he will!

The third vial began with the first triumphs of

Bonaparte; and the fourth closes with the close of his empire. A few verses sum up his history. And, united in his person, the third and fourth vials are not less intimately connected, or less clearly consecutive, even to contact, than any of the antecedent prophecies that follow in their order. *And the third angel poured out his vial upon the rivers and fountains of waters; and they became blood. And I heard the angel of the waters say, Thou art righteous, O Lord, which art, and wast, and shalt be, because thou hast judged thus: for they have shed the blood of saints and of prophets, and thou hast given them blood to drink, for they are worthy. And I heard another angel out of the altar say, Even so Lord God Almighty, true and righteous are thy judgments. And the fourth angel poured out his vial upon the sun; and power was given unto him to scorch men with fire. And men were scorched with great heat,—and blasphemed the name of God, which hath power over these plagues: and they repented not to give him glory.*

He who loveth God loves his brother also; but while the fiercest passions were at work, men fearlessly blasphemed the name of God. To swear like a dragoon, a trooper, or a tar, became proverbial expressions. Such at least, was not the spirit by which men were actuated on the former grand moral revolution in Europe,—even though the Reformation was followed by wars. And neither the civil wars and subsequent "commonwealth" in Britain, nor our glorious Revolution, were marked by such a brand of blasphemy. But when religious restraints as well as superstitious fears were dissipated by the revolution of France, execrations, almost at every word, gave free vent to the practical infidelity of the hardened hearts of men; devotional feelings gave way together with the softer affections of humanity; and none were ever more mindful of the glory of the God of heaven, than those who executed those judgments or partook of these plagues. The general irreligious character, or utter ungodliness of the time, is too manifest as well as too melancholy an illustration. It is not alone in such a death as that of Lasnes, duke of Montebello,—who falling in the battle of Asperne, replied with angry imprecations, when told that his wound was mortal, and "*blasphemed heaven and earth* that he should be denied to see the end of the campaign,"—that we may see exhibited the maddened spirit of the times: but blasphemy—the soldier's licence and the sufferer's resource was rife on earth, as if Europe had been a province of Pandemonium. And as touching the *not repenting to give God glory*, may it not be asked, even in our own land, where the light of the gospel is so widely diffused, and where our forefathers, in days of peril, assembled in the dens and in the caves to worship, and would have sacrificed their lives rather than forfeit their religious liberty, how many families called Christian, are there still in which the worship of God is not, how many parishes in which, as a practice beyond a mere form of hearing on the sabbath, it is scarcely known; and though happily now less rare than at the close of the revolutionary and imperial wars of France, which began with the open renunciation of the belief of a God, do not illustrations yet abound, by thousands on thousands, from the want alike of true godliness and righteousness, that men *repented not to give him glory?*

CHAPTER XXVIII.

FIFTH VIAL.

On the sounding of the fifth *trumpet*, (Rev. ix. 2.) the bottomless pit was opened; and there arose a smoke out of the pit as the smoke of a great furnace; and the sun and the air were *darkened* by reason of the smoke of the pit. Mahometanism arose; and the world was *darkened* by its doctrines, as well as punished by the arms of the Saracens. But, while also noting the *darkened* state of the minds of men, the fourth vial limits the description of the gross darkness conjoined with bitter miseries, peculiarly characteristic of the specific period, to *the kingdom of the beast*, or the dominions over which the papacy, on its re-establishment, still held its sway. And the state of that kingdom is described as full of darkness, and marked also by misery, blasphemy, and impenitence, without the designation or intervention of any external cause.

And the fifth angel poured out his vial upon the seat of the beast; and his kingdom was full of darkness; and they gnawed their tongues for pain, and blasphemed the God of heaven because of their pains and their sores, and repented not of their deeds. Rev. xvi. 10. 11.

Looking to change after change, and marking the succeeding forms of the time, in almanac notoriety and *manifest* evidence, we thus read in the chronology of remarkable events, in the year 1814;—"The allied grand armies cross the Rhine.—The French defeated at Toulouse; Bordeaux entered by the British; the French evacuate Spain, and *King Fer-*

dinand restored.—The allied armies enter Paris.—Bonaparte deposed.—The Bourbons restored, and a general peace concluded—The French evacuate Italy, Germany, and Flanders, and return within their ancient territory. *The king of Spain dissolves the Cortes, abrogates the new constitution, and all the laws favourable to the liberty of the subject;* REVIVES THE INQUISITION and the order of the Jesuits.—THE POPE RE-ESTABLISHED IN HIS DOMINIONS.*

In the beginning of the year 1812, when the Emperor Napoleon had under his immediate command or "entire control," armies amounting to one million, one hundred and eighty-seven thousand men, and when the Bourbons were in exile, Ferdinand in captivity, and the pope a prisoner, the wildest speculatist could not have dreamt, that, in 1814, the Bourbons would be restored, Ferdinand reinstated in his kingdom, and the pope re-established in his dominions. Yet though, immediately before, it had no existence but in name, and the imperial power of Bonaparte domineered over all, no sooner had that power ceased, than *the kingdom of the beast* reassumed its place in history, as it was the very next word in prophecy. And the dark and miserable state of the papal kingdoms, or wherever the domination of the papacy prevailed, is the precise and limited theme of the prediction.

Previously to the downfall of Napoleon, the state of Europe was that of uniform subjection to the one unvaried "Continental system." But after his fall, a marked contrast may be drawn between Protestant and Catholic states. There was peace externally over both. The high hand of the Holy Alliance was stretched over Europe, to check international wars, and insurrectionary movements. Over

---

* Edinburgh Almanac, 1818, &c. p. 32.

Roman Catholic kingdoms, popery was again associated with despotism. And there peculiarly, as the dark record of their fate gives proof, we are taught to look for darkness and misery. It might here suffice to mention the very names of Portugal, Spain, South America, Italy, and Ireland, as *contrasted* with Sweden, Denmark, North America, Holland and Scotland, to point to the chief regions of darkness and of woe.

From the days of Justinian to those of the French Revolution, during the *appointed time* in which *the saints of the Most High were to be tried, and the time and laws to be given into the hands* of the papal power, the suppression of light was the work of the papacy, and persecution the means. But they who kept the testimony of Jesus loved not their lives unto the death; to whatever bodily torture they were subjected, faith and patience were theirs; and it was the character of the witnesses of Jesus to praise and not to blaspheme the Lord. From the Revolution of France to the dethronement of Napoleon, except where at first they *who had the mark of the beast* were afflicted with *a noisome and grievous sore,* opinions were free, and, when superstition was shaken, infidelity abounded. And at the close of the era of marvellous and righteous judgments, which followed each other in rapid succession, constitutionalists, eager for civil liberty, took the place of the believers in Jesus, who laid down their lives for the faith, and became, in their stead, the victims of papal and despotic persecution. The inflicting power was the same, but the sufferers were different. Men were in *darkness*, while it was not the light of the gospel for which they struggled; and in their agony they found no comfort which they suffered not in the cause of religious liberty, nor looked to Jesus, who gives rest unto the souls of the weary and heavy laden who come unto him.

The nations were thirsting for liberty, without the moral aptitude of self-control which would have rendered it a blessing, when Bonaparte presented them with a vial of wrath, and coerced them by a military despotism before unknown in Europe. When that vial was exhausted, and he, who had held it, tasted its dregs in all their bitterness, and when his sword was broken, superstition came forth anew with her poisoned cup, and popery raised its *yoke* again over a portion of Europe; it sought to bind the mind as well as the body, and the struggle that ensued has marked its kingdom as full of darkness, and fraught with the bitterest miseries.

The very *darkness* that reigns over papal kingdoms precludes, in a great measure, the adduction of positive proof of the fact. The kingdom *of the beast* is so *full of darkness*, that sufficient light is wanting to decipher its intensity. And in default of documentary official evidence, where none is given, and of historical proof, not yet evolved till the thick darkness pass away, recourse must be had to individual testimony to disclose the power of the priesthood, where it prevails, the tyranny of the governments controlled by its influence, and the miseries of the prison-house under their joint domination. That domination is, perhaps, nowhere greater, nor may its effects be anywhere more clearly seen than in Spain and Portugal, which have discarded liberty when proffered for their acceptance, and rejected it when within their reach. From these countries, therefore, as well as from Italy, over which popery holds undivided sway, some illustrations may be drawn, how on the *pouring out of the vial on the seat of the beast, his kingdom was full of darkness;* and how *they gnawed their tongues for pain, and blasphemed the name of*

God because of their pains and their sores, and repented not of their deeds.

A work of great celebrity, "Rome in the Nineteenth Century," in which remarks on the state of society, &c. are incidentally introduced, in a series of Letters *written during a Residence in Rome in the years* 1817 *and* 1818, supplies us with ample testimony borne by an eye-witness, to the *darkness and misery* that pervaded Rome and Italy, at the *very period* to which prophetical history has brought us down—the very eve of the present day.

"All the riches and blessings with which the prodigality of Heaven has dressed the shores of Italy, have only served more effectually to rivet her chains. The highest gifted among the countries of the earth, she stands the lowest in the scale of nations. The strongest in physical power, she is trampled under foot by the weakest."* "The Romans passed beneath the yoke of despotism, never to be liberated. They have, indeed, known change of tyrants.[a] In a long succession of ages, they have been the successive sport of Roman, Barbarian, Goth, Vandal, Pope, and Gaul: but freedom has revisited the *Seven hills* no more; and glory and honour, and virtue and prosperity, one by one, have followed in her train. Long annals of tyranny, of unexampled vice, of misery and of crime,—polluted with still increasing luxury and moral turpitude, record the rapid progress of *Rome's debasement*."†

The fifth vial was poured upon *the seat* (θρονος, the throne, or *seat of* government) *of the beast*, and we may first look on the picture of wretchedness which *Rome itself*, the famed eternal city, presented to view, at the very period after the imperial power of Bonaparte was finally annihilated. It is not to Rome in its glory, but to a city surrounded by every symptom of decay and many tokens of judgment, and encompassed by *plagues*, that the traveller approaches, on entering, during the annual prevalence of the malaria, the renowned plain of Latium.

---

* Rome in the Nineteenth Century, 4th ed. pref. p. 20.
† Ibid. vol. i. p. 268.

"Between the Sabine hills on the east, and the Hills of Viterbo (Monte Ciminus) on the north, the bold ridge of Mount Soracte rose from the plain, insulated from every other height, the most picturesque, and, excepting the Alban Mount, the most lofty and beautiful of all the Amphitheatre of mountains that surround three sides of the plain of Latium. Far as the eye can reach, the Campagna stretches in every direction, to the base of these hills. To the west a wild sullen flat extends to the sea. A profusion of bushy thickets, and a few solitary trees, were scattered over the broken surface of this unenclosed and *houseless plain;*—for a plain it is—since, at the distance of sixteen miles, where we now stood, we distinctly saw Rome.

"Over this wild waste, no rural dwelling, nor scattered hamlets, nor fields, nor gardens, such as usually mark the approach to a populous city, were to be seen. All was ruin: fallen monuments of Roman days—grey towers of Gothic times—abandoned habitations of modern years, alone met the eye. No trace of man appeared, except in the lonely tomb, which told us he *had* been. Rome herself was all that we beheld. She stood alone in the wilderness as in the world, surrounded by a desert of her own creation—a desert which accords too well with her former greatness and her present decay. It may perhaps be soothing to the contemplation of the traveller, or the fancy of the poet, to see the once beautiful Campagna di Roma abandoned to the wild luxuriance of nature, and covered only with the defaced tombs of her tyrants, and the scarce visible remains of the villas of her senators; but it is melancholy to reason and humanity to behold an immense tract of fertile land in the immediate vicinity of one of the greatest cities in the world, pestilent with disease and death, and to know, that like a devouring grave, it annually engulphs all of human kind that toil upon its surface. The unfortunate labourers employed in the scanty cultivation occasionally given to the soil to enable it to produce pasturage for cattle, generally fall victims to the baneful climate. Amidst the fearful loneliness and stillness of this scene of desolation, as we advanced through the long dreary tract that divided us from Rome, a few wretched peasants, whose looks bespoke them victims of slow consuming disease, occasionally reminded us of the tremendous ravage of human life which this invisible and mysterious power is annually making."*

"Nothing is more striking to a stranger than the sombre air which marks every countenance, from the lowest in Rome. The faces even of the young are rarely lighted up with smiles: a laugh is seldom heard, and a merry countenance strikes us with amazement, from its novelty. Rome looks like a city whose inhabitants have passed through the cave of Trophonius.

"The country with the *unexampled* cold and drought of the spring, is dried up—vegetation is pined and withering; and there

---

* Rome in the Nineteenth Century, vol. i. pp. 99, 100.

is but too much reason to dread that the miseries which the poor have suffered during the last dreadful year of scarcity," (or 1816, the very *first* year after the *final* extinction of the empire of Napoleon,) "will be increased tenfold in the next. *Pestilence is already added to famine;*—the lower orders are perishing by hundreds of a low contagious fever, brought on by want, and *numbers have literally died of hunger by the waysides. This dreadful mortality at present extends all over Italy*, and the sufferings of the living are still more cruel and heart-rending than the number of the dead. You daily see human beings crawling on the dunghills, and feeding on the most loathsome garbage, to satisfy the cravings of nature. That this may occasionally be done to call forth charity, is unquestionable, but it is also done when no eye is visibly near; and *the extremity of misery*,—the *ghastly famine that is written in their looks*—cannot be feigned. The failure of those teeming harvests that usually cover the earth, spreads among the improvident and overflowing population of this country, *horrors of famine of which you can have no conception. The dying and the dead surround us on all sides;—the* VERY STREETS *are crowded with sick*, and the contagion of the fever is thought so virulent, that a cordon of troops is drawn around the Great Hospital of the Borgo San Spirito, to prevent communication with its infected inmates. From the returns it appears that *forty-six* per cent. die at the hospital San Spirito at *Rome*, whereas at Paris the average is only *seven* per cent., and in England it seldom exceeds four."* *And the fifth angel poured out his vial upon the* SEAT *of the beast.*

And his KINGDOM *was full of darkness, and they gnawed their tongues for pain*, &c. While Rome, more especially is *the seat of the beast, his kingdom* comprises the countries over which the dark dominion of the papacy still prevailed, and which superstition and despotism were again leagued to enslave. And that *kingdom was full of darkness.* The light of science, at least, began to dawn in Italy, under the reign of Napoleon; in Naples, under Murat; in Spain, alternately under King Joseph and the cortes; and in Portugal, under the protection of the British and the sanction of the king; and in all these countries religious opinions, after ages of darkness, had for a season been free. But on the re-establishment of the pope in his dominions, and of

* Rome in the Nineteenth Century, vol. iii. pp. 196, 197. Letter 79, dated 31st April 1817.

Roman Catholic despots on their thrones, incipient religious liberty was crushed, and the reign of darkness returned in all the *fulness* of its power. Superstition and infidelity acted and reacted on each other—while men were not prone to learn righteousness. The gross mummeries of the Romish church shocked reason, and men, making shipwreck of faith, were stranded on scepticism, and thought, for a moment, that they were safe. But wheh atheism appeared, not in theory but in action, and exhibited its horrors, any form of religion was deemed preferable to none; the mind, when overawed, clung to superstition anew, even as the shipwrecked mariner would cling to any plank. It is thus, perhaps, in some degree to be accounted for, that the gross darkness of the tenth century was partially revived in the nineteenth, and that if the latter be called "enlightened," it is not to those kingdoms where popery most prevails that we have to look for the proof. It is the prophetic characteristic of *the kingdom of the beast* to be *full of darkness*. And such darkness denotes where that kingdom is to be found.

And his kingdom was full of darkness. "Superstition prevails not only in Rome, but in all the states of the church.—A government wholly pacific like that of Rome, might console itself for its *political nullity*," (the judgment had already began to sit which was to take the power out of its hands,) "by encouraging and protecting letters, but an INTELLECTUAL DEADNESS *seems to pervade the Roman states*."*—*full* of darkness.

"The Roman nobility—read not, think not, write not.—The Italian noblemen, for the most part, are ill-educated, ignorant and illiterate."†

---

* Malte-Brun's Geography, vol. vii. pp. 678, 679.

† Rome in the Nineteenth Century, vol. iii. pp. 208, 219.—It is added, "I could give some curious proofs of this, but I content myself with mentioning one, which I witnessed the other night at the

"The fair sex in this country are generally extremely ignorant. They are occupied with pursuits of the most peurile vanity."* "After mass, the lower orders throng the streets in a state of complete apathetic *vacuity of mind*, and bodily inertion."† "There has actually been in Rome a trial for witchcraft, a grave formal trial for witchcraft, in the nineteenth century! I begin to think I must be mistaken, and that the world has been pushed back about three hundred years. But it was even so."‡ "I understand that *not one miracle happened during the whole reign of the French*, and that it was not until the streets were purified with *lustrations* of holy water *on the return of the pontiff*, that they began to operate again.§ But, with the pontiff, darkness returned, and the age of popish miracles revived." "Within this little month, (31st April, 1817,) three *great* miracles have happened in Rome. The last took place yesterday, when *all Rome crowded* to the capitol, to see an *image of the Virgin* opening her eyes." "When I behold crowds flocking to *kneel* before these talking and winking Maddonas, I cannot help asking myself, if this is really the nineteenth century? One would have thought that there had been miracles enough of late in Rome, to have satisfied any reasonable people; but the pope and a detachment of cardinals are going about every day after dinner in quest of more. They visit all the Maddonas in regular succession.—Private miracles, indeed, affecting individuals, go on quite commonly every day, without exciting the smallest attention. These generally consist in procuring prizes in the lottery, curing diseases, and casting out devils."‖ "Miracles and miraculous Maddonas

---

opera, when half a dozen dukes, marquisses, and counts, from different parts of Italy, who were in the box with us, began disputing whether Peru, which happened to be the scene of the piece, was in the East Indies, in Africa,—or, as one of them, for a wonder, was inclined to think—in America!"

* Ibid. vol. iii. pp. 224, 225. † Ib. p. 206.

‡ Ibid. p. 201. § P. 199.

‖ The mode of effecting this last description of miracle was communicated to me the other day by an abbe here: and, as I think it extremely curious, I shall relate it to you.

It seems that a certain friar had preached a sermon during Lent, upon the state of the man mentioned in Scripture, possessed with seven devils, with so much eloquence and unction, that a simple countryman who heard him, went home, and became convinced that these seven devils had got possession of him. The idea haunted his mind, and subjected him to the most dreadful terrors, till, unable to bear his sufferings, he unbosomed himself to his ghostly father, and asked his counsel. The father, who had some smattering of science, bethought himself at last of a way to rid the honest man of his devils. He told him it would be necessary to combat with the devils singly; and on a day appointed, when the poor man came with a sum of money, to serve as a bait for the devil, without which the father had forewarned him no devil could

abound nearly as much in Tuscany as in the Estates of the church, as I have good reason to know. At Mantua, a bottle of the blood of Christ is liquified every year, to the great edification of the compatriots of Virgil. The bottle containing this *real blood* of Christ, was dug up at Mantua in a box, about 200 years ago, with a written assurance that it had been deposited there by a St. Longinus, a Roman centurion, who witnessed the crucifixion, and became converted, and ran away from Judea to Mantua with this bottle of blood; and after lying sixteen centuries in the ground, the box, the writing, the bottle, and the blood were as fresh as if they had been placed there," (as in all likelihood they were,) "only the day before! But I might write a book of miracles, were I to relate the hundredth part of all that take place every year, nay, every day, in Italy."*

But other illustrations of the grossest darkness are supplied by the capital of the Roman Catholic world in the nineteenth century, such as the annals of paganism, in its darkest days, could scarcely have outrivaled, amidst all the manifold demonstrations which its records jointly with those of popery, supply of the deep debasement of the human intellect, before the prostrating power of dark superstition.

To renew our quotations from the testimony of an eye-witness to facts notorious and unquestionable, we read:—

"We were present to-day, (Sunday, January 18th, 1819,) at one of the most ridiculous scenes I ever witnessed, even in this country. It was St. Antony's Blessing of the Horses, which began on that saint's day, and I understand lasts for a week; but as this was a *festone*, I rather imagine we saw it in its *full* glory. We drove to

---

ever be dislodged, he bound a chain, connected with an electrical machine in an adjoining chamber,—round his body,—lest, as he said, the devil should fly away with him,—and having warned him that the shock would be terrible when the devil went out of him, he left him praying devoutly before an image of the Madonna, and after some time gave him a pretty smart shock, at which the poor wretch fell insensible on the floor from terror. As soon as he recovered, however, he protested that he had seen the devil fly away out of his mouth, breathing blue flames and sulphur, and that he felt himself greatly relieved. Seven electrical shocks, at due intervals, having extracted seven sums of money from him, together with the seven devils, the man was cured, and a great miracle performed. *Ibid.*

* Rome in the Nineteenth Century, vol. iii. pp. 193, 201.

the church of the saint, near Santa Maria Maggiore, and could scarcely make our way through the streets, from the multitude of horses, mules, asses, oxen, cows, sheep, goats, and dogs, which were journeying along to the *place of benediction*; their heads, tails, and necks decorated with bits of coloured ribband and other finery, on this, their unconscious gala-day. The saint's benediction, though nominally confined to horses, is equally efficacious, and equally bestowed upon all quadrupeds; and I believe there is scarcely a brute in Rome, or the neighbourhood, that has not participated in it.*

"An immense crowd were assembled in the wide open space, in front of the church, and from the number of beasts and men, it looked exactly like a cattle fair. At the door, stood the blessing priest, dressed in his robes, and wielding a brush in his hand, which he continually dipped in a large bucket of holy water, that stood near him, and spirted at the animals as they came up, in unremitting succession, taking off his little skullcap, and muttering every time,—'Per intercessionem beati Antonii abatis, hæc animalia liberantur malis, in nomine Patris et Filii et Spiritus Sancti. Amen.'

"The poor priest had such hard work in blessing that he was quite exhausted and panting, and his round face looked fiery red with his exertions. The rider or driver of the creature, always gave some piece of money, larger or smaller, in proportion to his means or generosity, and received an engraving of the saint and a little metallic cross; however, all animals might be blessed gratis.

"Several well-dressed people, in handsome equipages, attended with out-riders in splendid liveries, drove up while we were there, and sat uncovered while the benediction was given. Then, having paid what they thought fit, they drove off and made way for others,"† &c.

"There is a peculiar and more solemn sort of blessing given to two lambs, on the 21st of January, at the church of St. Agnese *fuori le murd*, from the sainted fleeces of which are manufactured, I believe, by the hand of nuns, two holy mantles, called *Pallj*, which the pope presents to the archbishops as his principal shepherds. It is incredible the sums of money that used to be given in former days, for the least scrap of these precious garments; but times are sadly changed, as an old priest pathetically observed to me. They still, however, carry a remnant of the Virgin Mary's own nuptial veil annually in solemn procession to the church of Santa Maria del Papulo, where it is still adored; and the marriage of Christ and St. Catherine is still celebrated with great pomp, on the anniversary of their wedding day, the 29th of January, at the church of Sainta Maria *supra Minerva*, and held as a grand festa. But the festa which pleased me the most, was that of the children. On the eve of the Twelfth Day, the *Crature*,‡ with trembling, min-

* Rome in the Nineteenth Century, vol. iii. pp. 193—201.
† Ibid. pp. 202, 203.
‡ The children.

gled with hope, anticipate a midnight visit from a frightful old woman, called the Befana, (an obvious corruption of *Epifania*, the Epifany,) for whom they always take care to leave some portion of their supper, lest she should eat them up; and when they go to bed, they suspend upon the back of a chair a stocking, to receive her expected gifts. This recepticle is always found in the morning to contain some sweet things, or rather welcome presents, which I need scarcely say, are provided by the mother or the nurse. There is here a dressed up wooden figure of La Befana, sufficiently hideous, the bug-bear of all naughty girls and boys."*

Thus, from the nobility to the mob, and from the churches to the nursery, all in Rome was *full of darkness*, which popes, cardinals, bishops, priests, monks, and friars, conspired to deepen, so soon as the reign of the empire was at an end, and that of the popery restored.

But wherever popery prevails, darkness has its dominion. Spain, wholly a Roman Catholic country, was once the most conspicuous for science of all the kingdoms of Europe—but science flourished there under the sword of the Mahometans, and not under the papal yoke.

On the invasion of the Moors, "the very name of science was forgotten, and the priests could hardly read the services of the temple. But these invaders introduced a high degree of civilization, and united with the most romantic bravery a passionate love of science and the arts. As the basis of national happiness and improvement, public schools were established in almost every town; and colleges, with well selected libraries, were splendidly endowed in all the principal cities under their dominion. In these the sciences of geography, experimental philosophy, optics, botany, natural history, and geometry, were cultivated with great success. The Moors were the first great improvers of chemistry; they excelled in astronomy, they enriched the medical art, which they had acquired from the writings of the Greeks with many important discoveries; and to them we owe both the science of arithmetic, and the invention of those numerical characters, which have been adopted by all European nations. Their most renowned universities were those of Seville, Cordova, and Granada; and such was the reputation which they had acquired, that crowds of learned

---

* Rome in the Nineteenth Century, vol. iii. pp. 204, 205.

men from various countries resorted to Spain to study those sciences which were nowhere else taught so successfully," &c.*

Is it then to such a country—the land too of Seneca, Quintilian, and Martial,—that in the "enlightened nineteenth century," we have to look for a portion or province of that *kingdom of the beast*, being wholly *his*, which, at the close of Napoleon's career, was *full of darkness*. In another page of its history, even after the gloom of superstition had been partially dispelled, quoting from the same authority, we read :—

"*Six years* of direful experience (from 1814 to 1820) had taught Spain what she had to expect from the uncontrolled will of *Ferdinand*. He *had subverted all her liberal institutions*, and had consigned to dungeons and to exile some of the bravest and most enlightened of her sons. During that period she had enjoyed repose, but it was the repose of *the grave, whose gloom* NO *ray of light is permitted to penetrate*,—a repose *fatal* to the industry, the *intelligence*, and the happiness of the people.† The inquisition was restored with its ancient plenitude of authority; and among its first acts were the publication of a long list of prohibited works, and a decree that all prints and pictures, as well as books, should be subjected to its previous censorship."‡

An incidental fact, however minute, may sometimes, as if by experiment, illustrate a truth more vividly than a general description.

"A priest," says Mr. Inglis, "with whom I was acquainted in Madrid, telling me one day that he had thoughts of going to London or Paris, to print an English and Spanish grammar, and a German and Spanish grammar, which he had written, I asked him why he did not print them in Madrid, since they were intended for the use of his own countrymen, especially as they could contain nothing political. His answer was, that *nothing was so difficult as to obtain a license to publish a book*, even although it contained no allusion to politics; 'and the better the book,' he said, 'the more difficult it is to obtain a license, and the more *dangerous* to publish, because government does not wish to encourage writing,

---

* Brewster's Encyclopædia, Art. Spain, vol. xviii. p. 341.
† Ibid. p. 309. ‡ Ibid. p. 304.

or even thinking *upon any subject*; and the publication of a good book sets men a-thinking.' This comprehensive reply describes, pretty nearly, the present state of literature in Spain, judging of it by the number and merit of publications."*

That the *darkness*, complete as that of the *grave*, which rests on Spain, denotes the total want of the light of revelation, which, wherever it shines, must ever dispel every shadow of idolatry, another illustration too fatallly demonstrates.

"Religion with this people is rather a business than a feeling, and their devotion consists merely in external ceremonies to which they are so habituated as to perform them almost instinctively, and the neglect of which would expose them to the horrors of the inquisition. In populous towns the inhabitants are frequently thrown into devotional attitudes by the sound of the little bell which precedes the priest who is carrying the consecrated wafer to a dying person. Its sound operates upon a Spaniard like magic. In whatever company or situation, in the street or in the house, he throws himself upon his knees, and in this posture he remains until the tinkling dies away in the distance. In the midst of a gay and noisy party this sound brings every one to his devotions; if at dinner, he must leave the table, and if in bed he must at least sit up. Even in the public theatres, as soon as the bell is heard, 'Dios, Dios,' resounds from all parts of the house, and every one falls that moment upon his knees. The actors' ranting, or the rattling of the castanets in the *fandango*, is hushed for a few minutes, till the sound of the bell growing fainter and fainter the amusement is resumed, and the devout performers are once more upon their legs anxious to make amends for the interruption."†

"The sale of the bulls of papal pardon and indulgence produces an immense revenue in Spain." "That the Spaniards, as a people, are ignorant, *supremely ignorant*, it is impossible to dissemble; but this comes from the control of education being altogether in the hands of the clergy, who exert themselves to maintain that ignorance to which they are indebted for their power."‡

The kingdom of Portugal is also wholly devoted to Catholicism, and there, too, the *darkness* is *full*. The belief of witchcraft is common to it with Italy.

---

* Spain in 1830, by H. D. Inglis, Esq., vol. i. pp. 261, 266.
† Laborde, quoted in Brewster's Encyclop. Ibid. p. 332.
‡ A year in Spain, vol. ii. pp. 327, 360.

And while beasts, besprinkled with holy water from the hands of a priest in the city of the pope, and under his eye, receive a benediction, to preserve them from evil; the priests in Portugal excommunicate the crawling vermin that infest the fields of wheat.* "The ecclesiastical establishment of Portugal is the *moral blight* and overwhelming curse of the country from north to south, and from east to west. A crafty priesthood intentionally keep the lowest orders of the people under a *degraded superstition*."† It, too, is *full of darkness;* there is no admixture of light, where there is none of Protestantism: as Popery abounds, darkness prevails. Of the darkness as well as misery of Ireland, it were superfluous to tell.

And they gnawed their tongues for pain, and blasphemed the God of heaven because of their pains and their sores, and repented not of their deeds.

"The *re-institution* of the *inquisition*, of the Jesuits, and of monastic orders in the nineteenth century, is a retrograde step in the progress of society."‡ By the re-institution of the *inquisition*, the most diabolical engine of oppression and torture was brought into action again. And justly may it be feared, that many a tale of bitter misery now untold, has yet to be disclosed. The re-establishment of female monastic orders is also another mode of imprisonment for life, and instances are recorded in which a forced adoption of the veil has led to frenzy, parricide, and despair. The order of Santa Theresa is the most severe."

"Its unfortunate votaries are doomed to unceasing midnight vigils and daily fasts; to penance, austerity, and mortification in every possible form, while all intercourse with their friends, all indulgence of the sweet affections of nature are as sedulously inter-

---

* Portugal in 1828, by William Young, Esq., p. 38.
† Ibid. pp. 36, 38.
‡ Rome in the Nineteenth Century, vol. iii. p. 174.

dicted as if these were crimes of the blackest dye. To all intents and purposes, to all the duties, pleasures, and hopes of this life, they are as completely dead as if the grave had already closed over them. And what is it but a living death, a more lingering mode of being buried alive? There is in Rome a convent, called, and justly called, the sepolto vivo, (buried alive,) in which are contumacious or fanatic nuns, from all convents—females condemned by the inquisition for too little or too much religion—and wives whose husbands and fathers have the means to prove they deserve, or the interest to procure the order for such a dreadful punishment. Instances have occured, where mere resistance to the will of a parent, or causeless jealousy conceived by a husband, have been followed by this *horrible vengeance.* None but its victims may enter, and none of them may quit it."*

But misery is not confined in Italy to the cells of the inquisition, or the dungeons either of a convent or a prison. Beggars and bandits are the scourges of Italy, and are as common in the kingdom of Naples as in the states of the church.† While swarms of begging friars infest the country, bands of robbers adopt other modes of pillage. "We hear fresh accounts every day (Rome, February 1818) of captives carried off to the mountains by the banditti, and the most daring outrages practised with impunity. The numerous bands of robbers which infest this country, by no means live either upon their depredations on travellers, or the ransom of their prisoners; their *grand resource is the plunder of the farmers,* particularly those who live among the hills, many of whom are extremely rich, not only in flocks and cattle, and such sort of rural property, but in money. The whole range of the Volscian hills, which extend from the Alban Mount far into the kingdom of Naples, and branch off into various chains, stretching up to the Appenines, and through the heart of Calabria, are all infested with banditti. The French would allow no robbers but themselves, and kept the country tolerably clear of

* Rome in the Nineteenth Century, vol. iii. pp. 187, 188.
† Malte-Brun's Geography, vol. vii. p. 704.

them; but *since* they went away, they have increased and multiplied."*

"Bad as the papal government is, indeed, it is by no means so bad as that beneath which a great part of Italy *is groaning*. Not so bad for instance, as Naples; or Piedmont; or Genoa, abandoned to the merciless gripe of Sardinia; or ill-fated Lombardy; or expiring Venice,"† &c. Italy, torn asunder by despots and Carbonari, and divided between priests and robbers, is full of bitter misery as well as of the blackest darkness. While intellectual darkness pervaded the Roman states, the time at which the vial was poured upon the seat of the beast was a season of pestilence and famine in Rome, and the "same dreadful mortality extended over all Italy."

"The Italians," to quote the farther testimony of the learned Sismondi, "partook of all the privileges of the conquerors: they became with them accustomed to the dominion of the law, to freedom of thought, and to military virtue,—secure that at no very distant period, when their political education should be accomplished, they would again be incorporated in that Italy, to the future liberty and glory of which they now directed their every thought.—Such was the work which the French accomplished by twenty years of victory; it was doubtless incomplete, and left much to be desired; but it possessed in itself the principle of greater advancement: it *promised* to revive Italy, liberty, virtue, and glory. It has been the work of the coalition to destroy all; to place Italy again under the galling yoke of Austria; take from her, with political liberty, civil and *religious freedom, and even freedom of thought*; to corrupt her morals; and to heap upon her *the ut-*

* Rome in the Nineteenth Century, p. 412.
† Ibid, p. 417.

most degree of humiliation. Italy is unanimous in abhorring this ignominious yoke; Italy, to break it, has done all that could be expected of her. The people have only their unarmed hands, and their masses unaccustomed to act together; nevertheless, in every struggle during these fifteen years in Italy, between the nation and its oppressors, the victory has remained with the people. At Naples, in Sicily, in Piedmont, in the states of the church, at Modena and Parma, unarmed masses have seized the arms of the soldiers; men chosen by the people have taken the places of the despots in their palaces. The Italians, everywhere victorious over their own tyrants, have, it is true, been *everywhere forced back under the yoke with redoubled cruelty* by the league of Foreign despots. *Italy is crushed—she is chained and covered with blood.*"*

Spain and Portugal, sunk in kindred ignorance, are associated with Italy in misery as in darkness. Of all the dark days of miserable Spain, naturally one of the first countries of Europe, but morally one of the most corrupt, that of the restoration of Ferdinand is one of the darkest. He who, while in exile, was an embroiderer to the Virgin, ceased not, when again a king, to maintain the authority of the church. "Before his return, he *had sworn* to maintain the constitution, but he no sooner found himself surrounded by the nobles and clergy, whose rights and privileges that constitution had in a great measure swept away, than his royal oath yielded to the ambitious wish of reigning *absolute sovereign* of Spain. He immediately annulled the constitution, and seizing the reins of absolute power, he established in all their deformity the abominations of the old government. His will again became the law; and,

* Sismondi's Hist. of the Italian Republics, pp. 364, 365.—1832.

supported by a cabal of crafty and interested zealots, he stalked forth as the cruel persecutor of all who had in any degree lent their aid in accomplishing his own restoration and the independence of their country. Sentences *of imprisonment, exile, or perpetual servitude,* were passed upon all the deputies of the Cortes who had shewn any zeal in the cause of freedom. Many distinguished leaders in the Spanish armies met with similar treatment, while others withdrew from persecution by seeking an asylum in foreign countries. The *yoke of despotism,* however, was not borne without *impatience.* Occasional irruptions showed that the flame of liberty might be smothered, but was not extinguished. An attempt of Porlier at Corunna to accomplish a revolution upon the principles of the *oppressed liberals,* was followed by others in Valentia, Catalonia, and Galicia, but were all attended with similar results, and *equally disastrous to their promoters.* The unfortunate issue of these designs checked for a time the spirit of opposition. If the term *absolute* can be applied to any monarch, the king of Spain *at this period* well deserved the appellation."*

Descriptive of the state of Spain, at the same period, the Annual Register, for successive years, bears the following melancholy record:—

1815.—"Perhaps no country in Europe is at present in a more *wretched* and degraded state than is Spain. It is really disgusting to dwell on the character of Ferdinand. The case of Ferdinand will abundantly prove how much evil a despotic sovereign may punish his subjects with, even when he is the most imbecile in intellect. It is not surprising that a man so weak, and so blind to his own interest, should be *the dupe of bigotted and cruel*

* Brewster's Encyclop. vol. xviii. p. 304.

priests, or that he should readily agree to *their design of establishing the inquisition.* In short, the state of Spain, viewed either in a political or religious light, appears to be *much worse now than it was even in the days of the most bigotted and tyrannical of the Philips.* Indeed, till the Spaniards are *more enlightened*, and less *under the dominion of superstition*, (kingdom of the beast, full of darkness,) it is in vain to expect from them any efforts to raise themselves to their just rank in the scale of European nations."

1817.—"The affairs of Spain still present a melancholy picture."

1818.—"The little that is known of the state of Spain is, that the finances are still in a wretched condition—that there are no means to send out the expedition to South America—that poverty and oppression gain ground, and that the inquision possesses more power than ever."*

1820.—"Much surprise was naturally excited that the Spaniards submitted so completely as they appeared to do, for such a length of time, (from 1814 to 1820,) to *the wretchedness of all descriptions with which they were overwhelmed.* Agriculture, manufactures and commerce nearly annihilated; the finances in a most dilapidated state; the most *enlightened* patriots, those to whom the monarch and the country were most indebted, *exiled* or in prison,—formed the picture of Spain."†

Spain is exclusively a province of the *kingdom of the beast*, and ruled by popery. Hence its yet impervious darkness, and miserable fate. Ferdinand himself is but the hound of the popish priesthood, and the liesh is in their hands. "The clergy is the great and dominant body in Spain, which

* Annual Register, 1818, p. 356. † Ibid. 1820, pp. 386, 387.

moves every thing at will, and gives impulse even to the machine of state. When we see a device of the Spanish government breathing a spirit of bigotted intolerance, we are not to ascribe it to this or that minister, but rather to some unseen bishop or father abbot behind the curtain. From these causes, then, and not from the sovereign will of a single individual, originate those persecuting decrees and apostolic denunciations which have brought on Ferdinand the appellation of bloody bigot, and all the hard names in the calendar of abuse."*

The disannulling of the constitution,—the re-establishment of the inquisition,—the absolute despotism of Ferdinand, himself the dupe of bigotted and cruel priests, led to the imprisonment, exile, or perpetual servitude of the bravest and most enlightened of her sons; and, notwithstanding abortive attempts for the recovery of liberty,—which served but to aggravate their pains and increase their bondage,—reduced Spain to a worse state than it was even in the days of the most bigotted and tyrannical of the Philips, and, under the dominion of superstition, overwhelmed it with miseries of all descriptions.

Of the little that, in a time so full of darkness, could be known of Spain, all was misery; and the spirit of priestly domination or of religious or political fanaticism that preyed on Spain, and of which the most enlightened of her sons were the victims, may be exemplified in the fact, that when the "priest party was restored to preponderance and power," after the brief but troublous supremacy of the Cortes, "it was publicly proclaimed from a pulpit in Madrid to be no sin to kill the child of a constitutional, though in its mother's womb."† And

* A Year in Spain, vol. ii. pp. 337, 345.

† Ibid. p. 9.

the inquisition was an engine of cruelty, and an instrument of torture, the very secresy and seclusion of which aggravated the agony, such as nothing but faith could overcome.

It is much to be feared that the minds of the Spaniards, whether tormentors or tormented, whether holding power by persecution, or daring the miseries of the dungeon in the hope of freedom, were divided between superstition and infidelity, and that there was no peace in the minds of the sufferers but what, as their hopes were earthly, the world could take away. "Imprisonment or perpetual servitude," the hard alternative and common doom, were enough to break the heart of which liberty was the idol, and proofs too conclusive abound, to show that miseries were superadded enough to cause them to *gnaw their tongues for pain.*

"The real condition of Portugal at the close of the peninsular war," or from 1814 to 1820, is thus described, in general terms.

"The extinction of the few native manufactories of the kingdom, the total loss of the lucrative commerce of Brazil, and the utter ruin of agriculture by the ravages of a cruel warfare, had all conspired to overwhelm the mass of the Portuguese population in distress and poverty. The return of a season of tranquillity, which should have healed the wounds left by foreign invasion and national misfortunes, had been permitted to exercise no real salutary influence. On the contrary, during the six years, the continued residence of the court in Brazil, with the exactions of an absentee nobility, the general corruptions of the institutions of government, and the misrule of the regency, had altogether *aggravated* instead of assuaging the sufferings of the nation. The clergy, and the harpies of administration, had alone flourished amidst the general calamity; the great body of the people, and especially the peasantry, were reduced to the lowest stage of penury and wretchedness."*

But, exclusive of this general description of the

---

* *State of Portugal*, p. 46.

wretchedness of Portugal, which admits not of denial, there is the testimony of witnesses who bore their part in the sufferings, and were the inmates of prisons; and whose case has not only excited the commiseration of a few, but commanded the attention of the British parliament and public. Sir John Doyle and Mr. Young were but two out of many thousands, who, on account of political offences, whether real or presumed, were immured in the dungeons of Portugal. And their right to a hearing in our land of liberty, and to protection as British subjects, though in a foreign kingdom, has exposed to view the horrors of Portuguese imprisonment, in a manner that otherwise could not have been divulged or credited. There darkness still has its seat. And the task is yet reserved for history, fully to disclose such abominations and barbarities. And in lieu of official documents, such as never can be given, and of historical records, which are yet wanting, recourse must be had to individual testimony; yet at no second hand, but of one who, for many years, was an eye-witness to what he describes, and who felt what he tells.

"I could mention facts," says Mr. Young, "which I have witnessed within these twenty years, that would make Englishmen turn with abhorrence from the pictures of villany which may be concealed under the cloak of religion. Many of these facts would be scarcely credible in a country not cursed with monks and friars."* "It should never be lost sight of, in speaking of the government of Portugal, that we are speaking of a set of men whose actions have one object, which they are all sworn to maintain as one man, that of acquiring absolute dominion over the minds and the properties of the entire community; and for the attainment of which object they prostitute the sacred name of religion, violate every moral and social tie, and are ready to sacrifice friend or foe to the attainment of their wishes." "It should always be borne in mind, that Miguel is the mere tool,

* Portugal in 1828, by William Young, Esq.

or political engine, of the principal jugglers of the college of Jesuits."*

"It is scarcely possible for language to describe the degree of *alarm, horror, and despair*, which the dreadful abuse of power produces among those of the Portuguese nation who have ever been suspected of entertaining any attachment to the constitutional charter. Suspicion is at all times sufficient to immure any man in a dungeon, on the accusation of one of the vilest even of the rabble of Lisbon."† Many thousands who now crowd the prisons of Portugal, owe their captivity to no higher offence than the hatred of some vagabond."‡

"There is no gaol allowance in any part of the country. It may appear strange in England, but when a man is locked up in Portugal, if he has no money to send for food, or no one brings him any, he may absolutely starve. None of the authorities ever inquire whether he has any means of subsistence: there is neither bed, blankets, nor even straw, unless the prisoner can buy it, and then he must pay the guards to let it pass to him. Among the many thousand unfortunate beings who are now confined in Portugal, great numbers of them are without money, or any other means of subsistence; and were it not for the charity of people in general, starvation would necessarily ensue. When the food, given in charity, is distributed, the persons who accept it form a line or a circle, according to circumstances, and sing in a loud voice a prayer to the Virgin Mary; this is a ceremony never omitted in any part of Portugal."§

"Every room or ward of the prison contains a juis (governor), a *mixinguero* (the governor's assistant), and a *varader* (a sweeper). These men are always selected from the greatest blackguards in the prison. The adjutant and sweeper acquaint the juis with every thing that happens, and very frequently with things which never exist but in their own heads; the juis tells the secretary or the jailor. The prisoners consequently have the utmost dread of these vagabond authorities, which the latter are aware of, and exercise their influence accordingly."‖

Such are "the horrors of Portuguese imprisonment," that their state is described as "bordering on frenzy or despair." "Men confined in these prisons appear, by degrees, to become other beings." Some are driven to actual madness, or "settled melancholy." "It was *truly dreadful to witness the*

* Portugal in 1828, by William Young, Esq. p. 123.
† Ibid. p. 176. ‡ Ibid. p. 156.
§ Ibid. pp. 110–12. ‖ Ibid. p. 115.

despair of some of those unfortunate victims of despotism. They would often be found sitting or lying in the dark passages of the prison, moaning and groaning; and when asked the reason, some would say, 'My father is dead of grief;' another, 'My poor wife is dead;' a third, 'My property is all confiscated, and I have nothing left; my family are begging in the streets; for myself, the only hope of subsistence is in the caridade." There were numbers in this melancholy condition, persons of property to-day, and to-morrow not worth a farthing."* When a man is put in the segrido, (or dungeon,) which is, and always has been in use in Portugal, it is usual to deprive him of all means of communication and self-destruction."†

Amidst the barbarities which ushered in the reign of Miguel, "the streets of Lisbon were crowded with soldiers, day and night, authorizing the mob to insult whoever they pleased, and those who made any resistance to be conveyed to prison. Each police soldier had *anginhos* (little angels, or *thumb-screws*) in his pocket; and I saw about this time, several respectable looking people escorted to prison with these instruments of torture affixed to them. *They often screwed them till the blood started from under the nails; I have heard them crying with agony as they went along.*"‡

Even in Roman catholic countries, the time is past in which civil and religious tyranny was tamely borne; and, from the multiplicity of victims guilty against the state, or liable to such suspicion, the land of despots has the semblance of a prison-house, in a form the most appalling.

---

* Young's Portugal, pp. 154, 155. † Ibid, p. 66.
‡ Ibid. p. 87.

PORTUGAL.

Victims of Don Miguel's cruelty.

"A recent publication gives, with the sanction of a well-informed native of Portugal, the following frightful list of Don Miguel's tyranny."—*Courier, July* 13, 1831.

Political offenders in the prison of Lisbon	3,600
at the fort of St. Julian	800
in the Reniche	400
Cascaes, Belem-Castle, and Trafaria	300
On board the hulks in the Tagus	600
at Oporto	2,000
In the different prisons of Tras-os-montes	1,200
In the province of Daura and Minho	2,000
Beira, including Almeida	5,000
Estremadura and Abrantis	3,000
Alerutejo, including Elvas	5,000
Algarve	1,200
Transported as convicts to Angula	400
to Cati Verde and other islands	500
to Cabinda, Agonche, Mozambique	700

Emigrants.

In the island of Terceira	7,000
In Brazil	2,000
In different parts of Europe	800
In France	1,800
In the Netherlands	1,000
In different parts of Europe	1,000
	40,300

"To this number may be added near 5,000 persons now concealed or wandering in different parts of the country, in order to escape persecution;—45,300 victims of *political vengeance and resentment*, out of a population amounting to 2,600,000, furnish the strongest proof of the government."

POLITICAL LETTER.

The liberty with which Christ would set us free, and which is the glorious calling of the Christian, is the only true freedom of the soul. Without it the tyrant is a slave, and with it the bondsman is free indeed. When it is felt and enjoyed, no manacles can fetter or depress the mind, no bolts of a dungeon can shut out the hope that is heavenly. When Paul and Silas, who had suffered the loss of all things for Jesus' sake, were cast into prison, after their clothes were rent off, and many stripes had been laid upon them, and they were thrust into the inner prison, and their feet made fast in the stocks, at midnight they prayed, and sang praises unto God. They accounted it all joy to suffer in the cause of their Redeemer. In the believer's reckoning, tribulation, as a trial of faith, is more precious than gold that perisheth; and it is the privilege of the Christian to rejoice evermore. Not loving their lives unto the death, the witnesses of Jesus could cast themselves into the flames. But the love of political liberty, however precious it may be, has no power to charm away the horrors of the dungeon; and to those to whom freedom, in a human sense, is the god of their idolatry, the restraints and privations of the prison-house, without the hope of release, are the bitterest of miseries, before which the heart, unsustained by faith, is broken, and all the powers of the mind give way. Instead of praying and singing praises unto God, there is "moaning and groaning," the voice of agony and despair: *and they gnawed their tongues for pain, and blasphemed the God of heaven, because of their pains and their sores, and repented not of their deeds*, verse 11th.

CHAPTER XXIX.

SIXTH VIAL.

The invasion of France by the armies of Russia, Prussia, Germany, Sweden, and Britain; the evacuation of Spain by the French and the entrance of the armies into France, and the abdication of Bonaparte; the restoration of the Bourbons, and the conclusion of a general peace; the evacuation of Italy, Germany, and Flanders by the French, and their restriction within their ancient boundaries, closed up, 1st, the *history of the French revolution;* 2d, of the *greatest of naval wars;* 3d, *of the wars of the directory and consulate of France;* and 4th, *those of the empire*—or, in other words, the first, second, third, and fourth vials of the wrath of God had been poured upon the earth. But the *plagues* were not at an end, nor had the *judgments* ceased. As these ended another began; and the *same* eventful year, 1814, which terminated, for a season, so many convulsions, was marked also—as even an almanac testifies—by the restoration of Ferdinand, the dissolution of the Cortes, the abrogation of the new constitution and of all laws favourable to the liberty of the press, the revival of the inquisition and of the order of the Jesuits, and the re-establishment of the pope in his dominions. The soldiers of Napoleon withdrew from Roman Catholic countries, and the priesthood reassumed its place. A system of coercion, and of the repression of liberty, was established by the sovereigns of continental Europe; and in suppressing revolution, freedom was stifled. But passive slavery was no longer the character of the time. A high and a hard hand could alone keep down freedom, or prevent the rising of anarchy. And, notwithstanding the league of monarchs, only six years elapsed—from 1814 to 1820—a period repeatedly referred to in the preceding extracts, till three revolutions burst forth in the Roman Catholic kingdoms of Europe, and gave to "the constitutionalists" in Spain, Portugal, and Naples a brief suspense from their bondage, which lasted in the two former kingdoms for the space of three years, when a counter-revolution in Portugal and the invasion of Spain by the French, under the Bourbons, rivetted the chains anew, and aggravated their woes.

During this very period—from 1820 to 1823—of the partially suspended operation of the fifth vial, the sixth vial, it would seem, *began* to be poured out. From a state of previous quiescence, those commotions of the Turkish empire then originated, which, followed as they have been by convulsion after convulsion, have already put its existence to the stake.

The locality of the third vial—that of the *rivers and fountains of waters*—is not more precisely determined by that of the third trumpet, defined in the same words, than the sphere of the fifth vial is identified with that of the fifth trumpet.

And the sixth angel sounded; and I heard a voice from the four horns of the golden altar which is before God, saying to the sixth angel which had the trumpet, Loose the four angels which are bound in the great river Euphrates. And the four angels were loosed which were prepared for an hour, and a day, and a month, and a year, for to slay the third part of men. Rev. ix. 13—15.

And the sixth angel poured out his vial upon the great river Euphrates; and the water thereof was dried up, that the way of the kings of the east might be prepared. Rev. xvi. 12.

The Turkish empire, under the same designation which it had previously borne, is here manifestly represented anew. Its early history and establishment in Europe, by the taking of Constantinople, have been already related. Its existence ceased not, nor did the woe pass away, when the period was completed during which the Turks were "*prepared* to slay;" but we have now to look on it again in another form, than sweeping over countries like a whirlwind, and overflowing them with *myriads of horsemen;* and the time is come that we have to resume its history, with the prophetic record before us, of a very different fate.

Symbolized by the Euphrates, the fall, and finally the dissolution of the Turkish empire, are marked by the drying up of *waters.* The significancy of the figure is interpreted in another vision. The *waters* which thou sawest are *peoples, and multitudes, and nations, and tongues,* Rev. xviii. 15. The extinction or subversion of the empire of the Turks, would be like the drying up of a great river—the people like the waters.

From first to last prophecy needs no comment but the history which it prefigured, or plainly foretold. The year 1820 was distinguished by three revolutions in the Catholic kingdoms of Europe, a brief intermission of the vial of wrath; but the darkness did not pass away, and the misery soon returned, and neither have yet disappeared from the *kingdom of the beast.* But, the scene being changed, we may look from the west unto the east, to see whether the fifth vial *began* to be poured out on the empire of Turkey, at the time when some rays of hope first seemed to penetrate the gloom that rested on the Roman Catholic kingdoms of Europe. Though their place be different, there is no historical chasm left between the fifth vial and the sixth.

The *Ottoman empire, by a long and unwonted good fortune*, found itself, *at the commencement of the era* (or of 1820) *freed at once from foreign war and domestic rebellion.* This opportunity it was determined to employ against one who had long been considered rather as an enemy than a subject. Ali Pacha became master not only of the whole of Albania, but of Suli, the ancient Epirus, and of Livadia or Thessaly. His dominion reached from the Adriatic to the frontier of Macedonia, and comprised a population of nearly two millions of souls. Considerable, however, as it was, it could ill enable him to contend with *the whole force of the Turkish empire, now* (1820) *united against him.** Ali and his sons were successively defeated; but the death of the Turkish commander-in-chief "spread a general discouragement through the army. A Turkish force, composed chiefly of tumultuary militia, soon *melts away*, when it is not fed by success and plunder. In the beginning of December, Chourschid (the Turkish general) found his army so reduced by desertion, and so destitute of supplies and provisions, that he was obliged to retreat to Arta. Ali again came forth, and could again cherish the hope of retrieving his fortune."†

"It is certain, that *the rebellion of Ali Pacha determined, more than any known event, the period of* (the Greek) *insurrection;* as if that monstrous spawn of despotism had been reserved to make, before he perished, one involuntary atonement to liberty for the outrages which he had employed his long life in inflicting upon her. Let us examine the facts for one instant. In the summer of 1820, Ali

* Annual Register for 1820, Lond. p. 316. † Ibid. 317.

declared his independence; and in September, the siege of Yanina commenced; in October, the landers called in their merchant ships; in November, the Suliots returned to their country from the Ionioan islands, and *raised the standard of rebellion*, in alliance with their former persecutor, against the Sublime Porte; in February 1821, Hourshid Pacha arrived before Yanina, from the Morea, *leaving that country almost destitute of Turkish soldiers*. Shortly after his arrival various Greeks who were in the service of Ali Pacha, left Yanina, and returned to their homes, where they hoped very speedily to be more actively employed; and in the first days of the April following, the insurrection did, in fact, break out at Patras."*

"In 1821, Turkey presented a scene of continued disorder. The successful resistance of the Pacha of Albania had given encouragement to the enemies of the Turkish yoke to venture upon open hostilities; and in the beginning of March, (1821,) insurrections broke out in various provinces of the empire."† Theodore, a native of Bulgaria, at the head of 10,000 insurgents, raised the standard of revolt in Wallachia. The Boyars, or chiefs, fled before them. They entered Bucharest, the capital, and took entire possession of it; and the "appearance of Bucharest was that of a town delivered into the hands of a merciless enemy, and daily scenes of disorders and atrocities took place." Prince Ypsilanti revolted in Moldavia; and "the news of his insurrection excited general consternation." "The alarm was raised to a still greater height by the intelligence of the insurrection *which had broken out in every part of Greece*. The people of the Morea were in arms: their chiefs had formed themselves into the senate of Calamata;

* Waddington's Visit to Greece, Introd. pp. 7, 8.
† Ann. Register, A. D. 1821, Preface, p. 247.

Candia had refused the usual tribute; the islands of the Archipelago had thrown off the yoke, and were fitting out fleets to cruise against their tyrants. The government and populace of Constantinople exhibited the most violent exacerbation."*

"Moldavia and Wallachia were reduced; but the insurgent Greeks were more formidable than ever. So early as the month of May, the Greek fleet had the command of the Archipelago. In June their naval force was estimated at 250 vessels, which formed four squadrons. The war in the Morea was a series of bloody skirmishes. The Greeks rose successively on a multitude of different points; and the Turks, unable to keep the field against their opponents, defended themselves in their fortresses. Many of these were reduced, generally through famine. The revolt had spread far to the north. Thessaly, Ætolia, Acarnania, and Epirus, were in a state of insurrection."† A national congress was convoked at Epidaurus.

"In September 1821, two irruptions were made into the Turkish dominions by the Persian princes Mahomed Ali Mirza, and Abbas Mirza. The former penetrated into the province of Bagdad; the latter into that of Erzerum. This invasion, occurring at such a moment, might have given a mortal blow to the Ottoman power in Asia. This year, (1821,) may be regarded as the date of the final extinction of the Mamelukes."‡

The Prince Royal of Persia, towards the close of summer 1821, having "marched a strong body of troops into the province of Wan, a district situated on the eastern banks of the Euphrates, the invaders advanced as far as the town of Bayazid, a considerable station on the road from Tebriz to Constantin-

* Ann. Reg. pp. 247, 248. † Ibid. pp. 254, 255. ‡ Ibid. p. 256.

ople; their farther progress, however, was stopped by the cholera morbus, which made its appearance in the army. The prince royal crossed the frontier towards the end of July 1822, with an army of 30,000 men, and marched upon Erzerum." He completely defeated an army of 52,000 Turks who fled in disorder from the field. "The prince royal followed up his successes, and advanced within two days march of Arzerum, but the cholera morbus is said to have again broken out in his army, and in such a manner as effectually to arrest its further advance."* "On the 13th of the same month a physical calamity came to consummate the general disorder of the empire. Aleppo, the capital of Syria, and one of the finest and most populous cities of the empire, was visited by an earthquake, which instantly overthrew a great portion of the buildings, burying thousands of its inhabitants under the ruins—at the lowest computation not less than 14,000 individuals perished. The shock was felt more or less in all the towns of Syria. Antioch is represented as having suffered scarcely less than Aleppo."†

The massacre of Scio, in 1822, roused, in a tenfold degree, the sympathies of Europe. The fire ships of the Greeks scattered the fleets of the Ottomans. A Turkish army penetrated into the Morea, but having been harassed in their retreat, and assaulted incessantly by the Greeks, repeatedly defeated, with the loss in one conflict of 2500 left dead upon the field,"—"it is calculated that of 26,000 or 30,000 men who in June had entered the Morea, there scarcely remained 10,000 at the end of August."‡

"In 1823, the war between the Greeks and the Turks continued to rage with undiminished fury."

* Annual Register, 1822, pp. 270, 272. † Ibid. p. 284.
‡ Ibid. p. 282.

After the death of Ali, "the pachas who, under the sultan, commanded in Albania, were at the head of a considerable force; but that force, instead of being employed in the subjugation of the Morea, found more than sufficient employment in checking the insurgent beys of Albania." Another Turkish army, partly by defeat and desertion, "ceased completely to exist." And the Greeks, becoming the assailants, made predatory inroads along the coasts of Asia Minor.

The year 1824 was peculiarly signalized by the triumphs of the Greeks both by sea and land. They continued to harass the Turks in Thessaly; completely routed, with great courage, the seraskier of Roumelia; contended in daily encounters with the army of Dervish Pasha, till it was utterly defeated and nearly annihilated. "In the various naval engagements, first with the Turkish fleet and in detachments alone, and then with the combined Turkish and Egyptian armaments, the Greeks were universally and completely successful. In the engagements of 16th, 18th, 26th, and 30th September, the Turks are said to have lost twelve frigates, twenty brigs, and more than eighty transports."*

While Turkish armies, whose chief bond of union is the love of plunder, thus successively "melted away" before the bands of intrepid Greeks, the Ottoman empire was threatened with new dangers. "Both the populace and the janisaries in Constantinople were in a state of great fermentation. In February 1825, four ortas of janisaries in which signs of insubordination had appeared, received orders to proceed to Thessaly, and join the corps opposed to the Greeks; but they unanimously refused to march."† The sultan of Turkey called in the

* Annual Register, A. D. 1825, p. 184.
‡ Ibid. 1824, pp. 200, 207.

aid of the Pacha of Egypt to suppress the revolt of Greece. The campaign of Bonaparte, in the land of the Pharaohs, had broken the power of the unruly Mamelukes; and the troops of Gaul had, by dire experience of its power, taught the Egyptians the use of military discipline, as practised in the modern art of war. Order had hence begun to be established in the basest of kingdoms. The unhappy dissensions of the contentious Greeks, so soon as for a moment they were free of a foreign enemy, laid that land of liberty open to the ravages of the disciplined soldiers of Egypt, whom all their fiery energy, though renewed, could not drive from their coasts. But Europe could not bear to see Greece crushed again, so soon as it was free. The Turks had executed their charge; and had for ages realized the character of *woe* to Christendom. But to them "the beginning of the end" was come; and the "last end of the indignation" in progress of accomplishment. And, like an exhausted executioner, their strength failed them, till self-defence against an aggressor passed their power. A great change had come over the spirit of the time, since Paleologus in vain implored Christendom to make an effort to save the empire of the Greeks. The cry of that bleeding people now resounded through Europe. And whatever it was the purpose of a worldly policy to effect, or the mutual jealousies that may have given birth to the scheme, the desolation which was spread over Greece by ruthless barbarians, though disciplined troops, combined in her behalf the great powers of Europe, who guaranteed her independence in defiance of the sultan and all his vassals.

While the Grand Turk was thus ignominiously bearded, as Mussulmen are wont to term them, by "the Christian dogs," the contrast between the time when the period was completed in which the four angels of the Euphrates were prepared to slay the third part of men, and that during which the vial of the wrath of God was poured upon the great river Euphrates, and the waters thereof were dried up, is strikingly illustrated in the fate of the Janisaries. In the last and fatal assault, which closed the siege of Constantinople, they rose "fresh, vigorous, and invincible," and the last of the princes and nobles of the empire fell beneath their scimitars. But the *sword* that was given to Mahomet and his successors *was* now no longer the weapon by which peace was to be taken from the earth. And the sultan sought in vain to "force on them a new system of discipline."* They revolted and rebelled, pillaged the palaces of the Porte, and committed the most frightful excesses throughout Constantinople. The *Sandschack Sherif*, or sacred banner of the prophet, which had not been displayed for half a century, was brought forth against them. And the faithful Moslems rallied around it. Sixty thousand men "surrounded the Etmedian, (15th July 1826), where the Janisaries were all tumultuously assembled in a dense crowd, and having no apprehension of such a measure; and the first intimation many of them had of their situation, was a murderous discharge of grapeshot from the cannon of the Topghees (artillerymen). Vast numbers were killed on the spot, and the survivors retired to their kislas, or barracks, which were close by: here they shut themselves up; and in order to dislodge them it was necessary to set the kislas on fire, as they refused all terms of surrender. The flames were soon seen from Pera, bursting out in different places; and that none might escape, the barracks were surrounded, like the Etmedian, with cannon, and the discharges continued

* *Turkey*, Brewst. Encyc. vol. xviii. p. 688.

without intermission. It is not possible, perhaps, to conceive any situation more horrible than that in which the Janisaries now found themselves; the houses in flames over their heads, and the walls battered down about them, torn to pieces with grape-shot, and overwhelmed with ruin and burning fragments. As it was determined to exterminate them utterly, no quarter was any longer offered or given, and the conflagration and discharge of artillery continued for the remainder of the day. At length, however, opposition ceased, when there was no longer any thing left alive to make it. The fire slackened and silenced, the flames were extinguished of themselves; and the next morning presented a frightful scene—burning ruins slaked in blood—a huge mass of mangled flesh and smoky ashes."* "The contests carried off, it is supposed, on both sides, about 30,000 persons."† "Every janissary taken in arms, or who was suspected of being concerned in the revolt, was strangled on the spot; and others less culpable were banished to Asia."‡ The order of the janisaries was abolished. In "the great fire of Constantinople," in the next month, six thousand houses in the most wealthy and magnificient part of the city were destroyed.§

The battle of Navarino was fought in 1827. "It continued with unabated fury during four hours. At the end of that period, the Turkish and Egyptian fleets had disappeared; the bay of Navarino was covered with their wrecks. The carnage on board the crowded ships of the enemy was destructive. In two of their ships of the line alone, two-thirds of their crews were killed or wounded."‖ The combination

* Walsh's Narrative of a Journey from Constantinople, pp. 88, 89.
† Ibid. p. 222.
‡ *Turkey*, Brewster's Encyclop. ib. p. 688.
§ Ibid.
‖ Ann. Reg. 1827, p. 318.

was as new and strange as the event was "untoward," by which British and French ships of war were allied with Russian, in destroying the naval power of the Turks. The battte of Navarino was "an event unexampled in the history of nations." And the unwonted league of France and England, to the formation of which jealousy of Russia may have somewhat conspired, was, by a remarkable fatality, the death-blow of the Turkish navy, and by giving the the command of the Euxine to the Russians, led to a new series of calamities to the Ottomans.

While the policy of Europe was directed to stay the threatened war, the sultan, by an act which "cut short all intermission," gave new proof to the truth of the proverb, with illustrations of which history is full, and Bonaparte is an example,—quem Deus vult perdere prius dementat—God first deprives of reason the man whom he has devoted to destruction. To call forth the fanatical fury of the Moslem population, as if to see whether Islamism had still the spirit or the fate to conquer, or was doomed to triumph or to fail in a war professedly religious, the sultan issued a despatch by the reis effendi, to all the pashas of the provinces, in which he avowed that his pretended negotiations with Russia "had been only devices to delay actual hostilities, till he should be able to sustain them," and that from the beginning "every thing announced that the answer to the proposition of the Franks would at last have to be given by the *sabre* alone."*

Russia declared war against Turkey on the 26th of April 1828. A Russian army, under Paskewitch, after having defeated the Persians and enforced peace, was in readiness on the *eastern* frontier of Turkey to invade its territories. Immediately on

---

* Ann. Reg. 1828, p. 222.

the declaration of war, "the sultan was attacked in his Asiatic pachalics; a Turkish army was put to flight; four entrenched camps were attacked, and taken possession of; the fortress of Achakalaki was reduced and occupied; and the conquerors took the city of Achalzik itself by storm, after an assault of thirteen hours, in the course of which the garrison of four thousand men were put to the sword. Paskewitch next overran, with little opposition, the pachalic of Bajazet, (Bayazid,) and was preparing to march against Erzerum, in the end of October, when the approach of winter put an end to the campaign."*

On the north, Turkey was invaded by a Russian "army of an hundred and fifteen thousand men."† The Turks fought with their ancient fury, as if they still had been prepared to slay. After desperate and long-continued sieges, Brailow was taken, and Varna surrendered. Other fortresses along the coast of the Euxine were yielded up to the Russians, and while their partial disasters led to new exertions, a way was prepared for the more splendid successes of the following year.

In 1829, the power of the Turkish empire was broken, though the empire itself was preserved. Literally and historically, without reference to prophecy, it might be said that "tidings out of the east and out of the north troubled" the Porte. On the east two Turkish armies were successively defeated; and Erzerum, the capital of Anatolia, fell into the hands of the invaders. And scarcely were these conquests won, when, after the fall of Silistria and of "the ports of the Euxine one after another" and the defeat of the grand visier, the Balkan was passed, and the head-quarters of the

* Ann. Reg. 1828, p. 222. † Ibid. p. 242.

Russians were soon in the city of Adrianople. "Experience was thus teaching the Turkish government in every direction, that it was involved in a struggle, in which continued resistance would only render ultimate ruin more inevitable and decisive."* "When the *Ottoman government* learned that the Balkan had been passed—that the Russian army was hurrying on from victory to victory, and that no force existed to bar their march to Constantinople, the true situation of their affairs was revealed to them. *The capital was in consternation.*"† The banner of the prophet, which had wrought the destruction of the janisaries, was unfurled in vain. And the sublime porte submitted to the terms of peace dictated by the Russian commander.

The sultan, ere the contest began, called forth the Turks to the defence of their faith, and proclaimed a religious war which was to decide the fate of Mahometanism. But it was destined to fall *without hand,* and the Russians did not destroy it, or subvert the empire of the Ottomans. Consternation had indeed seized the Turkish government, from simultaneous tidings out of the east and out of the north. But as, in "the fatal moment," Constantinople had been saved, when assaulted by the Turks, when the time of their *preparation* to slay was not complete, so in the moment of conquest and triumph, the progress of the armies of Russia was stayed at the very time when the empire of Turkey, in Asia and Europe, seemed to be prostrated before them. And although the conquest of Constantinople had long been accounted the main object of the policy of the Czars, it fell not by foreign foes.

From the testimony of a British officer who was

* Ann. Reg. 1829, p. 217. † Ibid. p. 218.

present on the scene, who "had arrived from England to join the army in the field and to see the operations of the campaign," and who had access to the tent and table of Marshal Diebitch, the Russian commander-in-chief, the true state of the Russian army at the close of their conquests, and after the taking of Adrianople, is illustrated by direct evidence.

"In the beginning of October (1829) there were only eight thousand effective men with the headquarters; for of the thirty thousand to the south of the Balkan, at least nine thousand were sick, and dying with plague and fever. The supposed loss this year was one hundred thousand men, and last year more, principally during the siege of Varna, and the disastrous retreat of Silistria. Thirteen thousand men kept up the communication between the coast, the Balkan and head-quarters, and chains of posts were judiciously established from the blockading army before Schumla, to guard against surprise from that quarter. However, the pacha of Scutari, from his head-quarters at Philippopolis, gave some trouble, and attacked the Russian foraging parties."* "As the pacha of Scutari continually threatened to attack, with his whole force, the Russian head-quarters, it was thought advisable to call in from the advanced posts at Kirklissi, &c., the division of Count Pahlen."†

Peace was preferable, even by the victors, thus circumstanced, to a prolongation of the war. The Russians, with the exception of part of an Asiatic province, agreed to abandon all their conquests. But liberty from the Turkish yoke was secured, by the temporary occupation of the Russian troops, to

---

* Captain Alexander's *Travels to the Seat of War in the East*, p. 127.
† Ibid. p. 129.

the principalities of Moldavia and Wallachia, inhabited by Christians of the Greek Church, and not a Turk was to be permitted to reside to the north of the Danube. The liberty and independence of Servia was also secured; and the region inhabited by Franks in the European dominions of Turkey, Greece being already free, having thus been released from the despotism of the sultan, the great body of the Turkish empire, over which Mahometanism prevails, was left to its destined or predicted fate. The pacha of Scutari, who hung on the rear of the Russian army, and whose threatened attacks induced the invaders to call in their advanced posts, soon after raised the standard of rebellion, and it remained to be seen in what other manner the *waters of the Euphrates* should continue to be *dried up*, or whether the time was come that the second woe should terminate and pass away like the first, by mutual destruction, and the Turks, like the Saracens, should kill each other.

In 1729, an army of 40,000 French landed on the African coast, defeated an equal numerical force of Turks and Arabs, took Algiers, converted a province of Turkey into a colony of France, and thus dried up one of the sources of the Turkish power.

But internal dissension soon succeeded to external war, to hasten, as it would seem, the ruin of Islamism. Reform is ill adapted to support a system of imposture, such as that of Mahometanism, even as it is also incompatible with the pretended infallibility of the Romish church. The changes introduced by the sultan were abhorrent to the feelings of the fanatical Turks, and prejudicial to the interests of the despotic pachas. And when the victories of the Russians had lessened the terrors of the bow-string, and the charm of the grand Seignor's power was broken, and Greece had set the example of freedom, revolt succeeded to revolt, and spread from one extremity of Turkey to the other. Since the termination of the Russian war, the Turkish empire, so prodigal in the gifts of nature, has been a scene in which incessant civil warfare has been conjoined with the ravages of the pestilence in completing the depopulation of the richest portion of the globe. No sooner has any partial revolt been suppressed, than another has burst forth with redoubled violence. Authentic accounts are not to be obtained from such a region. But little or nothing has been heard of from any of the provinces of Turkey but tidings of bloodshed and misery.

The commotions of Turkey began, after a season of unusual peace, by the suppression of Ali Pacha. Albania would not rise at his call, and he fell a victim to the wrath of the sultan, after Greece had arisen to be free. But when the Porte was seen to be but a power which enemies could overawe and subjects defy, Albania, joined by the western provinces of the empire, strove to assert its freedom, and a general insurrection seems to have ensued. Armies of insurgents, of whom the Pacha of Scutari was the chief, were combined against the sultan, and proclaimed the restoration of the Janisaries and of the old order of government, and the abolition of the new. Constantinople itself, it has been said, was threatened. And the revolt could be suppressed only by blood. The narrative of the war, furnished chiefly by the French and German newspapers, is too contradictory and indefinite to admit of detail. Albania was reduced to submission. But Bosnia, it would appear is still in open insurrection against the Porte. In Asia, as in Europe, revolt has been recently the order of the day. The pachas of Van and of Bagdad, on the Euphrates and Tigris, openly rebelled against the sultan; and now the pacha of

Egypt, after having by his ill-fated obedience called the great powers of Europe to the liberation of Greece, seems to divide with his former sovereign the remaining strength of the empire.

Of the *drying up of the waters of the Euphrates*, or of the great and rapid depopulation of Turkey, and of the great miseries and mortality of which it is now the scene, imperfect and very incomplete as are the records, there is yet appalling and unquestionable proof.

"The circumstance," (says Mr. Walsh, who arrived at Constantinople in 1821, and remained several years in the suite of Lord Strangford, the British ambassador,)—"*most striking* to a traveller passing through Turkey, is its *depopulation*. Ruins where villages had been built, and fallows where land had been cultivated, are frequently seen with no living thing near them. This effect is not so visible in larger towns, though the cause is known to operate there in a still greater degree. Within the last twenty years Constantinople has lost more than half its population. Two conflagrations happened while I was in Constantinople, and destroyed fifteen thousand houses. The Russian and Greek wars were a CONSTANT DRAIN on the Janisaries of the capital; the silent operation of the plague is continually active, though not always alarming;—it will be considered no exaggeration to say, that within the period mentioned, from three to four hundred thousand persons have been prematurely swept away in one city in Europe by causes which *were* not operating in any other,—conflagration, pestilence, and civil commotion. The Turks though naturally of a robust and vigorous constitution, addict themselves to such habits as are very unfavourable to population—the births do little more than exceed the ordinary deaths, and cannot supply the waste of casualties. The surrounding country is therefore *constantly drained* to supply this waste in the capital, which nevertheless exhibits districts *nearly depopulated.* If we suppose that these causes operate more or less in every part of the *Turkish empire,* it will not be too much to say, that there is *more* of human life *wasted,* and less supplied, than in *any other country.* We see *every day,* life going out in the fairest portion of Europe; and the *human race threatened with extinction,* in a soil and climate capable of supporting the most abundant population."*

"The Ottoman empire, by a *long* and unwonted good fortune, found itself freed at once from foreign wars and domestic rebellion." But we have seen how since that period a *vial of wrath* has been poured upon it, without any mitigation of calamities or interval of repose. But almost coincident with the commencement of these troubles and commotions, and partly operating in conjunction with them, a new power of destruction, more destructive and depopulating than them all, arose on the opposite extremity of the empire, as the Turkish armies began to melt away before the revived energies of the Greeks. In 1821, the cholera broke out at Bassora, which is situted at the head of the Persian Gulph, on the river Euphrates. "The disease lasted fourteen days in this city—which is the great market of Asiatic produce destined for the Ottoman empire—in which time it carried off from 15,000 to 18,000 persons, or nearly one-fourth of the inhabitants. From Bassora it was carried by the boats navigating the Tigris as far as Bagdad, and there it destroyed *one-third of the population.* From Bagdad the cholera ascended the Euphrates as far as the town of Annah, on the borders of the desert which separates Syria from Arabia. The disease died away at the approach of the winter

---

* Walsh's Narrative, pp. 22—24.

1821. In the spring of 1822, it broke out suddenly in the neighbourhood of the Tigris and Euphrates, and now threatened the Syrian territories fram another quarter. In seven months the cholera had extended its ravages from Caramania to Judea," &c.*

The ravages of the plague have succeeded along the Euphrates in the Turkish dominions, to those of the cholera. And the accounts, while more minute, are not less appalling. And in lieu of other or historical evidence, we may quote from that which the newspaper press presents openly to our view, and also from the testimony of an eye-witness of the dire and frightful desolation.

"In the short space of eight weeks, nearly 50,000 of the inhabitants of Bagdad have perished by the plague. The commission of the *destroying angel* has been awfully severe. To the horrors of disease were added the desolation of a flood, and the consequent impossibility of escape. Silently and in darkness did the pestilence walk through this deserted city, undisturbed in the work of death, daily dismissing thousands to their last account, and leaving the wretched survivors mourning over the loss of those with whose life their enjoyments and their hopes of happiness were enwrapped. The streets were no longer the scene of busy traffic, and were only disturbed by the passing funeral, or by the piteous cries of infants, or of children who were left destitute without home, parents, or friends.

"*Bagdad. Dreadful depopulation.* Mr. Kitto, who was for some time at Malta under the Church Missionary Society, but accompanied Mr. Groves to Bagdad, has sent home most affecting details of the ravages to which that devoted city has been subjected. The PLAGUE prevailing to a fearful extent among the inhabitants, part of them attempted to escape into the country, but were arrested by a sudden INUNDATION of the Tigris, by which numbers perished, and the rest were driven back into the city. Thousands were falling under the deadly influence of the pestilence, when the water made a breach in the walls, and swept away many of the habitations. The wretched inhabitants were crowded together, and compelled to take refuge even in houses left desolate by the plague. When, at length, it pleased God to stay the hand of the *destroying angel*, it was found that out of 80,000 human beings, not more than 25,000 survived! But the SWORD followed quickly in

---

* Quarterly Review, No. 91, pp. 178, 179, 196. Caledonian Mercury, 13th October 1831.

the rear of these desolating judgments. The plague had scarcely ceased, and the waters subsided, when troops arrived in the name of the sultan, to depose the pacha: fierce and bloody contests succeeded before a temporary calm was restored."*

The testimony of another witness bears the same melancholy record.

"Bagdad, April 22, 1831. Surely every principle of dissolution is operating in the midst of the Ottoman and Persian empires—plagues, earthquakes, and civil wars.—The pacha's palace is left open without a soul to take care of any thing: his stud of beautiful Arab horses are running about the streets. May 5—Inquire what you will, the answer is, 'The city is desolate.' The son of one Mollah told me to-day, that in the quarter where he lives no one is left; they are all dead. At Hillah, the modern Babylon, (population 10,000,) there is, Seyd Ibrahim told me to-day, scarcely a soul left; and the dogs and wild beasts alone are there feeding on dead bodies."†

"After the ravages of the plague had ceased, Bagdad was entered sword in hand, and carried by storm by the sultan's troops."‡

The chief seats or reputed holy cities of Mahometanism, did not escape. The Bombay Gazette (10th August 1831) has the following paragraph. "We have heard with the utmost dismay and sorrow, that Mecca, Medina, and Jidda have been *completely depopulated* by a dreadful disease, the nature of which is not yet known. Fifty thousand persons have been carried off by it, among whom we may mention the governor of Mecca. It broke out at the beginning of May, when all the pilgrims had collected at Mecca, in consequence, it is supposed, of the want of water. The government here have most prudently, while such an uncertainty exists as to the nature of the disease, ordered all vessels from those parts to be placed in quarantine."

Asia Minor and Egypt have also been visited by a depopulating pestilence. In Alexandria, Cairo,

* Missionary Register, London, November 1831, p. 512.
† Ibid. January 1831, pp. 55, 56.
‡ The Courier, 28th November 1831.

and Smyrna, hundreds died of the cholera every day. And although the accounts vary in detail, all denote a terrible mortality. Earthquakes, floods, pestilences, have been added to wars and internal commotions, such as might shake the stability of the firmest government—if any were verily stable in these days of general pestilence and peril: but least of all does the empire of Turkey seem competent or fated to withstand such shocks, and to survive much longer such accumulated calamities. Yet the question now is, whether there be facts enough indicative of decay, disorganization, and death, which shew that since the boding calm that preceded the year 1820, while the last plagues are coming on the earth and in the course of fulfilment, the vial of wrath has already left tokens that it has began to be poured upon the great river Euphrates. There is, we apprehend, many a sign to shew; and many a sign to be still seen. And having been brought to this point by the whole course of antecedent events, as historically recorded, we would now draw the conclusion, as we have endeavoured to establish the premises, in other and better words than our own.

"The gradual wasting of the strength of the Ottoman empire is strikingly foretold in Scripture, under the emblem of *the drying up of the great river Euphrates, that the way of the kings of the east may be prepared.* No prophecy could be in a course of more striking fulfilment; and as simultaneously with the accomplishment of this prediction, the 'marks' of the last days are becoming daily more strongly impressed on the men, and opinions and events of the present generation, it peculiarly becomes the church to be standing on her watch-tower, looking with interest, sobriety, faith, and hope, on the things which the Lord is bringing on the earth."*

---

* Record.

It has been the single object of the writer throughout the preceding pages to trace the accordance between history and prophecy through past ages to the present day, that, *in this respect*, the signs of these times may be seen. It is not his purpose here to point to "other marks of the last days," or to look to the signs of other times, beyond those which history has brought already into view. But that such "marks" are daily impressed upon the events of the present generation, the renewed signs may perhaps be already rising into view. We have seen the river Euphrates flowing from its sources in the mountains, and *overflowing many countries*, till at last it has begun to be dried up. The drying of its waters is preparatory for the way of the kings of the east. They have not yet passed over its channel, which is still drying up; but if by the kings of the east, the Jews or Israelites be designed, some sign may be seen that the *preparation* of their way is begun.

The angel, in revealing the last vision of Daniel, thus announced its purpose. "I am come to make thee understand what shall befall *thy people in the latter days*." And comparing things spiritual with spiritual, we read in reference to the fall of the empire of the grand seignior, of which Judea forms part,—*And tidings out of the east and out of the north shall trouble him: and he shall go forth with great fury to destroy, and utterly to make away many. And he shall plant the tabernacles of his palaces* (or the tents of his camp, or pavilion) *between the seas in the glorious holy mountain; yet he shall come to his end, and none shall help him. And at that time shall Michael stand up, the great prince which standeth for the* CHILDREN OF THY PEOPLE; *and there shall be a time of trouble, such as never was since there was a nation, even to that same time:*

and at that time THY PEOPLE SHALL BE DELIVERED, *every one that shall be found written in the book.*

The event cannot yet be determined; nor is the *mode* of the fulfilment of the prophecy a matter of revelation; in its appointed time once fully come, it will then speak and not lie: and all, perhaps, that can yet be seen, if even that be discernible by our feeble sight, is some sign of the declared process of preparation. It is at least worthy of remark and observation, that while perfect religious freedom has been bequeathed to the numerous Jews in the territory of Algiers by the conquest of the French, while they now are there governed by rulers of their own choice and of their own nation, a new thing for many ages to their race, and while the kingdoms of Europe have gradually been relaxing, and in repeated instances wholly abrogating, the severe penal laws long enacted and enforced throughout Christendom against them, the very Turks have changed their tone from that of persecutor to protector of the outcast children of Abraham, the sultan has proclaimed their religious toleration and liberty, and the son of the pacha of Egypt, who holds *Judea* in immediate possession, has abolished every restriction against their free entrance into Jerusalem. These at least are signs of the times, in conjunct reference to the gradual wasting of the strength and depopulation of the Ottoman empire, and to the laws of Christians and Turks in reference to the Jews, such as never before have been seen. The decree of religious toleration issued by the Porte, and the subjoined firman of the governor of Dgiddah (Jiddah) may yet have their place in a historical commentary on the text which seals the doom of the Turkish empire, and perhaps betokens the consequent restoration of the Israelites to the land of their fathers. Without the aid of any speculation, it may yet be reserved for themselves to prove their claim to the title of *kings of the east*. God will do his work, his strange work, and bring to pass his act, his strange act. If the commencement be strange, what may not the conclusion be? We give the quotation fully, as it here comes timely to our hand.

"JERUSALEM REFORMED.—And by a Turk! In the month of February, Ibrahim Pacha, the governor of Dgiddah, addressed the following firman to the mollah, the sheikh, and the other magistrates of Jerusalem:—'Jerusalem contains temples and monuments which Christians and Jews come from the most distant countries to visit. But these numerous pilgrims have to complain of the enormous duties levied upon them on the road. Being desirous of putting an end to so crying an abuse, we order all the Mussulmans of the pashaliks of the Saide, and of the districts of Jerusalem, Tripoli, &c. to suppress all duties or imposts of that nature, on all the roads, and at all the stations, without exception. We also order, that the priests who live in the buildings belonging to the churches in which the gospel is read, and who officiate according to the ceremonies of their religion, be no longer compelled to pay the arbitrary contributions which have been hitherto imposed upon them.'"*

It would seem, from many words of prophecy, that the kingdoms of the earth must yet pass through the fiery ordeal of national judgments, before it can be fully written, JERUSALEM REFORMED. Of Zion the Lord saith—Behold I have graven thee on the palms of my hands; thy walls are continually before me. Thy children shall make haste; thy destroyers and they that made thee waste shall go forth of thee, &c. Isa. xlix. 15, 16. Mahomet, or Mahometanism,

* Extracted from the Caledonian Mercury, 7th May 1832.

as symbolised by the little horn of the he-goat, magnified himself even to the prince of the host, and the PLACE OF THE SANCTUARY *was cast down. And an host was given him against the daily sacrifice by reason of transgression, and it cast down the truth to the ground; and it practised and prospered. Then I heard one saint speaking, and another saint said unto that certain saint which spake,* HOW LONG *shall be the vision concerning the daily sacrifice, and the transgression of desolation, to give both the* SANCTUARY *and the host to be trodden under foot? And he said unto me, Unto* TWO THOUSAND THREE HUNDRED DAYS; *then shall the sanctuary be* CLEANSED, Dan. viii. 11, 14. The first event which is expressly specified and defined in the things noted in the scripture of truth is the fact that the *fourth king* of Persia, after the days of the prophet, *by his strength through his riches stirred up all against the realm of Grecia*, Dan. xi. 2. Xerxes *began* his march from Asia in the year 481 before the Christian era, and in the following year he entered Greece and passed Thermopylæ, August, 480. And having seen how the intermediate history was all developed in the words of Daniel and the revelation of Jesus Christ, till we have come down to the period that the extinction of the Turkish power seems manifestly in progress, till Mahometanism is falling without hand, and Mahometans, no longer a woe to Christendom, killing one another, till the free exercise of the Christian religion is proclaimed in Jerusalem, and the way of the Jews open without penalty or restraint to Jerusalem again, and the sultan has issued the decree of equal toleration to every faith, and the Turkish empire so depopulated that we need not to wait till the great river Euphrates shall *begin* to be dried up, may we not look again to the times and the seasons that are passed, and see whether the period may not be commenced for the cleansing of the sanctuary as well as of the sitting of the judgment? We have seen how, after a time of previous repose, uninterrupted and accumulating calamities have beset the Turkish empire, "melted away" its armies, "drained" its population, and depopulated its cities, since the year 1820. And now it can cost the reader but a glance to mark the measure of the period down to that year from the invasion of Greece by Xerxes,

480*
1820

2300 years.

After great part of this treatise was written, it was the author's strong conviction, that the time was not yet come when the prophetic periods 1260, 1290, and 2300 years could be ascertained. That conviction, however, has almost, if not altogether, given way, before the obvious analogies which history presents in regard to times now *past*. And he would now submit to the judgment of the reader which decision is the more rational, that the following striking coincidences are or are not accidental.

After, from the time of the Reformation, the seven thunders had uttered their voices, the angel

* If the year 481, before Christ, in which Xerxes began his march towards Greece, be adopted as the period of the commencement of the 2300 years, they would have expired in the year 1819, thirty years after the beginning of the French Revolution. That the full period of two thousand three hundred years was to be *completed* before the sanctuary should begin to be cleansed, seems to be implied in the prediction. "How long shall be the vision concerning the daily sacrifice, and the transgression of desolation, to give both the sanctuary and the host to be trodden under foot? And he said unto me, Unto two thousand and three hundred days; THEN *shall the sanctuary be cleansed.*" Dan. viii. 13, 14.

lift up his hand to heaven and sware that *time*, or delay, would be no longer, and that the mystery of God should be finished. And the last of the seven thunders was the immediate prelude to the French revolution, the first of the last plagues, or the noisome and grievous sore that fell upon the men which had the mark of the beast, when the judgments of God were made manifest.

Identified with the same period by the same act, or the oath of the angel, or more than an angel, a time, times, and half a time was the measure of the period to the end of these wonders. The time, times, and a half are also identified with the thousand two hundred and sixty years, during which the witnesses testified, clothed in sackcloth, the church was fed in the wilderness, and the papacy wore out the saints of the Most High, and thought to change times and laws; after which the judgment was to sit, to take away his dominion, and consume and destroy it unto the end. And from the time that persecution was authoritatively established in the church, and the times and laws given into the hands of the pope, and his spiritual supremacy fully sanctioned and enforced by the emperor Justinian—from 529 to 533—twelve hundred and sixty years intervened until the beginning and completion of the French Revolution 1789—1793, which moulded the times and laws after another fashion than papal domination, and speedily disannulled the Code of Justinian.

In the year 1790, the first after the twelve hundred and sixty years were *completed*, the religion of the church of Rome "*no longer*" (*that* time should be *no longer*) "interested the national legislators of France. A civil institution was framed for the clergy, declaring them *totally independent* of the *see of Rome*," (see, as above, p. 448) and four thousand five hundred religious houses were suppressed.

And from that time *thirty* years elapsed from the pouring out of the first to the pouring out of the sixth vial, or from the sitting of the judgment to the cleansing of the sanctuary, being the measure of the difference between the 1260 and the 1290 years, and the completion of the full period of 2300 years from the invasion of Greece by Xerxes, the first specified event in the vision, to the drying up of the great river Euphrates, denoting the dissolution of the Turkish empire.

Whether these seeming coincidences, prophetic and historical, give full warrant for determining that the cleansing of the sanctuary, at the close of the 2300 years, and the termination of the 1290 years, are coincident with the pouring out of the sixth vial, the writer dares not venture to assert. A farther period of 1335 days, or years, is spoken of in the close of the prophecies of Daniel, and of that period when completed, as if on very purpose to quash any premature or presumptuous speculation, it is only said in general terms, but of which the blissful significancy will be none the less, Blessed is he that waiteth, and cometh to the thousand three hundred and five and thirty days. Till that period, or the full and final developement of the whole scheme of prophecy, the times and the seasons may not be perfectly seen in all their due relations and proportions, even till these shall be fully completed, and providential and prophetic histories shall at last bear witness, that the word of God, in the history of man as well as in the creation of the world, is perfect work.

Having, in the preceeding pages, attempted to trace the fulfilment of historical predictions from the Babylonish captivity to the present time, and having reached the period of the pouring out of the sixth vial, or of the drying up of the waters of the great river Euphrates, that the way of the kings of the east may be prepared, we here pause, on the completion of our purposed task, and can only ask the reader to look into the scriptures, and to see, as new events arise, what the Lord is doing on the earth, and how, through the greatness of his power, his enemies shall be constrained to submit themselves to Him. But surely we may take up the words of Daniel and Nebuchadnezzar, and say, "Blessed be the name of God for ever and ever; for wisdom and might are his: and he changeth the times and the seasons: he removeth kings and setteth up kings: he giveth wisdom to the wise, and knowledge to them that know understanding: He reveals the deep and secret things: He knoweth what is in the darkness, and the light dwelleth with him.—How terrible are his signs! and how mighty are his wonders! His kingdom is an everlasting kingdom, and His dominion is from generation to generation."

There is not a flower of the field, nor a star in the firmament, but what displays, by their beauty and structure, the wisdom and the power of God, who hath clothed the lily, and garnished the heavens. He is to be glorified throughout all his works. And even the wrath of man, though it worketh not the righteousness of God, shall be made to praise him. The whole of history is an illustration of his word. And kings and conquerors may be said to wear their crowns for a season, to cast them all at last at the feet of Jesus; and, though they denied the fealty, to testify from generation to generation the dominion of him to whom all power is given in heaven and in earth.

Under the sixth vial it is said, and the warning is given before the seventh angel pours out his vial into the air. *Behold I come as a thief. Blessed is he that watcheth and keepeth his garments, lest he walk naked, and they see his shame.* "I will stand," said the prophet, "upon my "*watch*, and set me upon the tower, and will watch to see what he will say unto me, and what I shall answer when I am reproved. And the Lord answered me and said, Write the vision, and make it plain upon tables, that he may run that readeth it. For the vision is yet for an appointed time, but at the *end*, it shall *speak* and *not lie*: though it tarry, wait for it; because it will surely come, it will not tarry. Behold, his soul which is lifted up is not upright in him: but the just shall live by faith," Hab. ii. 1–4. It is at the *end* that the vision speaks; and then it is seen that it does not lie. The providence of God alone can determine the mode of its fulfilment. And it is, to the last, his *strange work* that the Lord shall do. Farther than what is written in his word nothing can be said—and it still may be questionable whether the *order* of what is written there be yet so plain that he may run that readeth it.

The downfall of the Turkish empire, and of the papal power, the restoration of the Jews, accompanied by a time of universal and unparalleled commotions, the conversion of Israel, the universal diffusion of the light of the gospel, the establishment of the reign of righteousness, followed at last by peace upon the earth, seem to be truths so plainly written on the table of prophecy, that they who look on it with an unjaundiced eye cannot but see them clearly, even though running while they read.

But it ever behoves us to remember that secret things belong unto the Lord, and that his ways are not as our ways. In regard to symbolical predictions, no professed theologian, we think, can cope with the unconscious historian in the interpretation of the *past*. And, after having waited for three centuries subsequently to the conclusion of them all, till Gibbon *fully* expounded the significancy of the first six trumpets, and also for the same long period, till, if such even yet be the proper appellation, the name of the *angel of the reformation* was known, it would scarcely be a demonstration of bringing into captivity every thought to the obedience of Christ, were our souls to be lifted up in high speculation or bold dogmatizing concerning visions yet unexpounded by events, or were we to maintain that any peculiar *mode* of interpretation should be held a matter of faith, as to what shall be—or what shall not be—when at the *end* the vision shall *speak* and *not lie*, and refute all the fallacies that marred its form, and perhaps, at best could but mimic its effect.

In regard to the *order* or course of the fulfilment of predictions yet to be accomplished, respecting which the terms *I come quickly* augur not long delay, or comparing scripture with scripture, it may perhaps appear, from the similarity of the description as well as congruity of the time, each being unparalleled and each completing the respective vision, that the pouring out of the seventh vial, and the battle of Armageddon, to the preparation of which it is subsequent, the sounding of the seventh trumpet, the treading down of the wine-press, and the opening of the sixth vial, are all co-temporaneous. The connexion also may perhaps be established, between the pouring out of the sixth vial and succeeding visions, which succeeding events have yet to interpret.

And the sixth angel poured out his vial upon the great river Euphrates; and the water thereof was dried up, that the way of the kings of the east might be prepared. And I saw three unclean spirits like frogs come out of the mouth of the dragon, and out of the mouth of the beast, and out of the mouth of the false prophet. For they are the spirits of devils, working miracles, which go forth unto the kings of the earth, and of the whole world, to gather them to the battle of that great day of God Almighty. Behold I come as a thief. Blessed is he that watcheth, and keepeth his garments, lest he walk naked, and they see his shame. And he gathered them together into a place called in the Hebrew tongue Armageddon. And the seventh angel poured out his vial into the air; and there came a great voice out of the temple of heaven, from the throne, saying, It is done. And there were voices, and thunders, and lightnings; and there was a great earthquake, such as was not since men were upon the earth, so mighty an earthquake, and so great. And the great city was divided into three parts, and the cities of the nations fell; and great Babylon came in remembrance before God, to give unto her the cup of the wine of the fierceness of his wrath. And every island fled away, and the mountains were not found. And there fell upon men a great hail out of heaven, every stone about the weight of a talent: and men blasphemed God, because of the plague of the hail: for the plague thereof was exceeding great. Rev. xiv. 12.

After a description of the death and resurrection of the witnesses, it is added—

The second woe is past; and, behold, the third woe cometh quickly. And the seventh angel sounded; and there were great voices in heaven, saying, The kingdoms of this world are become the kingdoms of our Lord, and of his Christ; and he shall reign for ever and ever. And the four-and-twenty elders, which sat before God on their seats, fell upon their faces, and worshipped God, saying, We give thee thanks, O Lord God Almighty, which art, and wast, and art to come; because thou hast taken to thee thy great power, and hast reigned. And the nations were angry, and thy wrath is come, and the time of the dead, that they should be judged, and that thou shouldst give reward unto thy servants the prophets, and to the saints, and them that fear thy name, small and great; and should destroy them which destroy the earth. And the temple of God was opened in heaven, and there was seen in his temple the ark of his testament: and there were lightnings, and voices, and thunderings, and an earthquake and great hail. Rev. xi. 14.

And the angel thrust in his sickle into the earth, and gathered the vine of the earth, and cast it into the great wine-press of the wrath of God. And the wine-press was trodden without the city, and blood came out of the wine-press, even unto the horse bridles, by the space of a thousand and six hundred furlongs. Rev. xiv. 19.

And I beheld, when he had opened the sixth seal, and, lo, there was a great earthquake: and the sun became black as sackcloth of hair, and the moon became as blood: and the stars of heaven fell unto the earth, even as a fig-tree casteth her untimely figs, when she is shaken of a mighty wind: And the heaven departed as a scroll when it is rolled together: and every mountain and island were removed out of their places. And the kings of the earth, and the great men, and the rich men, and the chief captains, and the mighty men, and every bond man, and every free man, hid themselves in the dens, and in the rocks of the mountains: and said to the mountains and rocks, Fall on us, and hide us from the face of him that sitteth on the throne, and from the wrath of the Lamb: For the great day of his wrath is come, and who shall be able to stand? Rev. xi. 12—17.

There seems, however, according to the spirit of prophecy, to be a marked order of events between the pouring out of the sixth, and this consummation of the seventh vial. In immediate connexion with the opening of the sixth trumpet, it is recorded, as previously alluded to, p. 216, that the final judgment was first to be suspended till the servants of God should be sealed in their foreheads.

And after these things I saw four angels standing on the four corners of the earth, holding the four winds of the earth, that the wind should not blow on the earth, nor on the sea, nor on any tree. And

I saw another angel ascending from the east, having the seal of the living God: and he cried with a loud voice to the four angels, to whom it was given to hurt the earth and the sea, saying, hurt not the earth, neither the sea, nor the trees, till we have*

---

* God maketh his angels spirits, and his ministers a flame of fire. In his infinite wisdom and power he executeth judgment and justice on the earth, by means inscrutable to mortals. In his judgments against the Egyptians, (Ps. lxxviii. 49, 45.) "He cast upon them the fierceness of his anger, wrath, and indignation, and trouble, by sending *evil angels* among them. He made a way to his anger; he spared not their souls from death, but gave their life over to the *pestilence*." Evil *angels* are here associated with the *pestilence*. The Lord sent a *pestilence*, upon Israel, (2 Sam. xxiv. 16.) after David had numbered the people, "and there *died of the people*, from Dan even to Beersheba, seventy thousand men. And when the *angel* stretched out his hand upon Jerusalem to destroy it, the Lord repented him of the evil, and said to the *angel* that *destroyed the people*, It is enough; stay now thine hand." The people *died* of the *pestilence*, but the *angel* was said to *destroy* them. When Sennacherib besieged Jerusalem, "the *angel* of the Lord smote in the camp of the Assyrians, an hundred fourscore and five thousand, and when they arose early in the morning behold they were dead corpses," 2 Kings xix. 35. The *angel* mentioned in the text, may therefore denote some form of judgment. It comes not to cause, but to stay *war*: it is not local, or attached to a spot, like famine, but comes from a specified region, and therefore moves on like the pestilence that walketh in darkness. And of these three forms, war, famine, and pestilence, in which God pleads with all flesh, it would seem (if any) to be the last, or pestilence—which we thus see from scripture to be sometimes identified with the name, and to form the commission, of an angel, or messenger.

It descended not from heaven, like a blessing on the world; but the region from which it was seen *ascending*, or coming from a distance, is, in one word, the *east*.

It is also a manifest visitation of God—*having the seal of the living God*. It is nothing of man's creation, as either originating in their will, or dependent on their influence, or regulated by their wisdom or controlled by their power. It has *the seal of the living God*, an attestation of coming from his hands. The commission which it bears is from the Lord. When the prophet Gad, by the word of the Lord, said unto David, "Thus saith the Lord, I offer thee three things; choose thee one of them, that I may do it unto thee.—Shall seven years of famine come unto thee in thy land? Or wilt thou flee three years before thine enemies, while they pursue thee? or that there be three days pestilence in thy land?

sealed the servants of our God in their foreheads. And I heard the number of them that were sealed; and there were sealed an hundred and forty and four thousand of all the tribes of the children of Israel. Rev. vii. 1—4.

And David said unto Gad, I am in a great strait; *let us fall into the hands of the Lord*—for his mercies are great, and let me not fall into the hand of man. So the Lord sent a *pestilence* upon Israel." It came more immediately from the hand of God, without the instrumentality of man. And thus may the *pestilence*, more than less direct judgments, be said to have *the seal of the living God*—even as also the death which it wrought was said to be the act of an angel.

The angel, or messenger, that ascended from the *east*, having the seal of the living God, also cried with a *loud voice*—and his voice reached unto the *sea*. He came not unknown or unheard—he was seen in his progress *ascending from the east*—his *voice* was *loud* that all nations might hear, and his course was not stayed, till his influence was felt on the sea.

But the era of his coming, and the object to be fulfilled by that messenger of God, are not doubtful or undeterminate,—the one being obvious from the connexion with prophecies which mark the order of succession, and the other being expressly specified. *And I saw another angel ascending from the east, having the seal of the living God: and he cried with a loud voice to the four angels to whom it was given to hurt the earth and the sea, saying, hurt not the earth, neither the sea, nor the trees, till we have sealed the servants of God in their foreheads.* The purpose for which the messenger from the east appears at the marked and critical era of his coming, when all human things on every side were threatened with universal commotion, was to stay the tempest which was ready to burst upon the earth, as by the *blowing of the four winds of heaven;* and the purpose also for which that tempest, of universal war, is held back for a season, is, that the work of destruction may be suspended till the servants of God are sealed in their foreheads. Its period is therefore prior to that event, which itself takes precedence of others, before the seventh vial be poured out, and yet under the *sixth* it is said,—Behold I *come quickly*. It is one of the first precursors of the last and great catastrophe. Its immediate object is to stay a general or universal war, not in one country only, but in all. And is it not possible, that instead of looking for its coming, we may see it already, and hear its voice in every land, as Europe has been appalled by its ascent from the east,—marked before it came, and, though walking in darkness, tracked by destruction,—and Paris, which escaped unscathed by Cossacks, and many other cities as well as countries have been smitten by it,—till rumours of war have already been drowned by the voice of the war-suspending messenger,—'the pestilence,'—'the *new* disease,'—'the

Passing from scripture to scripture of obvious similarity of import, we read distinctly the order and succession of events from the sealing of the witnesses to the treading of the wine-press.

And I looked, and, lo, a Lamb stood on the mount

Asiatic cholera,'—'the destroying angel,' or 'the angel of death,' as it has often been termed, which *has* ascended from *the east*.

'Coming events cast their shadows before them.' If it yet shall prove, when the commissioned work is fully done, and the vision shall have spoken at the *end*, that such is the significancy of the symbol, a farther illustration may then be given, as has frequently heretofore been manifest, that the immediate judgment is often accompanied by a herald of the next. We have already seen how, in ascending from the east, and with no doubtful application, the pestilence, which has since reached to Europe, and whose voice has been heard on the sea, was none of the least effective of the agents in depopulating some of the cities and provinces of Turkey, or in drying up the waters of the Euphrates. Even on the banks of that river, if such be its charge, its farther object began to be fulfilled. It terminated the war between Persia and Turkey. "The Persian army, after having been attacked by the disease, was forced to retreat, and to *make peace* with the Turks."*

The seat of its origin was the east, from whence it was seen to ascend. "In the month of August 1817, at Jessore, about a hundred miles to the north-east of Calcutta, *the pestilence* AROSE; spreading from village to village, and destroying thousands of the inhabitants, it reached Calcutta early in September. It extended hence into Behar, *depopulating many large cities*, until the inhabitants fled to other spots, Benares, Attahabad, Goruckpore, Lucknow, Cawnpore, Delhi, Agra, Muttra, Meerat, and Bareilly, all suffered in succession; and it is remarkable, that it did not appear in these districts at the same time, but, leaving one, it soon showed itself in another."† "The partial irruptions of cholera in the principal towns of the presidency of Bengal, amount to two hundred in fourteen years, namely, from 1817 to 1830; in that of Madras, the number is one hundred and seventy-eight in the same period; in the presidency of Bombay, it amounts to fifty-five, thus making a total of four hundred and thirty-three visitations of the cholera in the cities of Hindostan in fourteen years. During this short period, Calcutta has been attacked fourteen times, or once every year, Madras nine times, Bombay twelve times."‡—"The cholera traversed the peninsula, east to west, from the bay of Ben-

* Quarterly Review, No. xci. p. 186.
† Hawkin's Hist. of the Cholera, p. 168.
‡ Ibid. 168. Quarterly Review, No. xci. pp. 172, 173.

Sion, and with him an hundred forty and four thousand, having his Father's name written in their foreheads. And I heard a voice from heaven, as the voice of many waters, and as the voice of a great thunder; and I heard the voice of harpers harping

---

gal to the bay of Cambay, a distance of four hundred and fifty leagues in less than a year; from north to south, three hundred leagues in nine months. It took less than two years to travel from the Persian Gulph to the shores of the Mediterranean.—The cholera attacked Astracan on the 20th of July; it ASCENDED the Volga to Twer, a distance of five hundred and fifty leagues, in little more than two months. Its *progress* was equally rapid at the very same time along the Don to Woronetz; and no less so on the banks of the Dnieper; so that in six months the disease had traversed Russia from the Caucasian provinces to the government of Twer and Yarastaf, a distance of seven hundred leagues."*

Thus, by a marked "rate of progression," was the cholera seen *ascending from the east.* Having thus *ascended* from the east, it occupied the whole extent of the regions to the *east* of Europe,—and its ravages have already spread from thence over a large portion of the continent. In the space of little more than a single year, it came, in a direct line from the *east* to the west in 1831, for for the space of two thousand miles, from Moscow to Riga, Dantzic, and Hamburg,† reaching to the *sea*, and passing the ocean, touched the shores of Britain. The full extent of its ravages over Europe, it is to be feared, have yet to be seen.

A sparrow cannot fall to the ground without the Father. And ranking in the midst of *judgments*, that fearful messenger of destruction, ascending from the east, is not without the seal of the living God, of which it has been said, "We have witnessed in our days the birth of a *new pestilence*, which, in the short space of fourteen years, has desolated the fairest portions of the globe, and swept off at least fifty millions of our race. It has mastered every variety of climate, surmounted every natural barrier, conquered every people."‡

The war between Persia and Turkey was stayed by the cholera, as it was ascending from the east. And already, perhaps, it may not, in some measure, have been without its effect in suspending a general or universal war. It reached Moscow in 1830, at a period when Europe, as described by the Premier of Great Britain, was "a magazine of combustibles, which the slightest spark might set into a blaze from one end to the other."§ The efficacy of the

* Ibid. 168. Quarterly Review, No. xci. pp. 186, 187.

† See Chart of its progress, Literary Gazette, Nov. 12, 1831.

‡ Quarterly Review, No. xci. p. 170.

§ Speech of Earl Gray on the Belgium Treaty, 26th January, 1832.

with their harps: And they sung as it were a new song before the throne, and before the four beasts, and the elders: and no man could learn that song, but the hundred and forty and four thousand, which were redeemed from the earth. These are they which were not defiled with women; for they are virgins. These are they which follow the Lamb whithersoever he goeth. These were redeemed from among men, being the first-fruits unto God and to

---

cholera in quenching, for a time, the threatened or incipient conflagration, may not yet be determined. But it reached Poland at an hour, when the eyes of all Europe were fixed on that country as the probable arena for deciding the controversy between liberty and despotism. The western nations were inspired with a greater terror than that of the Russian arms. And instead of armies rushing to the contest, all intercourse was restricted, or cautiously regulated, with the infected spot. The cholera first touched Britain at a perilous hour of political commotion. And when Russia denationalized Poland, and converted it into a subjugated province, the tidings reached Paris simultaneously with the cholera, and the French Chambers were dispersed without a word of remonstrance. The commission of the destroying angel—if such it be—is yet but in progress of fulfilment. And if it bear the seal of the living God, who shall let it? But who may not hear his voice and profit by the warning, when such a messenger has come for the suspension of weightier judgments, till the servants of the living God be first sealed in their foreheads?

The angel, or messenger, having the seal of the living God, ascended from the east, to stay the universal war till the servants of God should be sealed in their foreheads. And they that were sealed were of all *the tribes of the children of Israel.* To those who despise not the day of small things, and who look to that which the Lord is doing on the earth, the following information—a new thing since the days of the apostles,—may not be deemed uninteresting or unimportant.

"*Hebrew-Christian Church.*—Under this appellation a few Jews, who have embraced Christianity, have, for some time, formed themselves into a distinct community, conceiving that their brethren after the flesh will more readily unite with such a body than with those who were born Christians. They assembled first upwards of three years since, in a weekly prayer meeting; after a short time they met for worship on the Lord's day, first in a room, and afterwards in a small chapel, hired for the purpose; and are now seeking assistance to establish themselves in a more commodious place of worship."—*Missionary Register, March* 1832, p. 239.

the Lamb. And in their mouth was found no guile: for they are without fault before the throne of God. And I saw another angel fly in the midst of heaven, having the everlasting gospel to preach unto them that dwell on the earth, and to every nation, and kindred, and tongue, and people, saying, with a loud voice, Fear God, and give glory to him; for the hour of his judgment is come: and worship him that made heaven, and earth, and the sea, and the fountains of waters. And there followed another angel, saying, Babylon is fallen, is fallen, that great city, because she made all nations drink of the wine of the wrath of her fornication. And the third angel followed them saying, with a loud voice, If any man worship the beast and his image, and receivd his mark in his forehead; or in his hand, the same shall drink of the wine of the wrath of God, which is poured out without mixture into the cup of his indignation; and he shall be tormented with fire and brimstone in the presence of the holy angels, and in the presence of the Lamb: and the smoke of their torment ascendeth up for ever and ever; and they have no rest day nor night, who worship the beast and his image, and whosoever receiveth the mark of his name. Here is the patience of the saints: here are they that keep the commandments of God, and the faith of Jesus. And I heard a voice from heaven saying unto me, write, Blessed are the dead which die in the Lord, from henceforth and for ever: Yea, saith the Spirit, that they may rest from their labours, and their works do follow them. And I looked, and behold a white cloud, and upon the cloud sat one like unto the Son of man; having on his head a golden crown, and in his hand a sharp sickle. And another angel came out of the temple, crying with a loud voice to him that sat on the cloud, Thrust in thy sickle and reap: for the time is come for thee to reap; for the harvest of the earth is ripe.

And he that sat on the cloud thrust in his sickle on the earth; and the earth was reaped. And another angel came out of the temple which is in heaven, he also having a sharp sickle. And another angel came out from the altar, which had power over fire; and cried with a loud cry to him that had the sharp sickle, saying, Thrust in thy sharp sickle, and gather the clusters of the vines of the earth; for her grapes are fully ripe. And the angel thrust in his sickle into the earth, and gathered the vine of the earth, and cast it into the great wine-press of the wrath of God. And the wine-press was trodden without the city, and blood came out of the wine-press, even unto the horse-bridles, by the space of a thousand and six hundred furlongs. Rev. xiv.

He is not an old man who may have seen the first of the seven last plagues, and in whose days one vial of wrath has been poured out after another, from the French revolution to the rapid dissolution, now seemingly in progress, of the Turkish empire. Hitherto, in past judgments, men have not repented to give God glory. But in the great earthquake, or revolution, in which are slain of names of men, or men of note, seven thousand, it is said, *and the remnant were affrighted, and gave glory to the God of heaven.* The whole history of the world affords clear and experimental demonstration, that sin is the ruin of any people: while the word of a gracious God declares, that at what instant a nation shall turn from their evil, the Lord will repent of the evil that he thought to do unto them. He hath testified of his hatred of sin, and of his willingness to save, by the death of his Son upon the cross. He hath no pleasure in the death of a sinner, and his word of mercy ever is, Turn ye, turn ye, why will ye die? With the consummation of his controversy with the nations, in near if not immediate prospect, the world is now come to this pass, that by judgments, if not by the signs of them, men shall know that God is the Lord, either by abiding his wrath when he riseth to shake terribly the nations, or by learning to fear His great and glorious name, who hath power over these plagues, and who executeth justice and judgment on the earth. The destroyers of the earth are devoted to destruction. And ere the indignation be overpast, a time of trouble is at hand, such as the world has never witnessed. The only safety, whether for the youthful or the hoary head, is to be found in the way of righteousness. The righteousness that is of faith, is the watch-tower of the Christian, built upon a sure foundation. Though the heavens and the earth shall be shaken, the hope of the righteous shall not perish with the convulsions, nor, even at last with the wreck of the world. All things shall be shaken, that the things which cannot be shaken may remain. And when men's hearts shall fail them with fear, and for looking after those things that are coming upon the earth, it is the glorious privilege of the faithful in Jesus, and an act of obedience enjoined by him as their Master, to lift up their heads, and to know—from those very things which shall appal the world, and cause the ungodly to say to the mountains and rocks, Fall on us, and hide us from the face of him that sitteth on the throne, and from the wrath of the Lamb,—that the kingdom of God is nigh at hand, and their redemption draweth nigh. Now, when it may be seen that the *judgments* of God have been made *manifest*, the words of the prophet may be heard and laid to heart, Sow to yourselves in righteousness, reap in mercy; break up your fallow ground: *for it is time to seek the Lord*, till he come and rain righteousness upon you. And having seen how the Revelation of the Lord Jesus Christ unveils the past history of man, and how all human power is nothing at last but an illustration of his word, we may look to the glory that excelleth, and to the Lord who, blessing his people by redeeming them from all their iniquities, saves them from the wrath to come, and is preparing for them a kingdom that can never be moved,—and give the more earnest heed to his own warning, so suited to the time, "Take heed to yourselves, lest at any time your hearts be overcharged with surfeiting and drunkenness, and cares of this life, and so that day come upon you unawares. For as a snare shall it come on all them that dwell on the face of the whole earth. Watch ye, therefore, and pray always, that ye may be accounted worthy to escape all these things that shall come to pass, and to stand before the Son of man." Luke xxi. 34—36. And under the sixth seal, this is the counsel of the same Saviour, "Behold, I come as a thief; blessed is he that watcheth and keepeth his garments, lest he walk naked, and they see his shame." Rev. xvi. 15.

FINIS.

TABULAR SUMMARY,

WITH

DATES AND REFERENCES.

CHAPTER I.

CHAPTER II.

DANIEL'S VISIONS OF THE GREAT IMAGES AND OF THE FOUR BEASTS, INTERPRETED KINGDOMS.

CHAPTER III.

DANIEL'S VISION OF THE RAM AND THE HE-GOAT.

* The era of the Lagidæ commenced in this year,—the very year of the death of Alexander; that of the Seleucidæ in 311, before Christ.

CHAPTER VI.

CHAPTER VII.

CHAPTER VIII.

THE INVASION AND OPPRESSION OF THE PAPAL KINGDOMS, BY THE KINGS OF THE SOUTH AND OF THE NORTH; OR BY THE SARACENS, AND, SUBSEQUENTLY, BY THE TURKS.

THE BOOK OF THE REVELATION OF JESUS CHRIST.

CHAPTER IX.

INTRODUCTION TO THE BOOK OF THE REVELATION, AND THE OPENING OF THE FIRST SEAL, 168–184.

CHAPTER X.

THE SECOND SEAL.

MAHOMETANISM.

CHAPTER XI.

THE THIRD SEAL.

POPERY IN THE DARK AGES.

CHAPTER XII.

THE FOURTH SEAL.

INFIDELITY.

CHAPTER XIII.

FIFTH AND SIXTH SEALS.

The depressed and persecuted state of the true church of Christ in past ages.

A.D.		Page
452	Invasion of Northern Italy by Attila . .	244
461–467	Sedition of the Roman army at Fortona, in Liguria, or Piedmont. Ricimer reigns over Northern Italy, at Milan. Great mortality in the countries around the Po . . .	252

CHAPTER XVII.

FOURTH TRUMPET.—*Scene, the third part of the sun, &c. smitten.*

Extinction of the imperial power of Rome.

476 or 479	Extinction of the western empire by Odoacer. Xeno sole emperor; but imperial power not discontinued over Rome	259
493	Theodoric, the Ostrogoth, subdues Italy, takes Rome, assumes the Purple, and reigns over Italy, &c.	260
541	Extinction of the consulship	261
552	——————— Senate	261
	Subsequent restoration of the western empire by Charlemagne, A.D. 800	264

CHAPTER XVIII.

FIFTH TRUMPET, OR FIRST WOE.

Fall of a great star upon the earth. Opening of the bottomless pit. Darkening smoke out of the pit. Locusts out of the smoke. Mahometanism. Saracens.

591–616	Reign and magnificence of Chosroes, king of Persia. He invades the Roman empire, and besieges Constantinople	269
622	Rise of Mahomet. Mutual destruction of the Roman and Persian empires. First expedition of Heraclius against the Persians, and the commencement of the Hegira, or Mahometan era, same year	271
627–628	Flight of Chosroes. He is deposed and murdered	272

A.D.		Page
632	Invasion of Syria by the Saracens. Propagation and rapid progress of Mahometanism	273
	Saracens commanded not to touch the grass of the earth, &c. but to destroy idolators	283
	Prophetic and historical marks and description of the Saracenic woe	287
718–767	Empire of the caliphs—prevalence of their conquests. Foundation of Bagdad	292
936	Fallen state of the caliphs of Bagdad	294

CHAPTER XIX.

THE SIXTH TRUMPET, OR SECOND WOE.

The four angels that were bound in the river Euphrates, loosed—prepared for a day, a week, a month, and a year, or 396 years, 103 days—intermediate history—armies of horsemen—siege of Constantinople, the capital of the eastern Roman empire—establishment of the authority of the Turkish paschas—continued impenitence of the papal kingdom of Europe.

	The empire of the Turks identified with the King of the north, Dan. xi, 44. &c.	298
980–1038	Emigration of the Turks—they defeat the Gaznevides, and subdue Persia	301
1057	The sultan invested by the caliph	302
1065–1071	The conquest of Armenia and Georgia by the Turks. The Roman emperor defeated and taken prisoner	304
1076–1096	Division of the Turkish Empire into four sultanies. Conquest of Jerusalem by the Turks	305
1096–1295	The Turks *bound* in the Euphrates by the crusaders	318
1227–1295	Conquests of the Moguls	318
1299–1326	Reign of Othman, and *loosing* of the Turks	310
	Conquests of the Ottomans	312
	Period of preparation, 396 years, 103 days	314
	Purpose for which the Turks were prepared	318
	Retrospective view of the history of the Turks from the investment of the sultan by the Caliph, to the taking of Constantinople, and final submission of the eastern Roman empire	321
1353	Establishment of the Turks in Europe	322
1396–1402	Bajazet defeated the confederate Christian armies, and threatened the destruction of Constantinople, but was conquered by Tamerlane	323

A.D.		Page
1421	Reunion of the Ottoman empire .	323
1451	Mahomet II. on his ascension to the throne displays hostile intentions against Constantinople	325
1453	Period of preparation completed on the fortieth day of the siege, and the fate of Constantinople could no longer be averted . .	327
1453	The siege of Constantinople, and its fall .	336
	The eastern Roman empire dvided into Turkish pachalics	346
1453–1500	The papal kingdoms of Europe continue idolatrous and impenitent. Gross vices of the Roman Catholic clergy at the close of the fifteenth century	347

CHAPTER XX.

Another mighty angel descends from heaven clothed with a cloud—a rainbow upon his head—his face as the sun—his feet as pillars of fire—a little open book in his hand—his right foot on the sea—and his left upon the earth—he cried with a loud voice—when he had cried seven thunders uttered their voices—and when the seven thunders had uttered their voices, the angel sware that there would be time (delay) no longer. The era and the symbol of the reformation.

1517	Reformation commenced	363
	Significancy of the similitudes. Translation of the Scriptures—book from heaven opened .	366
	The maritime countries of Denmark—Sweden—Britain—Holland—chief seat of the reformation	368
	Protestant States of Germany	372
	The angel cried with a loud voice, as when a lion roareth. The Reformation a most momentous event, and glorious moral revolution	371
1555	Reformation consolidated by the pacification of Passau	374
	Seven thunders, denoting wars, uttered their voices, after the Reformation was established	374
1569–1607	I. THUNDER.—Civil and religious wars in Holland and Zealand against Spain. Holland cast off the Spanish yoke. War against the Hugenots in France. War between Britain and Spain. Destruction of the Spanish Ar-	

CHAPTER XXI.

CHAPTER XXII.

Vision of the Woman clothed with the Sun, &c. History of Christianity. The Conflict of the Church, 409–424.

CHAPTER XXIII.

The First and Second Beast. Imperial and Papal Rome.

CHAPTER XXIV.

THE SEVEN VIALS OF THE WRATH OF GOD, AND SEVEN LAST PLAGUES. THE JUDGMENT SITS ON THE PAPACY TO TAKE *away its dominion, &c.* THE JUDGMENTS OF GOD ANNOUNCED AS MADE MANIFEST.

FIRST VIAL, *French Revolution.*

CHAPTER XXV.

THE SECOND VIAL.—*Scene, the Sea.*

CHAPTER XXVI.

THE THIRD VIAL.—*Scene, the Rivers and Fountains of Waters*, 486—536.

CHAPTER XXVII.

FOURTH VIAL.

CHAPTER XXVIII.

FIFTH VIAL.

CHAPTER XXIX.

SIXTH VIAL.

Euphrates, or Ottoman Empire.

A.D.		Page
1821–1824	Insurrection of Greece, and its independence of the Porte	613
1825–1826	Revolt and destruction of the Janisaries	618
1827	Battle of Navarino	619
1828	War with Russia	620
	General revolt throughout Albania	625
1821–1831	Ravages of cholera and plague, and the depopulation of the eastern provinces of Turkey	627
	The commencement, as supposed, of the cleansing of the Sanctuary, (the place of which was trodden down by the Turks,) in the year 1820, on the expiry of the 2300 years mentioned by Daniel	634
	Vial continues to be poured out	639
	Order of predictions not yet fulfilled	645

APPENDIX.

L'an 1057.
Bondari
D'Herbelot.

Après cette victoire, Thogrul-begh reprit* le chemin de Bagdad. Il s'embarqua sur le Tigre, et se rendit par eau à la porte de Racca, où il monta à cheval, et fit son entrée dans Bagdad. Lorsqu'il fut parvenu au palais du Khalif il descendit de cheval et marcha à pied accompagné des E'mirs qui le précédoient sans armes. Le Khalif étoit assis derrière son voile noir, ayant sur ses épaules l'habit noir nommé Bourda, et dans sa main le bâton du Prophête. En s'approchant du thrône, Thogrul-begh baise la terre et se tint debout pendant quelque tems, après quoi il monta vers le thrône, suivi du premier Ministre du Khalif et d'un Interprête. Il s'assit sur autre thrône, et on lût en sa presence l'acte par lequel le Khalif le reconnoissoit maitre de tous les E'tats que le Dieu Tres-Haut lui avoit confiés, et gouverneur de tous les Mussulmans. On le revêtit de sept robes d'honneur, qu'on lui mit l'une sur l'autre; on lui donna des esclaves des sept contrées differentes qui formoient l'Empire des Khalifs; on lui couvrit la tête d'un voile d'étoffe d'or tout remplit de muse; ensuite on lui mit deux couronnes, l'une pour l'Arabie, et l'autre pour la Perse. Le Khalif lui donna *une épée* toute garnie d'or. Après cette cérémonie Thogrul-begh retourna à sa place, et voulut baiser la terre, mais on l'empêcha, et il baisa deux fois la main du Khalif. Caim-b'amr-illah lui fit present d'une seconde épée, et ils les mit toutes les deux E'tats, on le proclama ensuite Roi de l'Orient et de l'Occident.

C'est ainsi que le Khalif se donnoit un maitre. Depuis que l'on avoit établi anciennement un E'mir-el-omara, ou Lieutenant-Général de l'Empire, les Khalifs étoient accoutumés à se depouiller eux-mêmes de toute leur autorité en faveur de cet officier, et réduits en quelque sorte à une pension, ils se contentoient des respects que le peuple leur rendoit comme au Souvrain Pontife de la Religion *Mussulmanne. Thogrul-begh succèdoit dans cette charge aux Bouides qu'il venoit de détruire.—Histoire Général des Huns, des Turcs, des Moguls, &c. Par M. Deguignes, de l'Académie Royale, Interprête du Roi pour les Langues Orientales et I. R. S. Suite des Mémoirs de l'Académie Royale des Inscriptions, et Belles-lettres.* Tom. iii. l. 19. pp. 197-8.

---

* Samedi 25 de Dzoulcaada l'an 448.

32101 065973941

Lightning Source UK Ltd.
Milton Keynes UK
UKHW020412190821
389088UK00002B/178

9 781298 650269